Lizzie Borden took an axe
And gave her mother forty whacks.
And when she saw what she had done,
She gave her father forty-one.
– Fall River, Massachusetts Nursery Rhyme

THE BORDEN ALPHABET

A... was the August the murder took place.
B... Bordens murdered by blows in the face.
C... was the Crime in all its detail.
D... was the Daughter at once put in jail.
E... was the Evidence not in her favor.
F... was the Few little facts that might save her
G... was the Gown all covered in pain.
H... doubtless the Hatchet, tho' some said "it ain't."
I... was the Inquest they held all in vain.
J... was the Jury who most went insane.
K... was the Kind of woman she was.
L... was the Lawyer who pleaded her case
M... for Money the motive explain?
N... surely the Note they looked for in vain.
O... was the Officers of the police
P... was the Pardon and speedy release.
Q... was the Queries and Questions each day.
R... was the Russell who gave her away.
S... was the Sentence, oh! How she did fear it.
T... was the Ten months she waited to hear it.
U... is the Unfinished story it makes.
V... is the Villainous interest one takes.
W... for Who it is nothing explains.
X... the Unknown ever remains.
Y... would still bother us if we would let it.
Z... is our Zeal as we try to forget it.

Dead Men Do Tell Tales Series

ONE AUGUST MORNING

THE TRUE STORY OF LIZZIE BORDEN

BY TROY TAYLOR

American Hauntings Ink & Whitechapel Press

This Book is Published By:
Whitechapel Press
American Hauntings Ink
Jacksonville, Illinois | 1-888-446-7859
Visit us on the Internet at http://www.whitechapelpress.com

First Edition – June 2015
ISBN: 1-892523-95-7

Printed in the United States of America

Note from the Author:

This is a book that is filled history, mystery and lies. You'll find lies on almost every page – but they are not lies of my own making. The "true story" of Lizzie Borden is filled with more lies than any reader can possibly imagine. The police lied, in court and out of it. The prosecutor lied. The defense attorneys lied. The witnesses lied, often knowing quite well they were doing so. The reporters lied – and then lied some more, and then lied even more after that. Neighbors lied. Writers and historians lied and made up whole portions of the Borden story without a second thought.

And Lizzie Borden lied.

With that said, I have tried to wade through the weird stories, bizarre claims, missing minutes, outlandish theories, and wild stories.

Any mistakes found within these pages are mine and mine alone.

Most likely, someone lied to me.

PREFACE

The August afternoon was unbearably hot, especially for Massachusetts. The temperature had climbed to well over 100 degrees, even though it was not yet noon. According to the newspapers, the previous day, August 3, had been the hottest day of 1892. The rooms of Borden house, located at 92 Second Street, were stifling and filled with stale air. It had recently been a house of sickness, with several members complaining of stomach ailments, and the oppressive feeling of illness seemed to linger in the atmosphere.

The various members of the household – Andrew Borden, his wife, two daughters, a maid, and a visiting uncle – had slowly gone about their days. The discomfort of the stomach sickness that had plagued them left the family feeling listless. One of Borden's daughters, Emma, was not at home. She had gone away to visit friends. His other daughter, Lizzie, had slept late, while Borden, his wife, and John Morse, the brother of his late first wife, had eaten a small breakfast, prepared by the maid, who was still suffering from the recent illness.

John Morse left the house early to visit a niece and nephew and Andrew Borden soon followed. Borden's second wife, Abby, went upstairs to make up the room that Morse had slept in the night before. Morse was a frequent visitor to the Borden home, traveling from Dartmouth, Massachusetts, several times each year to visit his late sister's family and to conduct business in the prosperous town of Fall River. Before she went upstairs, Abby asked Bridget Sullivan, the family's maid, to wash the windows. In the meantime, Lizzie had come downstairs to the kitchen, where she had coffee and a cookie but did not eat. Bridget went outside the house and threw up in the backyard, her stomach still churning from whatever the household had been suffering from.

Around 9:30, Abby Borden came downstairs for a few moments to retrieve some fresh pillowcases and then went back upstairs. It was the last time that she was ever seen alive – except for by her killer.

As Bridget went about her daily chores, taking time to wash the windows and chat with the girl who worked next door, she came inside just before 10:00 a.m. to see Mr. Borden returning from his office. She let him into the back door, just as Lizzie was coming downstairs. Lizzie told her father that Abby had gone out – she had received a note from someone who was sick.

Borden, still in his heavy morning coat, was not feeling well. He let out a sigh as he reclined on the mohair-covered sofa in the parlor, leaning back so that his boots were resting on the floor and not soiling the upholstery of the couch. In a short time, he drifted off to sleep, never suspecting that he would not awaken.

He also did not suspect that, above his head, his wife was lying in a pool of blood on the floor of the upstairs guestroom. He had no way of knowing that the hand that had taken her life was just about to take his life, too. Even if he had known these things, by way of some macabre premonition, there is no way that he could have guessed that his killer would never be brought to justice.

As the mantel clock ticked quietly in the parlor, Bridget Sullivan was being overcome by the nausea that had been troubling her all morning. The heat of the day, combined with the strenuous nature of her chores, had left her feeling very ill. At around 10:45 a.m., she excused herself to go upstairs to her room and rest. She had just closed her eyes when she heard a voice calling out from downstairs.

It was Lizzie. "Come down quick!" she cried. "Father's dead! Somebody's come in and killed him!"

That shrill cry marked the start of a series of haunting events that remain unresolved and mysterious to this very day.

1. THE HOT AUGUST MORNING

The case of the Borden murders has fascinated those with an interest in American crime for well over a century. There have been few cases that are as compelling to us as the hatchet murders of Massachusetts businessman Andrew Borden and his wife, Abby. This is partly because of the gruesome butchery of the crime but also because of the unexpected character of the woman who became the leading suspect in the case. Borden's daughter, Lizzie, was not a homicidal maniac, but a demure, respectable, and, some would say, "spinsterish" Sunday School teacher. Thanks to this, the entire town was shocked when she was charged with the murder of her parents. The fact that she was found to be not guilty of the murders, leaving the case to be forever unresolved, only adds to the mystique and fans the flames of our continuing obsession with the mystery.

Who killed Andrew and Abby Borden? No one knows for sure. I believe that I can build a pretty good case that it was not Lizzie, but if not her, then who was it? We'll explore all of the suspects later in the book, but in the end, it may just be impossible to say. The case has never been solved and, after all of these years, it's unlikely that it ever will be.

Could this be the reason that the Borden house in Fall River is considered one of America's most haunted houses?

Andrew Jackson Borden was one of the leading citizens of Fall River, Massachusetts, a prosperous mill town and seaport. The Borden family had strong roots to the community and had been among the most influential citizens of the region for decades. At the age of 72, Borden was certainly one of the richest men in the city. He was president of one of the town's largest banks and sat on the board of directors of three others. He was a commercial landlord with considerable holdings, including a new three-story building in the center of downtown. He was a director of three of the major cloth mills that supported the economy and work force of Fall River, and which had put the city on the map as a thriving industrial town. He was more than halfway to becoming a millionaire, in an era when a million dollars was an amazing sum.

Fall River, Massachusetts, 1877

The Borden name carried with it great respect. The Bordens were among the earliest settlers of Fall River. A member of the Borden clan was present with the group that joined Anne Hutchinson when she was ousted from the Massachusetts Bay colony for heresy in the 1600s. By the early 1700s, third generation Bordens owned everything on both sides of the Taunton River in the Fall River area. According to local legend, it had been Andrew's grandfather who had named the town Fall River when it was founded. In 1892, there were more than 125 families of the Borden name living in the community.

Fall River, located about 50 miles south of Boston, owed its existence to a quirk of nature and a rushing stream the Indians called Quequechan. The stream began as an outflow from two substantial lakes, North and South Watuppa Ponds, on a plateau in the east, fell 125 feet in less than a mile before going underground. The waterfall created waterpower on its way down the hills to Mount Hope Bay. Men of industry, like Andrew Borden's forebears, recognized the possibilities of the rushing waters and the water wheels and, later, steam engines, they built brought about the cotton mills, and created the boom times that allowed the business owners to prosper. Until the Civil War, Fall River was a prosperous, but relatively unassuming city. The war, however, was what made it great. The city developed great cloth mills and a major cotton industry so that, by day, there was a persistent hum of spindles, and by night, a teeming force of mill hands.

Not all of the early families of the area embraced land and industry. Some looked to the sea for their fortunes, and shipbuilding and fishing industries grew up there.

The ship owners of New England and Fall River developed a three-corner trade route between New England, Africa, and the southern colonies. New England-manufactured rum was carried to Africa to exchange with native chiefs for their spoils of war: African men and women. They were transported as cargo to the American colonies in the south to exchange for molasses and cotton. The molasses brought to New England could be distilled into the rum necessary for the first corner of the "triangle." The cotton was also essential to the booming textile industry.

Many of the Bordens farmed and lumbered the land, which was allowed by the colony's English rules so that cheap raw materials could be sent back to established industries at home. This system produced little profit for the colonists and even less promise of a prosperous future, so they revolted against it. Not the least of these rebels were the Bordens.

In the Battle of Fall River, a British landing party, supported by naval cannon, invaded the community in 1778. It came ashore at the mouth of the Quequechan and fought its way uphill to what later became City Hall Square, where it was stopped by a renegade group of rebels under the leadership of Colonel Joseph Durfee. The British retreated back to their ships, but set fire to everything in their path as they fled. They burned the Borden mills and home and left behind two dead and several wounded.

But the Durfees and later the Bordens became mill owners once again. Colonel Durfee is credited with the first successful local venture into textiles. The Borden fortune in both cash and land came early, developed mainly by "nerve, grit, and cheek," which were evidently Borden characteristics.

Immigrant workers provided the labor for the textile mills and other industry in Fall River. Commerce and industry flourished and life was good – at least for those in charge. The minimum workday for laborers was 14 hours – although just 10 on Saturday – and the minimum hiring age was seven, if the child could be trained. The various ethnic groups and nationalities in Fall River hated each other, and those who owned the industry perpetuated the hatred because it kept up the competition for cheap labor. French Canadians settled in the east end of the city, while the Portuguese were in the south end. There was no west side of the city because of the Taunton River and the looming mills.

The north side of the city was the most important, as it had been dubbed "the Hill." The Hill was actually the uppermost reaches of the bluffs that rose, first gradually and then rapidly, from the east bank of the Taunton River. In the nineteenth century, The Hill was what we could consider to be a "gated community" today. The poor, the foreign, and the serving class were allowed to pass through and work on The Hill, but they were not allowed to live there. In 1892, this was where the society people of Fall River lived and where the wealthy kept their homes.

Andrew Borden could have purchased and lived in almost any house that he wanted in Fall River, including among the prestigious homes of The Hill, but he chose

Andrew Jackson Borden

a modest place on Second Street. Andrew's need to hold onto his money can be traced back a single generation within his family. All of the early Bordens had prospered, for the most part. Andrew's father, though, was one Borden who did not fare so well. He was a fish peddler, and Andrew had sworn that he would do better. He began as a carpenter's helper and soon advanced to a career as an undertaker in partnership with Frank Almy. They advertised as the sole dealers for Crane's Patented Casket Burial Cases, which were guaranteed to preserve the remains of a loved one longer than any other – a claim that would be difficult to prove.

Andrew Borden was a tall, thin, and dour man and while he was known for this thrift and admired for his business abilities, he was not well-known for his humor, nor was he particularly likable. He worked 14-hour days, saving, scrimping, hoarding, and re-selling. It was typical of him that on the day that he was murdered, he had picked up a broken, discarded lock that he had found in the street, wrapped it carefully in a bit of paper, and carried it home in his pocket.

Once he began making money in the undertaking business, Andrew's investments extended to other parts of the city's economy. He owned one of Fall River's banks and interests in others. His properties began on South Main Street, just yards from the city's banking center, and he collected his many rents personally. It was not uncommon to see him on his rounds with a basket of eggs. They came from one of his farms and he offered them for sale on his rounds, his rent book in one hand and basket of eggs in the other.

About two years before his death, Andrew used some of his savings to achieve his proudest personal goal. He erected a large office and commercial building in the heart of Fall River's business district. He named it, fittingly, the A.J. Borden Building. He owned it – along with all of his other property outright – and he loved telling anyone who would listen that he never borrowed a cent from anyone, nor had he ever signed a note.

Andrew lived with his second wife, Abby Durfee Gray and his daughters from his first marriage, Emma and Lizzie, in a two-and-a-half story frame house. The Durfee name carried the same weight in the business and social circles of Fall River as the

Borden name did. It was just as old and equally respected. From among the daughters of the family, Andrew had married Abby. It was his second marriage and her first. To Abby, Andrew's proposal must have seemed a fantastic stroke of good luck. She was old by the standards of the era, unattractive and undesirable. In her autopsy report, her weight was listed between 210 and 220 pounds. To Andrew, the marriage was strictly a convenient means of securing a housekeeper and a nursemaid for two young daughters. For reasons never questioned, there were no children from this union. There is no reason not to believe that, in their separate ways, each found in the marriage exactly what he or she was seeking. When she died, Abby was 65-years-old and was a retiring, almost reclusive, woman who preferred staying at home to just about any other activity.

Abby Durfee Borden

Andrew had fathered, at five-year-intervals, three daughters by his first wife, Sarah Morse. Emma was the first. The second, Alice, lived just two years. Lizzie was the last, the youngest daughter. Perhaps because he had wanted a son to carry on his name, he gave Lizzie the middle name Andrew. Two years after Sarah died, he married the spinster, Abby.

That there are no records of child abuse or neglect by Abby toward her stepdaughters, means very little because, in that era, short of killing a child as a discipline, anything was allowed if its intent was to produce character or "godliness." Even so, based on accounts that have survived over the years, Abby was a largely disinterested parent who loved and cared for her husband's children in the same manner in which they cared for her. In other words, none of the women in the house cared for one another very much.

The underlying tension in the house could be easily traced to the dictates and policies established by Andrew, who had what was often referred to as "habits of economy." The house in which the family lived, 92 Second Street, was a good example of those miserly habits. Located in an unfashionable section of town, it had been constructed as what was called a "railroad house," built soundly, but sparsely for two families. Separate entrances, one in front that opened onto the sidewalk, and another on the side that provided access to what would have been upper and lower apartments. Space-wasting walls were not included in the design, making it necessary to go from room to room to get to the front or back. Andrew, with his characteristically frugal nature, refused to have his house connected to gas mains.

The Borden House at 92 Second Street

Kerosene was good enough for the household, and he sternly restricted its use. Electricity was not yet commonly available, but telephones were. Andrew did not have one because he could see no use for it, or for the added expense.

There was no hot water in the house other than what a pot or tea kettle could produce. Most of the better wood and coal burning ranges of the time had water-warming reservoirs built in, but the Borden stove did not. When Andrew bought the house, it had running water. He stated that the running water on the second floor was an unnecessary luxury and the plumbing changed to cut it off and limit the water to a spigot in the basement. His only other concession to comfort was a coal-burning furnace, also in the basement. There were no bathrooms in the house.

Both of Andrew's daughters felt the house was beneath their station in life and begged their father to move to a nicer place. He never even considered the idea. The house at 92 Second Street was on the wrong side of a hill that divided the town as it thrust itself upwards from the rugged shoreline. In short, society lived up on The Hill; all others, lived below. That Andrew would not spend a portion of his considerable wealth for a luxurious home on The Hill was turned into a motive for murder by the prosecution in the court case that followed the Bordens' deaths.

The events that led to tragedy began early that morning. The maid, Bridget Sullivan, had been the first one up in the household that day, and her description of what had taken place provided the outline for those events.

Bridget was a respectable Irish girl who Emma and Lizzie both insisted on calling "Maggie," which was the name of a previous girl who had worked for them. At the time of the murders, Bridget was 26 years old and had been in the Borden household for three years. She was typical of the Irish immigrants who came to America during the industrial boom of the late nineteenth century. There is nothing to say that she was anything but an exemplary young woman, who had come to America in 1886. She had arrived first in Newport, Rhode Island, without family or

Bridget Sullivan

acquaintances. A year later, she moved to South Bethlehem, Pennsylvania, but eventually came to Massachusetts. Since 1889, she had occupied a small attic room in the third floor rear of the Borden house. Her duties included washing, ironing, cooking, sweeping, and general household work downstairs. Mrs. Borden, Lizzie, and Emma tended to their own rooms.

As she would later testify, Bridget liked her job, the family, and the town. She was an attractive, auburn-haired young woman who had many friends among the other servant girls in the community. She was generally happy, but the murders would shake her to the core. She did not stay in the house during the night of the murders, but did return the following day to spend the night in her room. It was her last night in the house. She left the following day and never returned.

She had risen that morning at her usual time of 6:00 a.m. She was already feeling sick when she got out of bed. She, as well as the family members, had all fallen ill the day before with bouts of vomiting and diarrhea.

She had come down the backstairs from her room at 6:15 and, bringing up wood and coal from the cellar, built a fire in the kitchen to start cooking breakfast. As she did every morning, she took in the milk can from a farm that Mr. Borden owned in Swansea and put out the pan to receive the iceman's morning delivery.

While she was busy with breakfast, John Vinnicum Morse, came downstairs, spoke to her, and went into the sitting room to wait for the others to appear. Morse, the brother of Andrew's first wife, had arrived the previous day for an unannounced visit. He was a frequent visitor to the house.

Mrs. Borden came downstairs at 6:30, using the back stairs from the master bedroom on the second floor, and Mr. Borden followed a few minutes later, carrying his chamber pot. There was no indoor toilet in the Borden home, only an earthen closet in the dirt floor cellar, so the emptying of chamber pots was a morning ritual.

The breakfast that was set out for Abby, Andrew, and John included mutton, which was served for a third day, mutton broth, johnnycakes, cookies, overripe bananas, and coffee. They ate while Bridget cleaned up the kitchen, waiting for the bell from the dining room that would signal that she was to clear away the dishes.

They lingered over breakfast, chatting for some time, and then John Morse left by the backdoor around 8:30. He was on his way to visit his relatives, who lived on Weybosset Street. Andrew accompanied him to the door, inviting him to return for the noon meal. After Morse left, Andrew locked the door behind him. It was a peculiar custom in the house to always keep doors locked. Even the doors between certain rooms upstairs were usually locked.

Mrs. Borden picked up her duster and puttered in the sitting room, while Andrew cleaned his teeth in the kitchen sink. It was, Bridget stated, a typical morning in the house.

At 9:00 a.m., Lizzie came downstairs with her chamber pot. She, too, had spent the night with stomach cramps and, understandably, did not want a heavy breakfast of old mutton and johnnycakes. She did take coffee and two small cookies. Two days before, Mr. and Mrs. Borden had been ill during the night and had both vomited several times. The illness spread to the rest of the household. It was assumed at first that the elder Bordens suffered from food poisoning because no one else in the family was affected. After Lizzie and Bridget also became sick, it might have been the onset of the flu – or something far more sinister.

Bridget, meanwhile, was also still sick. Barely finishing the breakfast dishes, she fled out the backdoor to vomit in the yard. When she returned to the kitchen a few minutes later, Lizzie had apparently gone back up to her bedroom. Mrs. Borden, still busy with the feather duster in the sitting and dining rooms, told Bridget that she wanted her to wash the windows that day, inside and out.

Andrew, dressed in the same black wool suit that he wore summer and winter, left for business downtown and to stop at the post office. Around the same time, Abby Borden went upstairs to make the bed in the guestroom that Morse was staying in. At 9:30, she came downstairs for a few moments and then went back up again, commenting that she needed fresh pillowcases.

Bridget had let the windows down in both rooms, went to the cellar for a pail and a brush, and then outside to draw water in the barn and start her work. While she was working, she paused for a few minutes to chat over the fence with the hired girl next door.

The backyard of the Borden House, where Bridget would become ill from stomach problems and where Lizzie later stated that she went to eat some pears.

Lizzie appeared at the backdoor and asked Bridget what she was doing. She told Lizzie that she would be washing windows outside for a while, and that Lizzie could lock the door if she liked, as there was water in the barn. But Lizzie didn't lock the door.

Bridget finished the outside of the windows at about 10:30, and then started inside. She heard someone rattling the front door and went to see who it was. It was Mr. Borden; he had forgotten – or misplaced – his key. There were three locks on the door, and as she fumbled to get them all open, she claimed that she said, "Pshaw!" However, it's likely that her expletive was stronger than she admitted, for she later testified that she heard Lizzie upstairs, laughing at the outburst.

Andrew went into the dining room and then into the sitting room, where he lay down on the sofa. He had the newspaper with him, but his pale face suggested that he was going to take a late morning nap. Lizzie came downstairs to ask if she had received any mail and to tell her father, "Mrs. Borden has gone out – she had a note from someone who was sick." Lizzie and Emma always called their step-mother "Mrs. Borden" and recently, the relationship between them, especially with Lizzie, was strained.

Andrew rose from the sofa and took the key to his bedroom off a shelf so that he could get into his room. This was done as a precaution because of a burglary the year before. In June 1891, a police captain inspected the house after Andrew Borden reported a crime. Andrew's desk had been rummaged through, and $100 and a watch and chain had been taken. There was no clue as to how anyone could have gotten into the house, although Lizzie offered the fact that the cellar door had been open. The neighborhood was canvassed, but no one reported seeing a stranger in the vicinity. According to the police captain, Andrew said several times to him, "I'm afraid the police will not be able to find the real thief." It is unknown what he may have meant by this and the statement was never explained.

After retrieving the key, Andrew went up the back steps. His room could only be reached by these stairs, as there was no hallway, and the front stairs only have access to Lizzie's room (from which Emma's could be reached), and the guest room, where John Morse had spent the night. There were connecting doors between the elder Borden's rooms and Lizzie's room, but they were usually kept locked. Andrew stayed upstairs for only a few minutes before coming back down and settling back onto the sofa in the sitting room.

Lizzie, who was dressed to go downtown when she came back downstairs, asked Bridget (or rather, "Maggie") if she planned to go out that afternoon. She said, "There is a cheap sale of dress goods at Sargent's this afternoon, at eight cents a yard. I'm probably going to pick up some material."

Bridget replied that she was probably not, since she was still not feeling well.

Lizzie added, "If you go out, be sure and lock the door, for Mrs. Borden has gone out on a sick call and I might go out, too." Asked who was sick, Lizzie said she didn't know. "She had a note this morning. It must be in town."

Lizzie took down the ironing board, set it up, and prepared to iron some handkerchiefs. She placed her irons on the kitchen stove to heat. It was now 10:50 a.m. and the heat of the kitchen was intense. The humid morning, the window washing, her chores, the hot kitchen, and an upset stomach all combined to make Bridget tired and queasy again. Feeling poorly, she told Lizzie that she was going upstairs to her attic room to take a short nap.

The stage was now set: Mrs. Borden was supposedly away from him visiting a sick friend; Andrew was resting peacefully on the sofa; John Morse was out of the house; Lizzie was preparing her handkerchiefs for ironing; and Bridget was resting in her room. The house was quiet, almost silent, but that stillness would soon be shattered.

Lizzie's narrative of the events that followed were later scrutinized by the police and prosecutors. Things had been largely as "Maggie" had described them, she said, with a few discrepancies as to exactly who was where and when, and what had been said and done.

Lizzie, who had been christened Lizzie, not Elizabeth, was Andrew's youngest daughter and his favorite. However, there were those who would say that he catered to her, not out of love, but for her iron will and her insistence at having her own way.

She was born on July 19, 1860, in the Borden house as 12 Ferry Street. Her mother died when Lizzie was two years old, and when she was four, Andrew married Abby, a spinster who, at the age of 40, had undoubtedly given up all hope of ever being married. Sarah Borden had been a young and attractive woman, while Abby was neither. She was a stocky woman, incapable of humor and of displaying either love or affection. But she had many qualities that Andrew prized: she was steady, moral, and undemanding; she was respectful, a good housekeeper, and knew when to leave a room when business was being discussed.

Lizzie A. Borden

Lizzie was 18 years old when she left Fall River High School and, in that era, little thought was given to her attending college. If she had, she would have excelled, but at that time and place, young ladies retired to their homes, learned and practiced domesticity, and waited for suitors to call. It should come as no surprise, though, that the prospect of courting in the cramped parlor of the shabby house on Second Street, under the glaring eyes of Andrew and the grim face of Abby, scared most young men away. There were a few callers – Lizzie was the daughter of the town's richest man – but they were not encouraged by her father and step-mother. Fewer and fewer young men called on her and, in time, they stopped coming altogether.

Her life as an adult in Fall River was unremarkable and there was nothing unusual about her beyond a pronounced reserve of bearing and coolness of demeanor. Her most striking feature was her large, wide-set eyes, alternately pale cerulean blue if you were her friend, gray and piercing if you were not. The width of her determined jaw kept her from being called a true beauty, but she was not unattractive in face, figure, or personality. She had red hair and a temper to match, and she was stubborn and set in her ways.

Lizzie belonged to the Central Congregational Church on The Hill and was unquestionably one of its most active members. She served in many capacities, on several committees, and on a number of church organizations. Lizzie was only 20 when she was named to the board of the Fall River Hospital, a significant honor for one so young. She became the head of the Fruit and Flower Mission, members of which were counterparts of the "candy-stripers" of the modern era. They visited the sick, the poor, and the homeless with gifts of food, books, and flowers. Her detractors would later say that her nomination to the board was in hopes of substantial donations from her father, but to say so was to deny the accepted knowledge that Andrew had never been known to give anything to charity.

By the time of the murders, Lizzie was 32. She had passed the age of youth and likelihood of marriage. She was known to have strong religious beliefs, and her inner shyness was masked by a positive presence and a composure that never seemed to be shaken by anything --- even the murders of her father and step-mother.

As Lizzie later explained to the police, she had spent a restless night, still bothered by the stomach troubles experienced by the rest of the household. She had felt better in the morning, well enough to think of taking some air by walking downtown to one of her favorite stores, Sargent's, to choose some material for a dress or two. She had dressed for the outing, she said, in a dress of blue cambric (a lightweight linen material) with a navy blue diamond figure printed on it. She had gone downstairs at about 9:30 and had taken only a cookie or two with coffee for breakfast. She had chatted with Mrs. Borden about inconsequential things and thought of ironing a few handkerchiefs, which she had rinsed out the day before.

Mrs. Borden had told her that she had received a note from a sick friend and was going out for a while to visit her. She would be picking up groceries for the evening meal – was there anything that Lizzie wanted? Lizzie told her that there was nothing that she particularly craved.

Father had come back from his trip to the post office and had brought no mail. She had told him of Mrs. Borden's going out and had set up an ironing board and put her irons on to heat. She admitted that she had not heard anyone deliver the note to Mrs. Borden. It had apparently come before she had risen or had arrived after she had busied herself in the kitchen. She had not heard anyone, nor had she actually seen the note.

While waiting for her irons to heat up, she had walked out into the backyard, hoping that it was cooler than the kitchen. With no purpose in mind, she had idly picked up a couple of pears from under the backyard tree, thinking that perhaps the fruit would settle her stomach.

While standing in the shade, she remembered that she planned to go to a church outing to Marion on Buzzards Bay on Monday morning. The idea of an hour or two fishing on the banks of the stream reminded her that the last time she was at the farm, her fishing lines had no sinkers, and that perhaps she should carry along some small pieces of iron or lead so she could fashion some new ones. She had gone into the barn and searched for some scraps of metal that she remembered had been there in a small box. She had found nothing downstairs, so she had gone up into the loft. She later stated that she was surprised to find it cooler in the loft, and she had idly searched for the lead pieces, eaten one of the pears, gazed out the window, and stayed, altogether, about 30 minutes, or perhaps it was 15 minutes, or somewhere in between.

As she was leaving the barn, she heard what sounded like a groan, she said, and had hurried to the backdoor. Finding it unlocked, she first rushed into the kitchen, and then to the doorway of the sitting room. She opened the door and stepped back in horrified shock. Her father was lying on the couch, his face covered with blood. She did not know if he was dead, nor did she examine the gashes on his head or see his eye, gouged out, dangling on his cheek, but she knew that his condition was serious.

"Maggie, come down!" Lizzie shouted from the bottom of the back stairs and up in her attic room, Bridget's eyes fluttered open. She had drifted off into a restless

The death scene of Andrew Borden

sleep, but the urgency of Lizzie's cries startled her awake. Bridget replied in a flustered voice, asking what was wrong.

"Come down quick!" Lizzie wailed, "Father's dead! Somebody's come in and killed him!"

As Bridget hurried from the staircase, she found Lizzie standing at the back door. Her face was pale and taut. She stopped the young maid from going into the sitting room and ordered her to go and fetch a doctor. Dr. Seabury A. Bowen, a family friend, lived across the street from the Bordens' and Bridget ran directly to the house. The doctor was out, but Bridget told Mrs. Bowen that Mr. Borden had been killed. The doctor's wife ran directly back to the house with Bridget. Mrs. Bowen asked Lizzie where she had been when the murder occurred, and she said she was out in the yard, heard a groan, and came inside. This was the first version she would give of her movements that morning – various others would follow.

Bridget was then sent to find a friend of the Borden sisters, Alice Russell, who lived a few blocks away. "Go and get her," Lizzie cried out, "I can't be alone in the house."

Alice Russell lived near the Borden home and she had long been a dear friend to both Lizzie and her sister, Emma. In fact, Lizzie had visited Alice just the night before and, for whatever reason, had chosen to pour her heart out to her about her worries and concerns with the family. It may have been a cry for help; a seeking of comfort for a troubled soul; it may have been anticipation of the events coming the next day that caused her to seek out Alice. We will never know. It was almost as strange as Abby's visit to Dr. Bowen the same day, professing worry that the family was being poisoned.

Lizzie told Alice that *someone* was planning to do *something*, with neither "someone" or "something" defined. That it would be done to the Bordens was implied, but it was no mere suggestion – it was going to happen, without a doubt. Because of the danger she sensed, Lizzie had written to friends near where Emma was vacationing and said that she had decided to join them as soon as she could. The earliest that she could leave town, however, would be Monday (this was Wednesday evening) because of a church committee meeting that was scheduled for Sunday afternoon. Alice saw the tension in Lizzie and encouraged her to leave Fall River. Lizzie admitted that she was under great stress. She went on to describe how the household were sick to the point that Lizzie believed they had all been poisoned. She echoed the same words that Abby had told Dr. Bowen that morning.

Lizzie continued to reveal to Alice more than was ever considered later at her trial. She stated that her father had an enemy, someone who caused him a lot of trouble, and was a danger to him. The prosecution later used these words to suggest that she was pointing the finger at herself, but this was obviously not the case. Lizzie truly seemed to believe that her father was in trouble.

She told Alice of an unknown man who had been on the property lately and some earlier break-ins that had occurred and about some pigeons that had been stolen. She also told her of a daylight burglary that had occurred during John Morse's last visit to Fall River. This was no mere break-in either. The Borden house was unusually secure for the era. Doors were triple-locked; basement windows had heavy screens; all other windows were well out of reach from the ground. The yard was also secure, including a rear fence that was approximately six feet high with barbed wire at the top and bottom. Neighboring houses were close on each side. The house was seldom unattended. Abby was almost always at home except for short shopping trips and supper with her sister every few months.

At the time the burglary took place, Abby was with Andrew on a visit to a Borden farm property on the other side of the Taunton River – a very rare event. However, the house was not empty since Emma and Bridget were both home. In spite of this – and in spite of the locked, double-locked, and triple-locked doors – the burglar made off with Abby's jewelry and gold watch, cash in bills and gold, and a booklet of street railway tickets. These items were taken from the elder Bordens' upstairs rooms, and nothing was reported touched in any other part of the house. Neither Emma nor Bridget heard, saw, or knew anything. John Morse testified that he had been in Fall River that day, but was not at the house. No one knows where Lizzie was, although many have assumed that she was at home. Her knowledge of the burglary was never questioned by the police.

Andrew reported the crime to the police, who dutifully investigated it. Lizzie volunteered that she had found the cellar door unbolted and wide open, and she gave the police a common nail that she had found in the lock. Within a few weeks, Andrew asked the police to drop the whole thing, suggesting that further investigation would be pointless.

From that day until the day of their deaths, Andrew and Abby's upstairs rooms were always locked during the daylight hours, but the key was left in plain sight on the mantle in the sitting room. Andrew never explained why he did this, but it can be surmised that he knew the theft had been carried out by someone he knew – likely in the same household – and this was his silent way of stating that he knew it.

For whatever reason, from that day on, not only was their bedroom door at the top of the rear stairs kept locked, the sole connecting door between their bedroom and Lizzie's was locked on each side and a chest of drawers was placed in front of it on their side.

After she unburdened herself to Alice, Lizzie gathered her things to return home. Her parting words to her friend were later called prophetic. She vowed that she would sleep with one eye open because she feared that someone would burn the house down around them. As she left, she reiterated, "I am afraid that somebody will do something; I don't know but what someone will do something."

Over the years, Lizzie's dire words have been largely dismissed. Most have come to believe that she was covering for herself in advance of the crime and the "someone" she allegedly feared was obviously Lizzie herself. But what if those doubters are wrong? What if Lizzie knew exactly who this "someone" was?

As the frantic scene in the Borden house spilled out of the back door, Mrs. Adelaide Churchill, a prim widow who lived next door, was looking out her kitchen window. She saw Lizzie in her agitated state and opened the window to call out and ask if anything was wrong. Lizzie responded by saying, "Oh, Mrs. Churchill, do come over! Someone has killed Father!"

Mrs. Churchill responded at once and, seeing that no one had called for medical help, went in search of a doctor. On the way, she passed John Cunningham, a news dealer, and asked him to please, quickly, run to the livery stable down the street and call the police. When Mrs. Churchill arrived at the Borden house, Lizzie told her that her father had been killed in the sitting room. The widow asked her where she had been when he was murdered and Lizzie stated that she had been in the barn, getting a piece of iron. She didn't know where Abby Borden was, offering that she had gone out to visit a sick friend. But she added, "But I don't know but that she is killed too, for I thought I heard her come in... Father must have an enemy, for we have all been sick, and we think the milk has been poisoned."

A call reached the Fall River police station at 11:15 a.m., but as things would happen, that day marked the annual picnic of the Fall River Police Department and most of them were off enjoying an outing at Rocky Point. Shorthanded, they would eventually respond with what numbers could be mustered. They were soon outnumbered by friends, neighbors, and curiosity-seekers. The cramped little house was teeming with activity, and a crowd of hundreds milled out on the street outside.

Adelaide Churchill and Alice Russell hovered over the ashen-faced Lizzie, alternately wiping her forehead with a wet cloth and cooling her with a straw fan. They gathered in the kitchen, out of the way of the policemen who shuffled together in the entryway, dining room, and the sitting room.

Patrolman George Allen, new on the force, had been the first officer on the scene. One look at the mangled corpse, and the fact that it had been one of the town's most prominent men, was all he had to know to realize that he needed help. He had quickly checked the front door to make sure that it was locked, hailed a friend from the crowd, Charles Sawyer, stationed him at the side door to secure the house, and ran off toward headquarters to report what he had found at the scene.

By this time, Dr. Bowen had arrived. As Officer Allen was rushing off, Lizzie, pale and apparently close to fainting, motioned him to the sitting room. "Father has been killed."

It took the doctor only a moment to confirm it. Andrew had been attacked with a sharp object, probably an ax, and so much damage had been done to his head and face that Bowen, a close friend, couldn't positively identify him at first. Borden's head was turned slightly to the right and 11 blows had gashed his face. One eye had been cut in half, and his nose had been severed. The majority of the blows had been struck within the area that extended from the eyes and nose to the ears. Blood was still seeping from the wounds and had been splashed onto the wall above the sofa, the floor, and on a picture hanging on the wall. It looked as though Borden had been attacked from above and behind as he slept.

Dr. Seabury Bowen

He returned to Lizzie. "Have you seen anybody around the place?" he asked her.

"No. No one."

"Where have you been? Where were you?"

"I was in the barn looking for some iron," Lizzie replied, and then gasped. "Oh, Doctor, I am faint!"

Alice and Mrs. Churchill helped her out of the chair in the stifling kitchen and supported her as they walked into the dining room. As Dr. Bowen covered the body of Andrew Borden with a sheet, Lizzie turned and asked if he would send a telegram to Emma, who was visiting in Fairhaven, and ask her to return home.

As they gathered in the dining room, Bridget suggested that perhaps Mrs. Borden was at the Whitehead home, the house of Abby's half-sister. Lizzie said she didn't think so, adding that it was possible Abby had come back; that she had heard a noise.

She ordered Bridget to go upstairs and check, but the maid refused to go alone. Mrs. Churchill offered to go with her. They went up the staircase together, but Mrs. Churchill was the first to see Abby lying on the floor of the guestroom. She had fallen in a pool of blood and Mrs. Churchill later said that she had been so savagely attacked that she only "looked like the form of a person."

Mrs. Churchill quickly returned to the dining room, her face the color of tepid milk.

"Is there another?" Alice Russell asked her.

"Yes. She is up there."

Officer Allen returned with reinforcements, Officers Mullaly, Doherty, and Wixon. Dr. Bowen had left and soon returned, the telegram to Emma having been

Death scene of Abby Borden

sent. When the officers came back to the house and learned that another body had been discovered, Officers Harrington and Medley and Assistant City Marshal John Fleet were dispatched to Second Street.

During the half hour or so that no authorities were on the scene, a county medical examiner named William A. Dolan passed by the house by chance. He looked in, and was pressed into service by Dr. Bowen. Dolan examined the bodies and after hearing that the family had been sick and that the milk was suspected, he took samples of it. Later that afternoon, he had the bodies photographed and then removed the stomachs and sent them, along with the milk, to the Harvard Medical School for analysis.

Abby Borden's body lay in the guest room at the top of the stairs, wedged between the freshly made bed and a small dresser. Like Andrew, her head had been savagely bashed in. A hairpiece, popularly used to enhance the coiffure or, in Abby's case, to cover advancing baldness, was found nearby on the floor. Dr. Bowen touched the back of her neck to test her body temperature and, likely by instinct, to feel for a pulse. She was quite dead. A cursory glance from the doctor seemed to show that Abby had been struck more than a dozen times, from the back. The autopsy later revealed that there had been 19 blows to her head, probably from the same hatchet that had killed Andrew. The blood on Abby's body was dark and congealed, leading him to believe that she had been killed before her husband.

The door to the guest room was discreetly closed. The investigation into Mrs. Borden's death would have to wait; priority went to the murder of the man of the house.

Office Mullaly had checked Andrew's body and found a silver watch and chain, a wallet containing $85, and 65 cents in loose change. He noted that a gold ring was on the dead man's little finger. If this had been a murder for money, the killer had failed.

He knocked quietly on the dining room door and, apologizing, asked Lizzie if there were either hatchets or axes in the house. Without hesitating, she told him there were both and directed "Maggie" to show him where they were in the basement. Bridget took him down to the cellar and pointed out two axes, as well as a claw-headed shingle hatchet. One of the axes was obviously bloodstained, and hairs still stuck to the blade. The hatchet was spotted with red, and Mullaly was certain that he had discovered the murder weapon. But Maggie had more to show him. From a shelf that was mounted on the chimney base, she took down a box and removed another hatchet from it. The officer now had more possible murder weapons than he knew what to do with.

Upstairs, Lizzie had retired to her room, where Alice and her friend, Reverend A. Buck, attempted to console her. She had changed out of the dress that she had been wearing and put on a pink-and-white striped wrapper with a gathered blouse. Dr. Bowen, still concerned that she might collapse from the excitement, sat with her for a few moments and then gave her a dose of a nerve sedative.

Assistant Marshal Fleet tapped on the door and Alice let him into the room. He asked Lizzie what time her father had returned home, and what happened after that. Lizzie told him of Andrew trying to get into the locked door, how he had looked pale and feeble, how she "assisted him in lying down," and that she had gone about the ironing of her handkerchiefs. When asked, she admitted that she did not know how long she was in the barn. It had been 30 minutes, or 15 or 20, she was not sure. She explained that she had been looking for iron with which to make fishing sinkers.

"Do you know anyone who might have killed your father and mother?"

Lizzie snapped at him. "She is not my mother, sir. She is my stepmother. My mother died when I was a child."

It was a true statement, simple and to the point, but it was a statement that would greatly affect the investigation that was to come, the trial, and the rest of her life.

2. "A SHOCKING CRIME"

The first public outcry of "murder!" in the Borden case had been given on August 4, at 11:15 a.m. By 2:15 that afternoon, a special edition of the *Fall River Daily Herald* was already on the streets. It was amazingly swift for a small town newspaper and it was undoubtedly prepared in a fury of activity. It contained a number of errors that would later be corrected, along with extensive and mistaken speculation as to what had exactly taken place, but it certainly captured the horror and essence of the crime. The issue sold out in a matter of minutes.

The initial headline promised details of a "shocking crime," and noted that the Bordens had been "hacked to pieces at their home" and had lost their lives "at the hands of a drunken farm hand." The police, the newspaper promised, were searching actively for the "fiendish murderer."

The story explained the where and how of the crime and noted that the Bordens were "hacked almost beyond recognition." It then offered a slightly off-kilter version of the events that surrounded the discovery of Andrew's body and the involvement of Adelaide Churchill. The article then went on to offer a *Daily Herald* reporter's account of what he saw when he entered the Borden house and walked into the parlor:

A terrible sight met his view. On the lounge in the cozy sitting room on the first floor of the building lay Andrew J. Borden, dead. His face presented a sickening sight. Over the left temple, a wound six by four had been made as if the head had been pounded with the dull edge of an axe. The left eye had been dug out and a cut extended the length of the nose. The face was hacked to pieces and the blood covered the man's shirt and soaked into his clothing. Everything about the room was in order and there were no signs of a scuffle of any kind.

The article then went on to reveal the state of Abby Borden's body in the upstairs guest room:

Upstairs in a neat chamber in the northwest corner of the house, another terrible sight met the view. On the floor between the bed and the dressing case, lay Mrs. Borden, stretched full length, one arm extended and her face resting upon it. Over the left temple the skull was fractured and no less than seven wounds were found about the head. She had died evidently where she had been struck, for her life blood formed a ghastly clot on the carpet.

Of course, the newspaper failed to mention how a reporter had gotten access to what should have been a closed crime scene, but obviously, things were done quite differently in those days.

The article goes on to mention the involvement of Dr. Bowen in the case, as well as the arrival of the police, and Lizzie's reaction, remarking that she was "so overcome by the awful circumstances that she could not be seen, and kind friends led her away and cared for her."

The squad of police that arrived conducted a careful search of the property for any trace of the killer. No weapon was found, the newspaper stated, and there was nothing about the house to indicate who the assailant might have been. There was a clue obtained, however. A Portuguese man whose name no one around the house seemed to know, had been employed at Mr. Borden's Swansea farm. He had a talk with his employer that morning about money that was due for his wages. Mr. Borden said that he had no money on him at the time, and to call on him later. Mr. Borden then went downtown, was shaved at Peter Leduc's barber shop at 9:30, and then stopped at the Union Bank, where he was the president. While there, he transacted some business and talked with Mr. Hart, the treasurer. Apparently, he had gone straight home after that. The newspaper then recounted what the police and reporters initially believed happened in the Borden house that morning:

He took off his coat and composed himself comfortably on the lounge to sleep. It is presumed, from the easy attitude in which his body lay, that he was asleep when the deadly blow was struck. It was thought that Mrs. Borden was in the room at the time but was so overcome by the assault that she had no strength to make an outcry. In her bewilderment, she rushed upstairs and went into her room. She must have been followed upstairs by the murderer, and as she was retreating into the furthest corner of the room, she was felled by the deadly axe. Blow after blow must have rained upon her head as she lay unconscious on the floor.

Hurriedly the murderer slipped down the stairs and rushed into the street, leaving the screen door wide open after him in his sudden flight. No sign of blood could be found on the carpet or on the stairs, not could any weapon be discovered anywhere. Nobody can be found who saw the murderer depart, and it is safe to conclude that he carried so small a weapon that it could be concealed in his clothing. Had he carried a gory axe in his hand, somebody's attention would have been attracted to it.

The article continued, detailing Lizzie's response to the "heavy fall and subdued groaning" in the house, even though Lizzie only told the police of the groan that she heard. The report stated that she rushed to the stairs and called for Bridget, who was washing windows on the third floor. At the time, Bridget was actually lying down in her room. It mentioned that Lizzie was in the barn when the attacks took place and adds that the killer worked so quietly that neither she nor Bridget heard anything out of the ordinary. After that, it continued with a somewhat inaccurate version of the events that followed, as well as more speculation:

...She found her father in the sitting room with a gash in the side of his head. He appeared at the time as though he had been hit while in a sitting posture. Giving the alarm, she rushed upstairs to find her mother, only to be more horrified to find that person laying between the dressing case and the bed, sweltering in a pool of blood. It appeared as though Mrs. Borden had seen the man enter, and the man, knowing that his dastardly crime would be discovered, had followed her upstairs and finished his fiendish work. It is a well-known fact that Mrs. Borden always left the room when her husband was talking business with anyone. A person knowing this fact could easily spring upon his victim without giving her the chance to make an outcry. Miss Borden had seen no one enter or leave the place. The man who had charge of her father's farm was held in the highest respect by Mr. Borden. His name was Alfred Johnson, and he trusted his employer so much that he left his bank book at Mr. Borden's house for safe keeping. The young lady had not the slightest suspicion of him being connected with the crime. As far as the Portuguese suspected of the crime was concerned, she knew nothing of him, as he might have been a man who was employed by the day in the busy season. What his motive could have been is hard to tell, as Mr. Borden had always been kind to his help.

The newspaper then went on to detail some of the investigations that were launched in the wake of the murders, including the search for the "Portuguese" at the farm in Swansea. When they arrived there, they found no trace of the man, but they did speak with a Charles Gifford, who assured them that no such laborer existed, or at least had worked on the farm. As far as he knew, the only man of Portuguese descent connected to the place was Alfred Johnson, Andrew's trusted foreman, who had been confined to his bed with an illness for several days. He admitted that a Portuguese day laborer might have recently worked on the farm, but he doubted it.

While at the farm, the police also looked into the possibility that the milk had been poisoned. Lizzie had already told them that everyone in the house had been sick with a stomach ailment that week. She feared that an enemy of her father's might have tried to poison them. A can of milk was sent to the Borden house from the Swansea farm every morning, and the can was left on the porch until Bridget retrieved it. There was ample opportunity for anyone with "foul designs" to tamper with the milk.

The article also revealed that a search of the barn that was located on the back of the Bordens' Second Street property found the outline of a man pressed down in the hay of the loft, as though a person had slept there for the night. The imprint had apparently been made by a man who was somewhat shorter than Mr. Borden, giving rise to the suspicion that the killer might have been hanging about the property for some time, hoping for an opportunity to commit murder. Could it have been the mysterious "Portuguese" the authorities were looking for? The police believed so. Detectives were dispatched to track down the foreigner. Others were sent to interview anyone who had seen anyone on the street that morning who did not "fit in." Rumors were plentiful among the curiosity-seekers, and detectives were assigned to check out every rumor.

The foreigner in question was quickly found. A "sturdy Portuguese" named Antonio Auriel was arrested in a saloon on Columbia Street, and was brought to the station for questioning. The frightened man protested his innocence and, fortunately for him, he had an alibi and an upstanding witness. He was released, but not without someone following him for the next few days.

The special edition of the newspaper brought even more people to Second Street. By midafternoon, hundreds had gathered. Although the water wagons had sprinkled all of the dry downtown streets to keep down the dust, it was another record hot day, and their efforts had done little good.

And the efforts of the men who watered the streets were not the only ones whose efforts were in vain that day. As the curious and the morbid milled outside the Borden house, gawking and speculating, the detectives inside of the house were finding little of substance. The unsatisfactory clues they compiled were developing into a murky picture of what had taken place that morning. No one seemed to know anything, and what they believed they knew, they found impossible to prove. Even so, the officials among them were convinced that the case would be solved.

None of the confident officers could have imagined then that the mystery would remain unsolved nearly 125 years later.

3. MYSTERIES, RUMORS & SPECULATION

There is no way to adequately explain the effect that the Borden murders had on the small town of Fall River in 1892. The newspapers certainly stirred up the passions of the residents, but it was not just the numerous stories that appeared in them. Talk on the streets, in the taverns, in the local shops and stores, and behind the closed doors of private homes swirled with the latest developments. The police gathered a number of clues, all of which led nowhere. A boy reported seeing a man jump over the back fence of the Borden property, and while a man was found matching the boy's description, he had an unbreakable alibi. A bloody hatchet was found on the Sylvia Farm in South Somerset, but the blood on the blade proved to be that of a chicken.

One of the many unexplainable things in the case (both then and now) was the shadowy role played by Lizzie's uncle, John Vinnicum Morse. His behavior throughout the dark events that plagued the family can only be described as very strange.

Morse's sister, Sarah, had married Andrew Borden 47 years earlier, when Borden was still young and struggling. Together, they had Emma, Lizzie, and little Alice, who had not survived. John and Andrew had started a furniture business together, but weren't very successful. At age 25, John had gone out west to seek his fortune. He settled for a time in Hastings Mill, Iowa, where he did very well in the horse trading business. He eventually returned to Massachusetts and established his home and business in South Yarmouth, near New Bedford. In August 1892, he came to spend a few days with the Bordens, but strangely, he had not brought a single piece of luggage, not even a comb, shirt, or toothbrush. He was welcomed, nonetheless, as he always was. Andrew was his closest friend and he often sought his advice on business matters.

Morse arrived, unannounced, at dinner time on August 3. Andrew was happy to see him and ordered another plate to be set for the meal. Morse had eaten and they had talked, he later told the police. He had then gone out on business, returning that night at 8:30. There had been more talk until 10:00, when all had gone to bed.

John Vinnicum Morse

He was up early the next day and departed about 9:00 a.m. with the promise that he would be back for the noon meal. He had been about town visiting his niece and buying a pair of oxen. Interestingly, he could trace his movements minute by minute and street by street, including the number of the trolley that he had ridden and the number on the cap of the conductor who had been on board. He had carefully built what was a detailed and unbreakable alibi. Whether or not that was what he was trying to do remains unknown.

When he returned at 12:00, he had apparently failed to notice the several hundred people milling about in front of the Borden house. He walked past the side door, where Officer Allen's large friend, Charles Sawyer, had been stationed. He spoke to no one to ask about the excitement. Instead, he pushed his way through the crowd and made his way into the backyard, where he absently picked up several pears and nonchalantly leaned against a corner of the barn. He showed no curiosity as to why Sawyer was guarding the door or why policemen were running back and forth frantically in and out of the house.

When he was finished with the pears (he later testified it was just one pear, but an officer who had watched him stated that it was three), he finally wandered over, identified himself at the door, and went into the house.

He told a reporter, "I opened the sitting room door and found a number of people, including doctors. I entered, but only glanced at the body. No, I did not look closely enough to be able to describe it. Then I went upstairs and took a similar hasty view of the dead woman. I recall very little of what took place."

He was in the house for a total of three minutes, and then left.

Was he in shock? Was he so stunned that he simply couldn't register what had taken place? Or did he care so little for this "closest friend" and the "dead woman" that he simply didn't care? Or, worse yet, was John Morse somehow involved in what had occurred? Was he so depraved that he was unmoved by the sight of the butchered corpses? Those questions, like so many others in the case, have never been answered.

Dr. William Dolan

Dr. William Dolan, who worked extensively with the police as the county medical examiner, was quite familiar with dead bodies, and he did not join in the speculation that was going on about how Andrew and Abby had met their deaths. Though the science of forensic medicine was not an advanced one in 1892, Dolan could tell by the dark, thick blood of Abby's wounds and the fresh, red flow from Andrew's that Abby had been dead for an hour or so before Andrew was killed.

If Andrew had died at 11:00, Abby had died at 9:30 or 10:00. It was a crucial revelation for it occurred during a span of time when nothing had been seen or heard. This caused Dr. Dolan to remember the mysterious note that Abby was supposed to have received. He asked Lizzie where it might be; it was important. But she had no idea. They had all searched for it in Abby's handbag and her sewing box. Alice suggested that perhaps she had tossed it into the fire.

Officer Harrington would testify that he had seen Dr. Bowen in the kitchen, reading a small piece of paper. When asked what it was, his reply had been, "Oh, it is nothing. Something about my daughter going somewhere." He had casually tossed it into the stove.

Was it important? Could it even have been the note that Abby allegedly received about a sick friend? Or was it something else? What secrets did Dr. Bowen have to hide? Once again, those questions have also gone unanswered.

There were a number of reports of unknown people around the Borden house on the day of the murder. Some even claimed to hear mysterious sounds on the night of August 3. Later, during Lizzie's trial, the first witness for the defense was Martha Chagnon, daughter of Dr. Chagnon, the Bordens' neighbor diagonally northeast behind them. As she also stated at the preliminary hearing, Martha testified that at about 11:00 p.m. on the night before the murders, she and her stepmother were disturbed by the sound of pounding on wood or on a fence. The noise came from the direction of the Borden fence and continued for four or five minutes. Her stepmother, Marienne Chagnon, was the second witness and repeated what Martha had said. In cross-examination, the prosecution muddled this testimony, forcing the two women to admit that they did not investigate at the time and that the noise could have come from some other source.

Oddly, the *Fall River Herald*, on August 8, 1892, had reported that "Mrs. Chagnon and her daughter, Martha, say that Wednesday night around 12 o'clock they distinctly saw a man jump over the fence into the Borden yard and subsequently heard a slight noise in the barn."

Which was it? Was the newspaper confused, or spicing things up for dramatic purposes? Or had their testimony changed? Or did they actually hear someone pounding on the Bordens' back fence? It's possible we will never know because even though the defense opened with their testimony, they failed to pursue it and never referred to it again. The prosecution spent considerable time neutralizing the testimony, but they, too, never referred to it again.

More reports came in of strangers seen on the day of the murders. One of the better known sightings came from Dr. Benjamin Handy and it was reported in the August 10 *Daily Globe:*

In connection with the great mystery a report is circulated upon which more or less importance may be attached. Dr. Handy says that while driving past the Borden house at about 10:30 or 10:40 on the day of the murder he noticed a man walking slowly by the house.

In his profession the doctor meets and passes many people, but he says that his attention as never attracted to a person on the street before as it was to this man. So much so was he struck by his appearance that he turned about in his carriage to obtain a second look at him.

He described him as being a man of about five feet four inches in height, of medium weight, and wearing a dark mustache. His face was deadly white but was round and full. The young man was apparently 24 years of age. This description tallies with that of a man whom Officer Hyde saw in the vicinity on the morning of the murder.

His description also answers to that of the man who is reported to have jumped on a wood team at Flint Village and asked to be conveyed to Westport. This man has had every opportunity to be miles away, but it is quite possible that if this same fellow was found something interesting would follow.

Another person seen around the Borden house on the morning of the murder was reported the next day, August 11, in the *Daily Herald:*

Another woman dropped into the case Wednesday afternoon, but she did not stay long. A lad who drives for Wilkinson, ice cream man, said he saw a woman come out of the Borden yard about 10:30 o'clock Thursday. Officers Harrington and Doherty went to work to find this woman, and they succeeded in discovering that Ellan Eagan was passing that way Thursday morning when she was seized with a sudden illness. She went into the first yard she came to, but it was Dr. Kelly's yard, which is next to the Borden house, and the boy was mistaken.

The "lad" who worked for Wilkinson was a Russian immigrant named Hyman Lubinsky. His initial reports were rejected by both the defense and the police for two reasons: his report of the time of the sighting was not consistent with the crime, and Ellan Eagan's innocent presence on the scene was a possible explanation for the woman he did see. The defense worked diligently on the testimony. Later, Lubinsky was promoted to the position of star witness to testify that he had seen Lizzie Borden outside her house at the time Andrew was murdered.

Dr. Handy was considered an important witness at the trial and told of the man he saw. Ellan Eagen, who was only mentioned by the defense in the summation of the trial, was never actually called to the stand even though, as the reader will see, her encounter is an important part of the story. She was the woman that the *Herald* said was seen by Herman Lubinsky. She did contact the police, but since she was so uneasy at giving her story to the authorities and since the officials got what they needed from Ellan to help build the case they had already developed against Lizzie, she was never given the opportunity to tell her whole story.

On the morning of the murders, Ellan passed by the Borden house on her way to Sargent's, where the store was having a sale on dress material. On the way, she had noticed Bridget washing the windows of the house, marveling that she was working outside on such a hot morning. After purchasing a bolt of cloth that would make two dresses (Mr. Sargent had sold it to her for the seven cents a yard, rather than the eight cents it was marked) and she started her walk back home along Second Street. As she started up the street, she realized it was hotter than she remembered. Although too hot to hurry, Ellan did walk a little quicker, for she felt rather sick.

As she neared the Borden house, she wondered if the silly maid was still washing the windows in the heat. No, Bridget was not in sight, but Ellan saw a man in the yard, just standing there. She tried to do the ladylike thing and avert her eyes, but she couldn't help staring at him. Something about him just seemed wrong. He was about hallway between the gate and the front stoop, and he was facing in her direction. He turned as if to go back in the direction of the house and so she could only see his left side and his back. His clothes were coarse and dirty, but he was wearing an overcoat – on one of the hottest days of the year. At first, Ellan thought his coat was burlap, then she realized he had a burlap bag over his shoulder and partially tucked under his arm. The overcoat was a long, duster-like covering. She looked at him for a long, uncomfortable moment and then he met her gaze. Ellan was shocked and scared and when the man took a step toward her, she ran.

As she hurried away, she sensed that something else was wrong – it was his smell. It was an odor like nothing she had ever experienced before. It was not sour, not sweet, not a manure smell, or sweat. It was thick and repulsive and impossible to describe. Her fright, the heat, the smell, they combine to make her sick. Gasping and sobbing, she sank to the ground. When her wits returned, she was under the shade of an elm tree on the cool, comforting grass. She realized that she had fainted, but didn't know how long she had been there.

Suddenly, she remembered what had frightened her and she looked all around. There was no one there. The man – the man she should refer to as the "devil" for the rest of her life – was gone. She felt a little foolish then. She had no idea why she had behaved in the way that she did. She looked around again and seeing nothing, she gathered her packages together, looked up and down the street one last time, and started home with a firm, determined stride. She had a dinner to prepare and ironing to do.

She heard the clock at City Hall chime eleven times. I'm very late, she thought.

The strange man that she had seen did not completely leave Ellan's mind. She remained troubled during the week that followed as the newspapers filled with stories about the murders – murders that must have occurred about the time that she had passed the house. Who was the strange man that she had seen, with the horrible odor that she was unable to describe? Unsure of what she had seen and how she could tell the police about a man that she never got a clear look at, Ellan decided that she would tell the police that she had seen Bridget outside, as the maid claimed, and mention that there had been a man in the yard. When the police caught him, as the initial newspaper reports said they would, Ellan would ask to look at him and see if he was the right one. It was a solid plan – but one that she never followed up on. When the arrest warrant was issued for Lizzie and not for the mysterious man she had seen, Ellan did not return to the police.

Whoever the man was, he vanished into history – or did he?

Throughout that day and the next, information poured into police headquarters from "volunteers" who genuinely wanted to help and from the inevitable amateur detectives and morbid attention-seekers. The police force, now back from the annual clambake at Rocky Point, were fully committed to the investigation.

On August 5, the *Daily Herald* updated its readers on the facts, rumors, and speculations in the case, noting that "further investigation unto the circumstances of the Borden murder shroud it with an impenetrable mystery. Nothing that has ever occurred in Fall River or vicinity has created such intense excitement."

With nothing more than rumors and theories to build a story from, the newspaper used all of the gossip that was spreading through town to simply ask questions and report the stories that were spreading through the town. Since almost the very moment the crime had been reported, Second Street had been crowded with curious people – and all of them were talking. The newspaper managed to fan the flames of speculation and question how such a bloody deed could be perpetrated in broad daylight, in a house on one of the busiest streets in town. No one had been seen entering the house, inside of it, or fleeing the place with bloodstains on his clothing. It was a perplexing mystery, but the newspaper was determined to list the suspects – or at least the characters in the strange story – because they were the people being talked about in the streets of Fall River.

John Morse, who had offered a reward of $5,000 for information leading to the killer, was described by the newspaper as "well known in the city where he was born and lived for many years." It made mention of his successful horse business and noted that while nothing definite was known about his affairs of the past week, he had told friends that he had brought a train of horses with him from Iowa to sell and that they were being kept in Fairhaven. When the police spoke with the niece that he had visited on the day of the murder, Mrs. Emery, she said that she had several callers during the day, and one of them was John Morse. He had left her home around 11:30 that morning, at least a half hour after Andrew Borden had been killed.

Emma Borden had returned home from Fairhaven on Thursday evening, summoned back to town by news of the murders. The details of the crime had not been told to her, and she was said to have been overcome by the recital of the events.

The newspaper article also returned to the question of the mysterious letter that Abby Borden was believed to have received on the morning she was killed. The letter, the newspaper reported, "has since disappeared." The explanation that was given was that, after reading it, Abby tore up the note and threw the pieces in the fire. Bits of charred paper were found in the grate, but not enough to give any idea about the nature of the note – or even if it was the note in question at all. No one in the house could offer any explanation as to where the note had come from. But, as the writer stressed, "since publicity has been given and considerable importance attached to it, it is considered probable that the writer will inform the family of the circumstances and thus remove suspicions." But, of course, that revelation would never occur. If there truly had been a letter, its contents were never revealed.

The newspaper story also stated, "Causes for the murder are arising so fast at the present time that it is nearly impossible to investigate them." One of the latest stories involved a tenant named Ryan, who occupied the upper floor of a house that was owned by Andrew Borden. He was so troublesome that he was asked to move, which resulted in a loud disagreement with Mr. Borden. Several people overheard him saying that he would like to see him dead. The police looked into the matter, but nothing came of it.

The owners of Griffith Bros., carpenters on Anawan Street, told a story that seemed important in the days after the murders. They were driving up Pleasant Street at about 11:00 on Thursday morning, when they saw a short, poorly dressed man walking rapidly along the sidewalk. Under his arm, with the handle down, was a large cleaver unlike anything they had ever seen before. It was large, like a tool that was used by fish dealers to lop the heads off the fresh catch, but it had a rusty appearance, like it had not been used for a long time. As the weapon with which the murders were committed had not been found, the carpenters surmised that the man might have been carrying the weapon that had killed the Bordens. The police looked into the sighting, but again, nothing came of it.

The final section of the story was the most telling in regards to what direction the police were going with their investigation. They had been following the case with leads from a dozen different directions and began to collect a chain of circumstantial evidence that was beginning to point in a troubling and startling direction. The newspaper reported:

The police have worked in other directions and have discovered things which bring them face to face with embarrassing difficulties. The poisoned milk theory had been investigated and an unsuccessful attempt was found to have been made to purchase a drug at a South Main Street store that may have something to do with a subsequent development in the case.

The police are guarding these facts and others of an important nature which they possess and a sensation is promised when the time comes to lay all the evidence before the public. The necessity of another search of the premises for the sake of bringing to light the weapon with which the deed was done is being urged. This will furnish an important link in the chain of evidence, and until it has been found it is doubtful whether any definite movement will be made.

A physician who took part in the autopsy told a reporter that if the dead body could speak they would disclose the fact that no mysterious stranger had been around to rob them of a life; that the person who committed the foul deed was at that moment not far from the scene and knew just where to lay hands on the weapon. When pressed for an explanation of these mysterious words, the doctor declined further to commit himself, saying that strong suspicions were not trustworthy as evidence.

And with these words, the first hints were revealed that the investigators in the case were looking for a killer that was far closer to home than any tenant with a grudge, or stranger who happened to enter the house with plans to rob the place.

These words were the first daring, almost scandalous suggestion that, absent any other motive, one had to look to the ones who benefited most from the deaths of Andrew and Abby Borden. This was an obvious pointing of the finger toward Emma and Lizzie. And since Emma had been in Fairhaven at the time of the murders, that left only the sister who had been at home.

The note that the police had "discovered things that bring them face to face with embarrassing difficulties" was another suggestion that something awkward had been discovered by the inquiry, but it was the unnamed physician's thoughts on what the corpses might say if they were able to speak that came very close, for the first time, to accusing Lizzie of murder.

4. SUSPICIONS OF MURDER

In the days that followed the Borden murders, crime did not come to a standstill in Fall River. Drunkenness, disorderly conduct, horse theft, assault, and other common offenses continued to occur while the police grappled with the complexities of the event that had occurred on Second Street.

After two days of almost nonstop duty, a major portion of the police force was exhausted, bewildered, and bickering among themselves. As reports began to pile up on Marshal Hilliard's desk at City Hall, he found them contradicting one another far too often. A separate stack contained sightings, confessions, letters of advice and abuse, threats, and telephone messages from the curious and the cranks. Albert E. Pillsbury, attorney general of Massachusetts, had been on the phone constantly pressuring Hilliard about any progress that had been made. On top of these copious piles were all of the booking slips, reports that had to be read and signed, schedules that needed to be made up, and all of the standard paperwork that was part of his daily routine. Needless to say, Hilliard was feeling overwhelmed.

On Saturday morning, he called a meeting at City Hall for all of the principal officers who had been working on the case. The meeting was to check on the progress of the case, and he was concerned to find that little had been made. Each of the investigators had his own theories about what had occurred, when it had occurred, and who might have been involved. The dozen men each reviewed their findings – and lack of findings – and recited the mysteries that remained unexplained. But none of them left out their speculations about the things that they could not prove.

Deputy Marshal Fleet, from the morning of the murder, believed that Lizzie had committed the murders. He seemed to come to this conclusion at the same time that she had told him that Mrs. Borden was her stepmother, not her mother. Officers Harrington and Medley shared his belief. The

City Marshal Hilliard

three men were close friends, so it was not surprising that they would agree with each other.

The second most popular suspect was John Morse. Was his unannounced arrival at the Borden house on the night before the murders just a coincidence? He had brought along no luggage, no toothbrush, no comb, no nightshirt, and yet, he planned to stay, he said, for a few days. His disappearance from the house just minutes before Abby was murdered, and his strange behavior when he returned just minutes after Andrew's body was found certainly seemed strange to most of the investigators.

The general public had their suspicions, too, even if the alibi that Morse offered was apparently airtight. On Friday night after the murders, Morse had slipped out of the house, unseen by the crowd gathered in front, evaded the police guarding the property, and made his way to the post office to, he said, mail a letter. There, he was recognized as he left, and an angry mob, estimated to be made up of between 400 and 2,000 people, surrounded him in the street. Whichever figure was correct, it was clearly a lynch mob, and Officer John Minnehan rescued him and got him back to the house and to safety.

The alibi of Emma Borden was checked, and then checked again. Two officers went to Fairhaven, where Emma had been staying for two weeks before the murders. Unquestionably, she had been there and she could not have sneaked back to Fall River on Thursday morning. She was eliminated from the suspect list.

Another favorite suspect was Bridget Sullivan – or more likely, Bridget and Lizzie together. It was hard to make a case for the poor maid alone, for there was no apparent motive for her to have killed anyone, other than that she had been paid off by Lizzie. That theory vanished when, later, after Bridget was arrested, her bail money was put up by the good Irishmen of the police department, and they secured her a job working for the department until the trial was set.

On Friday, the barn, house, and grounds were searched again and, this time, officers combed every inch of the place, leaving no stone unturned. A pile of scrap lumber next to the fence in the backyard was examined, board by board. In the barn, hay filled one corner of the ground floor and it was turned over, one forkful after another, into an opposite corner. The floor boards were ripped up. An abandoned well was cleaned out and searched. The ashes in the kitchen stove were sifted in search of a button, a hook, or traces of burned cloth. Five officers spent three hours opening and emptying drawers, cases, trunks, closets, and cupboards. Mattresses were overturned and dresses turned inside out and inspected carefully for bloodstains. They examined everything in the house, "right down to the slightest bump in the wallpaper," Dr. Dolan later wrote.

They found nothing incriminating in the house, in the barn, or anywhere on the grounds.

But there were far too many questions that remained unanswered. Many of them remain unanswered to this very day. The 30 minutes between the time that Andrew Borden returned at 10:45 a.m. and the cry of "murder!" that sounded at 11:15 is perhaps the most studied half-hour in American criminal history, and is also perhaps the most puzzling.

Prosecutor William H. Moody

Later, at Lizzie's trial, prosecuting attorney William H. Moody called attention to the haziness of those 30 minutes in his opening statement to the jury: "The time between Bridget's going upstairs and coming down again must be diminished on the one side by the time consumed by the washing of a window and a half in the sitting room and two windows in the dining room and the putting away of the cloth and water. On the other side, the half hour between eleven o'clock and half-past eleven must be diminished by the acts of Bridget and the acts of Mrs. Churchill and the acts of Cunningham."

But Moody had it wrong. The time to be examined was not the 45 minutes between 10:45 and 11:30, but rather the 30 minutes between 10:45 and 11:15, when the first telephone call was received at the Fall River police station. Moody had opened up the question as to what had actually taken place, but instead of following it by giving his version of the events, he opted to leave it up to the jury to decide what had happened. This made the time period even more mysterious. No one on the prosecution team ever mentioned that half-hour again. Someone should have, because a minute-by-minute examination shows that what was said to have taken place – or assumed to have taken place – could not have taken place at all!

There are two known points in which time can be marked in the sequence of events. Bridget testified at the inquest, and the preliminary hearing, before the grand jury, and at the trial that the City Hall bell had tolled 11:00 a.m. three minutes after she had reached her room to rest. She had verified the time by the clock next to her bed, which was later checked and found to be accurate. The police had received the call from John Cunningham, the news dealer, telling of a disturbance on Second Street at 11:15. In addition to the police record, he had noted the time himself, and his watch was also checked for accuracy.

During that 15-minute period, a number of known events took place; others can only be conjectured.

Using a stopwatch, historian David Kent calculated times and distances at the site, while following a scenario of known events. He allowed the minimum amount of time for the conversations and responses that took place, as well as the distances that were quickly covered. Each was assumed to have an immediate reaction, which was unlikely, but theoretically possible. He created a timeline, including minutes and seconds, for the events that occurred:

* Bridget goes to her room to lie down at 10:57 a.m.
* City Hall clock tolls the house at 11:00.
* Lizzie calls for Bridget to come down at 11:08.
* Bridget comes downstairs, is told of the murder, questions Lizzie, sent to find
Dr. Bowen.
* Bridget puts on her hat and shawl and crossed the street.
* Arrives at the Bowen house at 11:10.
* Mrs. Bowen comes to the door, is told of the murder, explains that the doctor is not home.
* Bridget crosses the street back to the Bordens'. It is now 11:11.
* Bridget tells Lizzie doctor is not home, has more conversation, is told to fetch
Miss Russell.
* Mrs. Churchill sees the commotion, looks out window, calls to Lizzie, is asked to come over.
* Mrs. Churchill leaves kitchen, goes out front door, over to the Bordens' side door. It is now 11:12.
* Lengthy conversation as to what happened and where Lizzie was, goes in sitting room, views body.
* At 11:14, Mrs. Churchill leaves to find another doctor, goes to Hall's stable at the end of the block.
* Meets John Cunningham, tells him of the murder, and asks him to call the police.
* Cunningham goes to find the nearest telephone.
*At 11:15, the call is made to police headquarters.

It is highly unlikely that any of these things could have taken place in less than the time that has been allotted for them. Accepting these times and actions as plausible, there is a maximum of only 11 minutes from the time that the City Hall bell tolled to the time when Lizzie called Bridget to come downstairs – a startlingly short amount of time.

During those 11 minutes – and that's starting at the exact moment that Bridget went to her room – Lizzie could not have gone to wherever the hatchet was hidden, returned to the sitting room, murdered Andrew, hidden the hatchet, inspected herself, combed her hair and washed away the inevitable bloodstains, gone back up to her room, changed clothes, hid the bloody garments somewhere, gone back downstairs, out to the yard, picked up pears, entered the barn, gone up to the loft, eaten the pears, come back down, returned to the house, and, finally, called out to Bridget. It is impossible, physically, to do all of those things in that short amount of time. But this time frame also leaves no time for a 30-minute, 20-minute, or even 15-minute trip to the barn – with or without allowing time for the murder and its aftermath. So, did this trip to the barn really happen at all?

Because the time the call was received at police headquarters cannot be disputed, there is only one possibility: Bridget did not tell the truth about hearing the City Hall clock and the series of events started earlier than 11:00 a.m. But why would Bridget lie? Since she testified that she checked her own clock when she heard the bell toll, her testimony could not have been a simple mistake; it would have had to have been an outright lie.

Who would gain by altering and constricting the time? Not Lizzie, for if it is left unexplained, it makes the trip to the barn and/or the murder of Andrew a virtual impossibility in such a short span. There simply would not be time for her to do either, let alone both.

The other 15-minute period mentioned by Moody, from 10:45 to 11:00, is equally vague and troubling.

Downtown, Andrew had stopped by a store, where carpenters Joseph Shortsleeves and James Mather were doing some repair work. Shortsleeves noted the time when Andrew left and started home – it was 10:45. It is reasonable to assume that it took him five minutes to walk three blocks to 92 Second Street, with another minute passing for Andrew to fumble with the locks and for Bridget to quit her work, walk to the front door, and let him inside. He took his bedroom key from a shelf and went upstairs. There is no explanation for why he did this, but it is a reasonable assumption that the trip up the backstairs, time for the purpose of his trip, and time to come back down to the sitting room, can be estimated at three minutes.

Lizzie came downstairs, asked about the mail, told him Abby had received a note and gone out, and walked with him to the sitting room, where he took off his coat, folded it on the couch, and began reading the paper. It was now 10:56 a.m.

Bridget finished washing two windows in the dining room and two in the sitting room, where Andrew was. She talked with Lizzie about Abby having gone out and the necessity of locking the doors. She wrung out her cloths, emptied her pail, talked with Lizzie about the likelihood of her going out, and retired to her room. According to the official timeline, all that was done in one minute, which is impossible.

The two quarter-hours have now over-lapped and made it questionable that Bridget could have gone to her room at 10:57. It is also difficult to believe that Andrew could have gone to sleep during all of the commotion of window washing and the conversation with Lizzie.

At some point, in someone's testimony, and in one account or another, the timeline had gone askew. Someone was mistaken, lying, or simply confused. There is no way that things could have happened as reported in the half-hour between 10:45 and 11:15. It was simply impossible. Thanks to this, it remains the most baffling 30 minutes in the annals of American crime.

In the midst of the police investigation, public interest in the crime was reaching a fever pitch. The specter of a crazed killer carrying an axe dripping blood and lurching through the streets of Fall River in search of more victims did not seem to be on the minds of the local citizens. This was a telling fact in itself. It was obvious to everyone that there was no madman on the loose – the crime had been committed by someone who knew the victims.

There was, it seemed, less interest in the brutality of the two murders than there was in the puzzle of the whole thing. How could the murders have been committed? What had been the motive? Could a killer have gotten into the house, killed the Bordens, and then escaped unseen? One daring reporter experimented on his own. He walked up Second Street and entered the Borden property, walked beside a grape arbor on the north side, behind the barn, across a fence to the property in the rear, across another fence, reentered the Borden property, and this time looked inside of the unlocked barn and came out to Second Street again, passing the side steps. He was unobserved by Morse, Emma, or Mrs. Churchill, who were all known to be home at the time.

While the reporters were carrying out secret missions, members of the general public had become armchair detectives, looking for their own clues in the rumors and stories that were going around town and in the leaked information that was coming out of the police department. The story of the Borden murders was being circulated by newspapers from coast to coast, but the event had stunned New England, and paralyzed the town of Fall River.

The big story that was now spreading around town concerned the Eli Bence development, which had been hinted at in the recent newspaper report and was the source of the department's "embarrassing difficulties." On Wednesday, the day before the murders, Abby and Lizzie were convinced that they were being poisoned by someone, likely an enemy of Andrew's. They surmised that the poison was in the baker's bread that they had bought, or in the milk that was delivered daily from the Borden farm. Andrew had also suffered stomach cramps and vomiting, but it was Abby who dressed early and went to see Dr. Bowen across the street. He questioned her about what the family had eaten recently and was undoubtedly appalled to hear that their meals had included warmed-over fish and some mutton that had been served as various dishes for three consecutive hot summer days. He assured Abby that there was nothing to be alarmed about. The family was making themselves sick with their poor diet.

This was the beginning of the "poison theory" that Lizzie told the police about on Thursday. After hearing her talk about poison, Officers Harrison and Doherty were sent to check all of the druggists in Fall River, New Bedford, and all points in between for recent purchases of poison – which could be easily bought over the counter in those days.

Eli Bence, a pharmacist at D.R. Smith's drugstore, on the corner of Columbia and South Main in Fall River, told them that a young woman carrying a fur cape had come into the store on Wednesday, the day before the murders, and tried to purchase 10-cents worth of prussic acid. She explained that she wanted it to kill the moths that were eating away at her sealskin cape. Bence told her that the poison could not be purchased without a prescription, and she had left. Even though Bence had

Druggist Eli Bence

never met Miss Borden, she was the young woman who came into the store that day, he said. A customer and another clerk also identified Lizzie as being in the store that morning, but she denied it. She later testified that she had not attempted to purchase the poison, and had not been at the drugstore that day.

How sure was Bence that the woman was actually Lizzie Borden? We will never know. Heated debate took place at police headquarters and among the general public about the druggist's identification. If it was Lizzie, wasn't her attempt to purchase poison proof that Lizzie had deadly intent against someone on the day before the murders? Or was her errand truly as innocent as she claimed? And, if so, why did she deny being in the drugstore?

In 1892, Fall River, Massachusetts, boasted three newspapers. The *Herald* in the morning and the *News* in the afternoon had been, until a few years before, the two principal papers that had kept generations of locals abreast of goings-on in town. But a few years before, the *Globe* had set up shop with the stated purpose of upsetting the market and wooing away subscribers from the other newspapers. It was patterned after the style of "yellow journalism" usually found in big cities, with lurid stories, graphic illustrations, and lengthy articles filled with wild speculation.

On Saturday, the second day after the murders, the *Globe* was loudly calling for Lizzie's arrest, printing stories expressing her guilt. It was along this same line that the newspaper would follow relentlessly throughout the investigation and trial, and for years after. All of the stories were slanted against Lizzie; many were manufactured. The *Globe's* police reporter was Edwin H. Porter, who would later use his stories as the basis for his book, *The Fall River Tragedy*, a "history" that was published in 1893. For a number of years, it was considered the best account of the mystery by many historians. However, in 1924, author Edmund Pearson discovered what Porter had done with this book. Literally from day one, Porter had decided that Lizzie was guilty of the murders. To sustain his belief, he had systematically abridged courtroom testimony and evidence that was favorable to her and highlighted only those things that supported his theory. Witnesses who testified favorably toward Lizzie were often missing from the book or, at best, appeared only as one who had "testified," without a word of what was said. Any sort of damning testimony against her was printed in lurid detail.

Knowledge of what Porter had done was unwittingly obscured when Lizzie, learning of the publication, was rumored to have bought up all but about 25 subscription copies, and had them destroyed. Initially, only a few people were aware of what Porter had written and were unaware of how he had distorted things. In time, however, scholars managed to track down the few copies in public libraries and other institutions, and his slanted research began to be used, copied, and passed along as accurate. While Edmund Pearson eventually discovered what Porter had done, he also believed that Lizzie was guilty and liberally adopted Porter's tactic of slanting the evidence. For every deviation from the truth that he corrected, he added one of his own. And the story of Lizzie Borden became as skewed as the poem that claimed she "gave her mother forty whacks."

And it all began with the *Globe* and Edwin H. Porter. The police beat writer had a field day with the Eli Bence development. He wrote, "The demeanor of Miss Lizzie Borden through the trying ordeal of being confronted with the man who says that she asked about the poison was that of contempt and scorn; in fact, her conduct as seen by the police has been strange."

The fact that no such "confrontation" took place didn't seem to bother Porter or the *Globe*, but it certainly made a good story.

While the Saturday morning meeting at City Hall for all of the lead officers investigating the case was taking place, some 4,000 people, sweating and shoving, had filled the area around Second Street. It took 20 policemen to maintain any kind of order at all. What had attracted them back to the spot? It was the morning of the funerals for Andrew and Abby Borden.

At 9:00 a.m., John Morse came out of the Borden house and chatted with the reporters who pushed their way up to the front of the crowd. He protested his innocence, shaken, perhaps, by his near escape from the lynch mob the evening before. He stated that he was giving the police his "full cooperation" and invited the "fullest investigation" of his alibi. Once again, Morse's behavior was strange. No other family members emerged from the house to chat leisurely with reporters and there seems to be no good reason why he had chosen to do so. There is no question that his alibi was strong, but the odd way that he acted – before and after the murders – remains troubling, even after all of these years.

The funeral service was to be conducted by Reverend Thomas Adams, of the First Congregational Church, and City Missionary Edwin A. Buck, a long-time friend of Lizzie's. When the two men arrived, they joined the 75 others who were elbow to elbow inside of the house. In the sitting room, the coffins were displayed side by side. Lizzie, escorted by Adelaide Churchill, had earlier come downstairs from her room. She stood next to Andrew's casket for a silent minute, wept, and kissed him on the lips.

After the casket was closed, an ivy wreath was placed on top of it. A bouquet of white roses, tied with a white satin ribbon, was placed on the lid of Abby's coffin. Scriptures were read, hymns were sung, but no eulogy was given.

At 11:00, Lizzie was the first to leave the house, leaning on the arm of undertaker James E. Winward. Those who had already accused her of showing no emotion at the time of the murder, or during the days of questioning, were later also to profess shock and indignation that she neither showed any emotion nor wore mourning black at the funeral. This was not the case, though. A female reporter from the *Boston Herald* was careful to describe what she wore: "A tight fitting black lace dress with a plain skirt and waist of equally modest cut and finish, while a dark hat, trimmed with similar material, rested upon her head."

As for her emotions, a *New York Times* reporter wrote: "Her nerves were completely unstrung as was shown by the trembling of her body and the manner in which she bore down on her supporter. When she reached the carriage she fell back exhausted in the cushions."

Emma, much calmer than her sister, followed. She walked quickly and took a seat beside Lizzie, and both fixed their eyes straight ahead. Neither of them glanced at the mob in the streets, nor did they seem aware of the raised hats and bowed heads along the route of the cortege as the two hearses and 11 carriages made their way through town to Oak Grove Cemetery. The burial service was private and only about 40 of the family's closest friends were invited to accompany the remains to the cemetery.

But the burial did not take place. A telegram from the state analyst, stopping the ceremony, had reached the cemetery moments ahead of the burial party. The last rites were halted, and the caskets were placed into a receiving vault.

The following Thursday, Dr. W.A. Dolan, assisted by F.W. Draper, with Dr. J.H. Leary and autopsy clerk Dr. D.E. Cone as witnesses, entered the cemetery vault, conducted a formal autopsy, and severed the heads of both victims, dispatching them to Harvard University for examination.

Mercifully, the family had no idea that this had happened.

As soon as the funeral party left the Borden house, police officers arrived to search the place again. It was the third consecutive day of searches. By now, Andrew Jennings, an attorney who had represented Lizzie once before, had been consulted. Aware of the possibility that Lizzie might be accused, Jennings was on hand to monitor the search. Once again, nothing criminal was unearthed.

The day before the funeral, Marshal Hilliard had called Hosea Knowlton, district attorney for the second district, and asked for a meeting on Saturday that would also

include State Police Detective George Seaver, Mayor John Coughlin, and Medical Examiner Dolan. While the funeral cortege moved along its route, and while the Borden house was being searched for the third time, the five men met in their unannounced session, which lasted until 6:00 p.m. They reached the consensus that Lizzie was probably the murderer of her father and step-mother.

Mayor Coughlin and Marshal Hilliard came to the Borden house later that evening and met with Lizzie, Emma, and John Morse in the dimly lit parlor. Coughlin told them that he had a request to make of them – that they remain in the house for the next few days.

Lizzie asked, "Why? Is there anybody in this house suspected? I want to know the truth."

Coughlin hesitated in his reply, and Hilliard said nothing. Lizzie asked again and

Prosecutor Hosea M. Knowlton

finally, the mayor replied, "Well, Miss Borden, I regret to answer, but I must answer yes. You are suspected."

Lizzie rose to her feet and calmly faced the two men. She said, "Then I am ready to go right now."

The two men were struck speechless, having no idea what to say. But one thing that they should have done was to remind Lizzie about her right to remain silent and to have an attorney present when questioned. While referred to as the "Miranda" warning today (based on a court case in the 1970s), those rights were guaranteed by the Constitution of the United States and were recognized in Massachusetts and all other states in 1892. But Marshal Hilliard failed to mention this protection against self-recrimination on that Saturday or at any time to follow. It would become a critical error.

On Sunday, the congregation of the Central Congregational Church held a joint service with the First Church, and every pew was filled to capacity. During the service, Reverend W. Walker Jubb prayed for divine intercession in solving the terrible mystery. After the morning sermon, he stepped out of the pulpit to speak directly on the subject that was on everyone's mind. The minister had no illusion about the fact that discussion before the service started had more to do with the murders on Second Street than with the wonders of God. His manner was deliberate and his voice calm and contained. He accurately captured the mood, perplexity, and frustrations of everyone who lived in Fall River, no matter what their religious faith.

He spoke to the people in the sanctuary:

I cannot close my sermon this morning without speaking of the horrible crime that has startled our beloved city this week, ruthlessly taking from our church household two respected and esteemed members. I cannot close without referring to my pain and surprise at the atrocity of the outrage. A more brutal, cunning, daring, and fiendish murder I have never heard in all my life.

What must have been the person who could have been guilty of such a revolting crime? One to commit such a murder must have been without heart, without soul, a fiend incarnate, the very vilest of degraded and depraved humanity, or he must have been a maniac. The circumstances, execution, and all the surroundings cover it with a mystery profound.

Explanations and evidence as to both perpetrator and motive are shrouded in a mystery that is almost inexplicable. That such a crime could have been committed during the busy hours of the day, right in the heart of a populous city, is passing comprehension.

As we ponder, we exclaim in our perplexity, why was the deed done? What could have induced anybody to engage in such a butchery? Where is the motive? When men resort to crime it is plunder, for gain, from enmity, in sudden anger, or for revenge. Strangely, nothing of this nature enters into this case, and again I ask – what was the motive? I believe, and am only voicing your feelings fully when I say that I hope the criminal will be speedily brought to justice...

Without speaking her name aloud, he then directed his remarks to police rumors, newspaper stories, and local gossip about Lizzie's eminent arrest.

I trust that the police may do their duty and lose no opportunity which might lead to the capture of the criminal. I would impress upon them that they should not say too much and thus unconsciously assist in defeating the ends of justice. I also trust that the press – and I say this because I recognize its influence and power – I trust that it will use discretion in disseminating its theories and conclusions, and that pens may be guided by consideration and charity. I would wish the papers to remember that by casting a groundless and undeserved insinuation that may blacken and blast a life forever, like a tree smitten by a bolt of lightning; a life which has always commanded respect, whose acts and motives have always been pure and holy. Let us ourselves curb our tongues and preserve a blameless life from undeserved suspicions. I think that I have the right to ask for the prayers of this church and of my own congregation. The murdered husband and wife were members of this church, and a daughter now stands in the same relation to each one of you, as you, church members, do to each other.
God help and comfort her.

But no one, God included, seemed to be looking out for Lizzie when it came to her being accused of her parents' murders.

On Monday morning, Marshal Hilliard met with Second District Court Judge Josiah C. Blaisdell behind closed doors and left his office with a warrant for Lizzie's arrest. What factors determined the probable cause in the case are unknown since no one else was present in the judge's chambers. As with all developments in the case, reporters learned of the meeting within minutes, and were told, "There will be action soon." They interpreted that assurance to mean an arrest was imminent – that very day. But, by 5:00 p.m., nothing had happened.

Hilliard and Prosecutor Knowlton, for whatever reason, had hesitated. It was likely, with a warrant finally in hand, Knowlton was struck by the enormity of what they were about to do. It seems almost impossible to believe that Hilliard could have obtained an arrest warrant with what the police and prosecution had in their possession that would point to Lizzie's guilt. There was no reason to believe that any additional evidence would be turned up, even though on that day the Borden house was scheduled to be searched for the fifth time. Every rumor, no matter how ridiculous, had been investigated; every lead run down, even though each led to nothing. They had no physical evidence; no weapon; no clear-cut motive. Yet, they were about to arrest a young lady of impeccable character, bearing a name that dated back to the very beginnings of the town, and to charge her with committing the most heinous crime in anyone's memory.

Hilliard and Knowlton surely must have questioned what they were about to do. Hilliard likely asked himself if his men had failed to find any clues, no matter how insignificant. Was there any other suspect that could be found or conclusion drawn from that missing clue? Hilliard was an experienced police officer, just as Knowlton was far from a novice prosecutor. He knew that he would be the man who became the face of Lizzie's persecution, as some people would likely see it. Did the police have a case that he could take to not only the jury in the courtroom, but the jury made up of the general public who would be scrutinizing everything that he did?

In the end, it was Knowlton who blinked. Before he would allow Hilliard to serve the warrant, he had to have more. He wanted a further inquiry of some kind, and some additional time for questioning. Knowlton decided to schedule an inquest to try and get to the bottom of things.

5. THE INQUEST

An inquest, according to the legal definitions of the term, is a judicial inquiry to determine the cause of a person's death. Conducted by a judge, jury, or government official, an inquest may or may not require an autopsy carried out by a coroner or medical examiner. Generally, inquests are only conducted when deaths are sudden or unexplained. An inquest may be called at the behest of a coroner, judge, prosecutor, or, in some jurisdictions, upon a formal request from the public. The verdict can be, for example, natural death, accidental death, misadventure, suicide, or murder. However, it was not an accusatory procedure, so attorneys were not needed to defend anyone. If the verdict reached during the inquest was murder, criminal prosecution was likely to follow and, at that point, suspects were able to then defend themselves.

Since attorneys were not used during an inquest, this would give Hilliard and Knowlton great latitude in their search for more facts and evidence with which to strengthen their case against Lizzie. They went back and forth about what exactly to call the inquest and settled on an "informal examination" of various witnesses, which they announced would be held the following morning at 10:00 a.m.

Lizzie's attorney, Andrew Jennings, knew there was nothing "informal" about the meeting. She was already under house arrest and had been told she was suspected of committing the murders. When she was served with a summons, ordering her to be present at the "examination," he asked for permission to attend with her. He argued at length to be able to represent his client. At this point, Knowlton admitted the meeting was officially an inquest, and Jennings was refused admission and asked to leave. Massachusetts Attorney General Albert Pillsbury had put himself into the case, likely for the publicity that it offered him, and he probably advised Hilliard and Knowlton that they could not carry off the subterfuge. Late on Monday, Knowlton released a press statement that simply said, "Inquest continued to 10 o'clock."

The inquest turned out to be a major event in Fall River. It was the next step in a series of major events that had begun with the first cry of "murder!" on the previous Thursday morning. From that

Fall River's Old Courthouse

moment, industry and commerce had virtually come to a halt in the city. Hundreds of people had closed off Second Street so that it was impossible to travel by carriage except in the early morning hours, or late at night. Many of the mills and businesses had been forced to close that Thursday because workers never returned from their lunch hours. It had been much the same ever since, and this was the sixth day. Crowds continued to mill about on Second Street, staring at the Borden house, and hoping that a policeman or a member of the family might enter or leave. On every corner, groups gathered, exchanging gossip or swapping new theories about the murders. When the word came on Tuesday that an inquest was to be held before Judge Blaisdell that morning, crowds rushed to the square and, within minutes, all of the approaching streets were closed down by the curious.

The inquest was to be held at the Old Court House, as it was called in 1892. It had been built in 1857 and named the Second District House. Located on Court Square, it was a gloomy, foreboding building of gray stone that housed Fall River's two firefighting units, which were huge, horse-drawn fire engines. At the rear was the police lockup and the remainder of the first floor was the city stable. The second and third floors were shared by the police and the court. There were sleeping quarters for off-duty policemen and offices for judges, clerks, and lawyers. There was a cupola on top of the building that held the town's fire alarm bell, which was rung by means of a rope that extended down to the street below.

A carriage approached the courthouse at 10:00 a.m. sharp and the uproar around the building swelled in volume. People jostled and pushed, hoping to catch a glimpse of one of the principals in the case. But if they hoped to see Lizzie, they were disappointed. The carriage contained Officer Patrick Doherty and the servant girl, Bridget Sullivan.

She was immediately rushed into the presence of Knowlton, Hilliard, Medical Examiner Dolan, State Police Officer Seaver, and Dr. Coughlin, Fall River's mayor. One can only imagine the anxiety the young, immigrant maid must have felt in the presence of these intimidating men. Reports later stated that she was "deeply distressed," burst frequently into sobs, and was barely coherent.

She was ushered first into Hilliard's office, where she was questioned for an hour or more before the group moved into the district court room and the inquest was officially started by Judge Blaisdell. There, she told of the breakfast, of washing windows, lying down in her room, and of Lizzie's frantic calls, which brought her back downstairs. Her testimony, as far as is known, revealed nothing that she had not already told the police.

That afternoon at 2:00 p.m., Lizzie took the stand at the inquest. District Attorney Knowlton's first queries plumbed for motive, one of the elements that he would have to prove to a jury if he hoped to obtain a conviction in trial.

Q. (Knowlton) Give me your full name.
A. Lizzie Andrew Borden
Q. It is Lizzie or Elizabeth?
A. Lizzie.
Q. You were so christened?
A. I was so christened.
Q. What is your age?
A. Thirty-two.
Q. How long had your father been married to your step-mother?
A. I think about 27 years.
Q. How much of that time have they lived in that house on Second Street?
A. About 20 years last May.

The inquest soon veered into what many believe remains a controversial area when Knowlton asked Lizzie how many children her father had. Lizzie responded, "Only two." When asked if there had been any others, she replied, "One that died." This referred to a sister who lived only a short time. But there are many who believe that Lizzie was lying about this, stating that Andrew Borden had fathered an illegitimate son by a woman named Phebe Hathaway. William Borden, the bastard son, was never publicly acknowledged or recognized by Andrew. However, it is believed that Knowlton was aware of the gossip and was letting Lizzie know that he knew of her half-brother. Or perhaps not. It may have just been a series of questions to establish who would inherit as the result of Andrew's death that theorists have turned into something else – namely that a conspiracy was afoot and Knowlton was aware of it.

But the testimony soon returned to Andrew Borden's money:

Q. Have you any idea how much your father was worth?
A. No sir.
Q. Have you ever heard him say?
A. No sir.
Q. Have you ever formed an opinion?
A. No sir.
Q. Do you know something about real estate?
A. He owns two farms in Swansea, the place on Second Street, and the A.J. Borden building and corner and the land on South Main Street where McManus is, then a short time ago he bought some real estate further south that formerly, he said, belonged to Mr. Birch.
Q. Did you ever deed him any property?
A. He gave us some years ago, Grandfather Borden's house on Ferry Street and he bought it back from us some weeks ago. He gave us $5,000 for it.
Q. Did you pay him anything when you took a deed from him?
A. No sir.
Q. Did you ever know of your father making a will?
A. No sir.
Q. Did he have a marriage settlement with your step-mother?
A. I never knew of any.

Knowlton had already established his position – that Lizzie had killed her father because of greed, and her fear that Andrew might be planning to leave his considerable estate to Abby. If that was allowed to happen, Emma and Lizzie would face years of poverty and, even worse, total subservience to their dour stepmother.

There was plenty of gossip going around that there had been protracted arguments in the family over money and property, but there was not nearly enough proof of such arguments to obtain a murder conviction. Knowlton was an experienced prosecutor, and he surely knew that, without witnesses and hard evidence, the motive for the murders had to be a clear and substantial one.

Q. Did you ever know of your father making a will?
A. No sir.
Q. Did he ever mention the subject of a will to you?
A. He did not.

Q. Do you know of anybody that your father was on bad terms with?

A. There was a man that came there that he had trouble with. I don't know who the man was.

Q. Tell all you saw and heard.

A. I did not see anything. I heard the bell ring and Father went to the door and let him in. I did not hear anything for some time, except just the voices: then I heard the man say, "I would like to have that place. I would like to have that store." Father says, "I am not willing to let your business go in there." And the man said, "I thought with your reputation for liking money, you would let your store for anything." Father said, "You are mistaken." Then they talked awhile and then their voices were louder and I heard father order him out.

Q. Besides that, do you know of anybody that your father had bad feelings toward or who had bad feelings toward your father?

A. I know of one man that has not been friendly with him: they have not been friendly for years.

Q. Who?

A. Mr. Hiram C. Harrington.

Hiram Harrington was Andrew's brother-in-law, married to his sister, Laurana. The root of their dislike for one another was not known, only that it had started many years before and had festered over time. With their very different personalities and ambitions, the two men had never gotten along. Harrington was a blacksmith, with no aspiration to go beyond his station in life. He had saved nothing and had invested nothing because he earned little more than what was needed for the absolute necessities. Andrew never felt that such a man was worthy of his sister. At some point years before, there had been "hard words" between them, and from that day, Hiram was not welcome in the Borden house, nor was Andrew ever known to visit his sister unless he knew that Hiram was not home.

On the day after the murders, Hiram spoke freely with reporters, and he immensely enjoyed his newfound fame. He presented his own version of what happened at Andrew's house and left little doubt that he believed Lizzie was the murderer. Implying an intimacy with Lizzie that he certainly did not have, Harrington told about a long "interview" that he had with her – that never took place. A legitimate reporter who was present when Harrington came to the Borden house said that he had been inside exactly three minutes. He told his editor, "Mr. Harrington is embittered against the family and does not hesitate to make startling statements."

And he was right. Harrington was a gold mine for the yellow journalist. He stated that the motive for the murders was "money, unquestionably money." He added, "I would not be surprised at the arrest any time of the person to whom in my opinion suspicion strongly points." While others present on the morning of the murders had described Lizzie at various times as crying, deeply agitated, or on the verge of fainting, Harrington said she was "very composed, showed no signs of emotion nor were there any traces of grief upon her countenance."

Of course, that's what the muck-raking reporters printed and, unfortunately for her and as untrue as it was, this image would hound Lizzie for the rest of her days. Victorian ladies were supposed to get the vapors, tremble, and swoon at times of adversity. The general public of the day, along with many who have written about her since, refused to forgive her for her shyness, her strong sense of propriety, and her unwillingness to show her deepest emotions to strangers.

Asked if he knew of any dissension within the Borden family, Harrington was quick to say that there was, although, he added, it has always been kept very quiet. He said, "For nearly ten years, there have been disputes between the daughters and their father and stepmother." The disputes had been bitter, he explained, and Lizzie did most of the "demonstrative contention." She was haughty and domineering and of a "repellant disposition," and he had heard many of the bitter things that she said of her father. Harrington added, for whatever reason, that he was positive, though, that Emma knew nothing of the murder.

For a man who was not allowed in the house while Andrew was alive, and who was not even invited to the funeral when he died, his insight into family secrets was extraordinary. He finally had his revenge for all of what he perceived as having been Andrew's slights against him.

Q. Do you know of anybody that was on bad terms with your stepmother?
A. No sir.
Q. Or that your step-mother was on bad terms with?
A. No sir.
Q. Did you ever have any trouble with your step-mother?
A. No sir.
A. Have you, within six months, had any words with her?
A. No sir.
Q. Within a year?
A. No sir.
Q. Within two years?
A. I think not.
Q. When was the last that you know of?
A. About five years ago?
Q. What about?
A. Her step-sister, half-sister.
Q. What name?
A. Her name is now Mrs. George W. Whitehead.

This, the prosecution would claim, was where it all began – the rumored troubles in Andrew's home, Lizzie and Emma's supposed hatred of their stepmother, and the awful prospect that she, not they, might become Andrew's heir.

Abby's stepsister, Sarah, had married George W. Whitehead, and it was neither a happy or prosperous union. They shared half of a nondescript house with Abby's mother. Mrs. Gray wanted to sell her half, but the few prospective buyers wanted the entire house, or nothing at all. Fearing that her stepsister might find herself homeless in her declining years, Abby had pressured Andrew into buying the house. To Andrew, $1,500 was not a great sum and, since he had never done anything for Abby except for marry her and thereby obtain a free housekeeper, he had arranged the purchase and put the house in Abby's name.

The prosecution believed that this was the basis of the "Abby-as-heir" theory, and he wanted to drive that point home during the inquest.

Q. Then you have been on pleasant terms with your step-mother since then?
A. Yes sir.
Q. Cordial?
A. It depends on one's idea of cordiality, perhaps.
Q. According to your idea of cordiality?
A. Quite so.
Q. What do you mean by "quite so?"
A. Quite cordial. I do not mean the dearest friends in the world, but very kindly feelings and pleasant.
Q. You did not regard her as your mother?
A. Not exactly, no; although she came here when I was very young.
Q. Were your relations toward her that of daughter and mother?
A. In some ways it was and in some it was not.
Q. In what ways was it not?
A. I did not call her mother.

The same statement that Lizzie had made in the hours after the murder to Deputy Fleet – which convinced him that she was a murderer – came back to haunt her once more. Later, too late, she would say that she meant no disrespect, only that she was suffering from the shock of the hour and had responded to relentless questioning by other policemen before Fleet. She did not say so, but it is likely that Fleet's belligerence had encouraged her snappish response.

It seems that the thought never came to anyone that, while a child at the age of four would not hesitate to call the wife of her father "mother," and adult might, without venom or hatred, prefer to call her by her Christian or married name. It was equally odd that no one took exception to the fact that Emma, who was a child of 14 at the time of the marriage, not only would never call Abby "Mother," but would not even acknowledge that she was "Mrs. Borden." The only way that Emma ever addressed her was "Abby."

In my opinion, Lizzie did not have any hateful feelings about her stepmother. More likely, she saw her as an intrusion into her life or, at the very least, that she did not matter all that much. She didn't consider her as her "mother," because she was almost a faceless entity in her life. Andrew, himself, seemed to have little use for her, other than as a housekeeper, and Lizzie likely felt the same. Abby was simply another person in the house, like Bridget Sullivan, who Lizzie and Emma insisted on calling "Maggie," because she didn't matter all that much to them either.

Q. What dress did you wear the day they were killed?

A. I had on a navy blue, sort of bengaline or India silk skirt with a navy blouse. In the afternoon, they thought I had better change it. I put on a pink wrapper.

Q. Did you change your clothing before the afternoon?

A. No sir.

Q. Where was your father when you came down on Thursday morning?

A. Sitting in the sitting room in his large chair.

Q. Where was your mother? Do your prefer me to call her Mrs. Borden?

A. I had as soon you called her mother. She was in the dining room with a feather duster cleaning.

Q. Where was Maggie?

A. Just come in the backdoor with the long pole and brush and getting her pail of water. She was going to wash the windows around the house. She said Mrs. Borden wanted her to.

Q. Did you get your breakfast that morning?

A. I did not eat any breakfast. I did not feel as though I wanted any.

Q. What was the next thing that happened after you got down?

A. Maggie went out of doors to wash the windows and father came out into the kitchen and said he did not know whether he would go down to the post office or not. And then I sprinkled some handkerchiefs to iron.

Q. Did your father go downtown?

A. He went down later.

Q. How long a job was that – ironing the handkerchiefs?

A. I did not finish them. My flats were not hot enough.

Q. Where were you when he returned?

A. I was down in the kitchen.

It is possible that Lizzie's memory of this detail of where she was when Andrew returned home was simply faulty, or it may be that it was a vital part of some important deception. No one knows either way, but Lizzie and Bridget disagreed in their answers.

Under relentless questioning, Lizzie said, at various times, that she was in the kitchen, dining room, or upstairs. She settled finally on the kitchen. Bridget recalled that she was upstairs and she was unshakable in this answer. She remembered because Andrew had trouble with the three different locks on the front door, and when Bridget also fumbled opening them, she had let out some sort of expletive. She remembered hearing Lizzie laugh at that, and she remembered the laugh coming from upstairs.

The significance of their different recollections is not known, but, apparently, there was one.

During the inquest, however, Knowlton was intent on placing Lizzie upstairs at the time he would maintain that Abby was murdered. Lizzie did not hesitate to say that she had been upstairs.

Q. Did you go back to your room before your father returned?
A. I think I did carry up some clean clothes.
Q. Did you stay there?
A. No sir.
Q. Did you spend any time up the front stairs before your father returned?
A. No sir.
Q. Or after he returned?
A. No sir. I did stay in my room long enough when I went up to sew a little piece of tape on a garment.
Q. How long had you been there?
A. I had only been upstairs just long enough to take the clothes up and baste a little loop on the sleeve. I don't think I had been up there over five minutes.
Q. Had you any knowledge of Mrs. Borden going out of the house?
A. She told me that she had had a note, somebody was sick, and said, "I am going to get dinner on the way," and asked what I wanted for dinner.
Q. Did you tell her?
A. Yes, I told her I did not want anything.
Q. Did you hear her come back?
A. I did not hear her go or come back but I suppose she went.
Q. When you found your father dead you supposed your mother had gone?
A. I did not know. I said to the people who came in, "I don't know whether Mrs. Borden is out or in; I wish you could see if she is in her room."
Q. You supposed she was out at the time?

A. I understood so; I did not suppose anything about it.
Q. Did she tell you where she was going?
A. No sir.
Q. Did she tell you who the note was from?
A. No sir.
Q. Did you ever see the note?
A. No sir.
Q. Do you know where it is now?
A. No sir.
Q. She said she was going out that morning?
A. Yes sir.

After that final question, the inquest was adjourned until 10:00 a.m. the next morning.

The crowd outside shuffled and grumbled in the scorching heat. They had expected an arrest and now there was yet another delay. The crowds slowly filtered away from the courthouse, many of them returning to mill about on Second Street, staring at the Borden house as if expecting some kind of answer to the mystery to appear.

The reporters were equally disappointed and adjourned to the local taverns to come up with some sort of story to send to their editors. By now, every major newspaper in every large city on the East Coast had at least one representative in Fall River, some of them accompanied by a photographer or artist. The only wire service, the Associated Press, had their man in the city, and some had come from as far away as New Orleans and San Francisco. They numbered at least 100. Word of the mystery had even reached as far away as London and Europe.

The newspapers – just like the people of Fall River – were divided about how they felt about Lizzie. In Fall River, the *Globe* kept up its daily demand for Lizzie to be arrested. The *Springfield Republican*, on the other hand, took an entirely different view:

All through the investigation carried on by the Fall River police, a lack of ability has been shown seldom equaled, and causes they assign for connecting the daughter with the murder are on the par with their other exhibitions of lack of wisdom. Because someone, unknown to them and too smart for them to catch, butchered two people in the daytime on a principal street of the city, using the brute force far in excess of that possessed by this girl, they conclude that there is probable reason to believe that she is the murderess. Because they found no one walking along the street with his hands and clothes reeking with blood, they conclude that it is probable, after swinging the axe with the precision of a butcher, she washed the blood from her hands and clothes.

In other words, the dogged pursuit of Lizzie as the killer by the police was the result of lazy investigative work. Sadly, it had to be a newspaper to point out one of the obvious flaws in the prosecution's case – how could she have committed the murders without getting a speck of blood on her body or clothing?

The inquest reconvened on Wednesday morning, around the same time that the August heat was broken by a thunderstorm. Instead of sweltering under the hot sun, the curious crowd that gathered now carried umbrellas. By 10:00 a.m., they had filled the square. They had expected someone to be arrested on Monday or Tuesday, and now that it was Wednesday, they were convinced that it was about to happen.

At 10:05, Lizzie took the stand and was reminded that she was still under oath.

Q. When you went out to the barn, where did you leave your father?
A. He had laid down on the sitting room lounge, taken off his shoes, and put on his slippers, and taken off his coat, and put on the reefer.

A "reefer," which is not a term commonly known by modern readers, was a double-breasted, sleeveless garment that was a less dressy equivalent of a smoking jacket. It is a commentary on Andrew's rigid formality that event on the hottest day of the year, he put on his reefer rather than simply relax in shirt sleeved comfort in the privacy of his own home.

Lizzie's statement that he had taken off his shoes and put on slippers is one of the anomalies of her testimony. When he died, Andrew was wearing black congress gaiters, ankle-top shoes with elastic gussets in the sides. Changing into his slippers was perhaps what he normally did when taking a nap at noon, and so Lizzie may have simply assumed that he did the same thing on this day. If there was a sinister motive behind this misstatement, no one ever picked up on it. Knowlton ignored it, or missed it, and pressed on. He was far more interested in Lizzie's minute-by-minute movements on that August morning.

Q. Whereabouts in the barn did you go?
A. Upstairs.
Q. How long did you remain there?
A. I don't know. Fifteen or twenty minutes.
Q. What doing?
A. Trying to find lead for a sinker.

Q. Can you give me any information how it happened at that particular time you should go into the chamber of the barn to find a sinker to go to Marion with to fish the next Monday?

A. I was going to finish my ironing. My flats were not hot. I said to myself, "I will go and try to find that sinker. Perhaps by the time I get back the flats will be hot." That is the only reason.

Q. Had you got a fish line?

A. Not here; we had some at the farm.

Q. Had you got a fish hook?

A. No sir.

Q. Had you got any apparatus for fishing at all?

A. Yes, over there.

Q. Had you any sinkers over there?

A. I think there were some. It is so long since I have been there. I think there were some.

Q. You had no reason to suppose you were lacking sinkers?

A. I don't think there were any on my lines.

Q. Where were your lines?

A. My fish lines were at the farm here.

Q. What made you think there were no sinkers at the farm on your lines?

A. Because some time ago when I was there I had none.

Q. How long since you used the fish lines?

A. Five years, perhaps.

Q. You left them at the farm then?

A. Yes sir.

Q. And you have not seen them since?

A. Yes sir.

And the questions went on and on from there, delving into pointless, excruciating details. Questions about the sinkers, lines, and poles went on for over an hour. It must have seemed to the few people allowed into the inquest that Knowlton was being paid by the question. Many wondered what point the prosecutor was trying to make in all of the haggling over what seemed a minor matter. After all, the purpose of the inquest was supposedly to look into the deaths of the Bordens, two of the town's most prominent residents, and not to worry about fish hooks and sinkers.

But Knowlton had a reason for picking away at Lizzie's story. Her trip to the barn had to be trivialized and, if possible, discredited altogether. If he could convince a jury that she had made up the story of visiting the barn, she could then be placed inside of the house at the time that Andrew was killed. Unlike Morse's alibi, Lizzie's was vulnerable to ridicule even if Knowlton could not actually prove that it wasn't true.

For another hour, he walked her through the events of the morning. The story that she and Bridget had told at least a dozen times was repeated in great detail. Few of the questions that she was asked was anything new, but one of them was:

Q. Did you have an apron on Thursday?
A. Did I what?
Q. Have an apron on Thursday?
A. No sir, I don't think I did.
Q. Do you remember whether you did or not?
A. I don't remember sure, but I don't think I did.
Q. You had aprons, of course?
A. I had aprons, yes sir.
Q. Will you try and think whether you did or not?
A. I don't think I did.
Q. Will you try and remember?
A. I had no occasion for an apron that morning.
Q. If you can remember, I wish you would.
A. I don't remember.
Q. That is all the answer you can give me about that?
A. Yes sir.

It is obvious to the reader what Knowlton was fishing for with this line of questioning – if Lizzie had been wearing an apron, then this might explain why she had no blood on her clothing after committing the murders. Even if she had, this would have been ridiculous. The murders had been brutal and bloody. Whoever had killed Andrew and Abby had been undoubtedly splattered with gore. An apron would not have protected Lizzie from the spray if she had been wearing one.

After realizing that his questions were leading nowhere, Knowlton then switched to the subject of axes and hatchets and how much Lizzie knew about either tool.

Q. Did you have any occasion to use the axe or hatchet?
A. No sir.
Q. Did you know where they were?
A. I knew there was an old axe down cellar; that is all I knew.
Q. Did you know anything about a hatchet down cellar?
A. No sir.
Q. Where was the old axe down cellar?
A. The last time I saw it it was stuck in the old chopping block.
Q. Was that the only axe or hatchet down cellar?
A. It was all I knew about.

Q. When was the last time you knew of it?
A. When our farmer came to chop wood.
Q. When was that?
A. I think a year ago last winter; I think there was so much wood on hand he did not come last winter.
Q. Do you know of anything that would occasion the use of an axe or hatchet?
A. No sir.
Q. Do you know of anything that would occasion the getting of blood on an axe or hatchet down cellar?
A. No sir.
Q. I do not say there was, but assuming an axe or hatchet was found down cellar with blood on it?
A. No sir.
Q. Do you know whether there was a hatchet down there before the murder?
A. I don't know.
Q. You are not able to say your father did not own a hatchet?
A. I don't know whether he did or not.
Q. Did you know there was found at the foot of the stairs a hatchet and axe?
A. No sir, I did not.
Q. Assume that is so, can you give me any explanation of how they came there?
A. No sir.
Q. Assume they had blood on them, can you give me any occasion for there being blood on them?
A. No sir.

Knowlton was still poking around for information. The questions that he asked meant nothing in themselves, but they opened up the opportunity for Lizzie to unwittingly reveal something that could be of interest. But nothing was revealed during the exchange. Lizzie did not deny all knowledge of axes and hatchets in the house, only a vagueness of how many and where they were.

As the questions continued, she once again said that Andrew had taken off his boots when he returned from downtown – but this time, she said that she saw him do it. Since she obviously had not, it is strange that Knowlton made no effort to pin her down on this point. If, instead of making an honest mistake, she was deliberately lying, this would have been an excellent opportunity to catch her in a lie. But, Knowlton passed over the slip and it was not mentioned again.

On Thursday, Lizzie was again called to the stand. Knowlton started in immediately on the Bence testimony that claimed she had gone to Smith's drugstore to purchase prussic acid on the day before the murders.

Q. Your attention has already been called to the circumstance of going to the drugstore of Smith's, on the corner of Columbia and Main Streets, by some office, has it not, on the day before the tragedy?

A. I don't know whether some officer has asked me, somebody has spoken of it to me. I don't know who it was.

Q. Did that take place?

A. It did not.

Q. Do you know where the drugstore is?

A. I don't.

Q. Did you go into any drugstore and inquire for prussic acid?

A. I did not.

Knowlton had, by now, questioned Lizzie for a total of 12 hours. In his mind, as he would later put it, her testimony had been "a confession," a conclusion that seems very hard to understand. But after a few more questions, he would be finished.

Q. Was the dress that was given to the officers the same dress that you wore that morning?

A. Yes sir.

Q. The India silk?

A. No, it is not an India silk. It is silk and linen. Some call it bengaline silk.

Q. Miss Borden, of course you appreciate the anxiety that everybody has to find the author of this tragedy, and the questions that I put to you have been in that direction. I now ask you if you can furnish any other fact, or give any other, even suspicion, that will assist the officers in any way in this matter?

A. About two weeks ago ---

Q. Were you going to tell the occurrence about the man that called at the house?

A. No sir. It was after my sister went away. I came home from Miss Russell's one night and as I came up, I always glanced towards the side door as I came along by the carriage way, I saw a shadow on the side steps. I did not stop walking but I walked slower. Somebody ran down the steps, around the east end of the house. I thought it was a man because I saw no skirts and I was frightened, and of course I did not go around to see. I hurried to the front door as fast as I could and locked it.

Seven days had now passed since the murders. Over the course of the three days that Lizzie had been in the witness chair, others had also been called and questioned: Bridget Sullivan, Drs. Bowen and Dolan, Eli Bence, Adelaide Churchill, Emma, Hiram Harrington, Uncle John Morse, and others. During that time, the crowds outside never diminished in size and every arrival or departure of a carriage caused a sensation.

When Knowlton had asked his last question and heard Lizzie's answer, he asked her to wait across the hall in the matron's room and not leave the building. After she was safely behind the room's closed door, a hurried conference was held in Knowlton's office. The warrant that had been sworn out for Lizzie's arrest was destroyed, and a new one was hastily written and dated so he could maintain that she was not under duress or jeopardy when she had been questioned. This ignored the fact that at one point in the inquest, he had lost his composure and snapped at Lizzie, "You did not answer my question, and you will, if I have to put it to you all day!" That made it difficult to maintain that she had voluntarily testified, but no one present argued the claim.

With a new warrant signed by Judge Blaisdell in hand, Knowlton and Hilliard left the courthouse, hailed a carriage, and set off for the home of Lizzie's attorney, Andrew Jennings. They informed him that they were prepared to arrest her and asked him if he would like to be present. Jennings stated that he did, and the three of them returned to the courthouse. They went upstairs to the matron's quarters, where Lizzie was lying on a couch. She immediately sat up when the three men entered.

Lizzie's attorney, Andrew Jennings

Hilliard told her, "I have here a warrant for your arrest, issued by the judge of the District Court. I shall read it to you if you desire, but you have the right to waive the reading of it."

Jennings, his lips drawn into a narrow line, advised Lizzie, "Waive the reading."

"You need not read it," she told the marshal. The warrant for her arrest made no reference to the murder of Abby; she was only accused of murdering Andrew.

Lizzie's reaction to the arrest warrant remains a bit of a mystery. Typical of his portrayal of her, Edwin Porter wrote of her "unemotional nature" and said "she did not shed a tear." Of course, on the same page, he also noted that all during the "open, fair, and impartial" trial, she had been "defended by her chosen counsel." Actually, the "trial" (inquest) had been closed and her counsel barred from the courtroom, so we should take his description of her reaction to the news of her arrest with a grain of salt. Other accounts say that her face was pale and filled with tears, and that she was almost "prostrated." Lizzie was said to give way to her feelings and she "sobbed as if her heart would break. Then she gave up to a violent fit of vomiting and the efforts to stop it were unavailing."

News of the arrest quickly spread to the mob packed in front of the courthouse. Each time the doors opened, people surged forward and were pushed back by the police. Emma was the first to appear, weeping and "suffering intensely," it was said, but Lizzie was not allowed to leave. She was searched by the matron and held in custody. There was no suitable jail cell in which to hold her, so sheets and covers were hastily obtained, and she was left alone in the matron's room for the night with the door firmly locked.

News of the arrest also spread throughout the country via telegraph, and the *Globe* printed headline: "Locked up! Lizzie Borden in Custody at Last."

You could almost imagine the triumphant smile that accompanied those black letters on the page.

6. "FLAP-DOODLE AND MISREPRESENTATIONS"

At 9:15 on Friday morning, August 12, a carriage pulled up at the side door of the courthouse. Emma and John Morse got out and went up the stairs. Reverend Buck was already present, waiting with Lizzie in the matron's quarters. At 9:30, Andrew Jennings entered the courtroom, asked for a sheet of paper, and sat, writing furiously. Lizzie entered the courtroom at 9:45, dressed as she had been the day before, in a dark blue suit and hat with a tiny spray of red flowers on the front. Emma had brought her a small valise of fresh clothing, but there had not been time for her to change.

Jennings rose from the table where he had been seated and addressed the court. Before Lizzie would plead, he announced, she wished to present the following:

Bristol ss. Second District Court. Commonwealth vs. Lizzie A. Borden. Complaint for homicide. Defendant's plea.

And now comes the defendant in the above entitled complaint and before pleading thereto says that the Honorable Josiah C. Blaisdell, the presiding justice of the second district court of Bristol, before which the complaint is returnable, has been and believes is still engaged as the presiding magistrate at an inquest upon the death of said Andrew J. Borden, the person whom it is alleged in said complaint the defendant killed, and has received and heard and is still engaged in receiving and hearing evidence in relation to said killing and to said defendant's connection therewith which is not and has not been allowed to hear or know report of, whereof she says that said Honorable Josiah C. Blasdell is disqualified to hear this complaint, and she objects to his so doing, and all of this she is ready to verify.

But before Jennings could argue the motion that Judge Blaisdell be removed from the case, the warrant had to be read and Lizzie's plea entered.

Commonwealth of Massachusetts, To Augustus B. Leonard, clerk of the second district court of Bristol, in the county Bristol, and Justice of the Peace:

Rufus B. Hilliard, city marshal of Fall River, in said county, in behalf of said Commonwealth, on oath, complains that Lizzie A. Borden of Fall River, in the county of Bristol, at Fall River, aforesaid, in the county aforesaid, on the fourth day of August, in the year of our Lord 1892, in and upon one Andrew J. Borden, feloniously, willfully and of her malice aforethought, did make assault and that the said Lizzie A. Borden, then and there with a certain weapon, to wit, a hatchet, in and upon the head of said Andrew J. Borden, then and there feloniously, willfully and of her malice aforethought, did strike, giving unto the said Andrew J. Borden, then and there, with the hatchet aforesaid, by the stroke aforesaid, in a manner aforesaid, in and upon the head of the said Andrew J. Borden, one mortal wound, of which said mortal wound the said Andrew J. Borden then and there instantly died. And so the complainant aforesaid, upon his oath aforesaid, further complains and says that the said Lizzie A. Borden, the said Andrew J. Borden in manner and form aforesaid, then and there feloniously, willfully and of her malice aforethought did kill and murder.

Signed, Marshal R.B. Hilliard

If the reader failed to make it through the long-winded, grammatically nightmarish, and linguistically-challenged jumble of "saids" and "aforesaids," he or she can be forgiven. To boil it down, the warrant stated that Lizzie murdered her father, Andrew, and she did it by striking him in the head with a hatchet. The "said murder" had been done "feloniously, willfully" and with "malice aforethought." Judge Blaisdell stated that she had to enter a plea in person.

In response to the clerk's question as to how she pled, Lizzie stood and replied, "Not guilty."

The clerk, apparently not clear about what she had said, asked the question again. This time, Lizzie spoke louder and repeated her reply, placing special emphasis on the word *not*.

With the formalities concluded, Jennings rose to argue his motion that Judge Blaisdell should recuse himself from the case. It was the kind of motion that attorneys often make, doubting that they will prevail. He would be arguing a point of equity, that it was unfair to a defendant to face the same judge at arraignment who was still presiding over the "inquest" that sent her there, and where her lawyer had been prohibited to represent her. He pressed his point by pointing out, "Your Honor sites her to hear this case, which is remarkable before you, when you have already been sitting on the case in another capacity. By all the laws of human nature, you cannot help being prejudiced from the character of the evidence which has been submitted to you. The Constitution does not allow a judge to sit in such double capacity, and it guarantees a defendant from a prejudiced hearing."

The position argued fairness, not a point of law, and Knowlton pointed this out. He knew of more than 20 cases that had been handled in this same manner, and he said, "It is your Honor's duty to hear this complaint."

Judge Blaisdell agreed. "The statutes make it my imperative duty to hold an inquest and upon the testimony introduced at that hearing, to direct the issuance of warrants."

Jennings sighed. "Then, we are ready for trial."

The audacity of proposing an immediate trial caught Knowlton off guard, and he moved for a continuance.

But Jennings shook his head. "We are anxious to proceed at once. We ask for a trial at the earliest possible moment."

Again, Knowlton pleaded that he was not ready, and an agreement was reached so that August 22 would be the date for the preliminary hearing. Since murder was not an offense that offered release on bail, Judge Blaisdell remanded Lizzie to the county jail in Taunton.

The square outside of the courthouse was in a frenzy as the morning proceedings came to an end. Word spread that Lizzie would be taken to Taunton on the 3:40 train, and the crowd seemed divided as to where best to get a glimpse of her from – the square on the railroad station. In the end, the crowds were about equally divided.

At 3:20, Lizzie appeared at the side door, accompanied by Reverend Buck, Marshal Hilliard, and State Officer Seaver. A clerk handed up her small valise of clothing and the carriage moved off. It was a straight drive from the courthouse to the station, and the route was lined with people, all craning their necks to catch a glimpse of the prisoner. Most of the crowd, however, was disappointed as the carriage took a circuitous route of side streets, leaving many curiosity-seekers struggling to catch up. A squad of police pushed back the crowd that was on the platform, waiting on the train, which was already 10 minutes late. Lizzie waited in the carriage with Reverend Buck until the "all aboard" call sounded.

Dressed in blue, her favorite color, and with her face partially covered by a veil, Lizzie boarded the train and entered the last coach, supported by the marshal and Reverend Buck. The blinds were drawn and the train pulled away, making the short run of less than 20 minutes to Taunton. Another mob waited for her there.

The matron of the county jail was the wife of the sheriff, Andrew J. Wright, who had been Hilliard's predecessor as the marshal of Fall River. As a child, Lizzie had played at their home with their daughter, Isabel. Mrs. Wright's welcome to the now famous prisoner was polite, but strained. She took Lizzie to the cell that would be her home for the next ten months, a square room of seven-and-one-half feet on every side. It included a chair, bed, and a wash basin. The Borden home might have been a modest one – much more modest than Lizzie and Emma wanted – but it was luxurious compared to the place that Lizzie found herself now.

No sooner had the cell door clanged shut behind her, but the clamor began from every reporter and artist assigned to the case to try and interview the prisoner. All of them were refused except for one, a Mrs. McGuirk, with whom Lizzie had served in charitable causes in Fall River. She was allowed to sit down with Lizzie and publish her interview in the September 20 edition of the *New York Recorder:*

"I know I am innocent and I have made up my mind that, no matter what happens, I will try to bear it bravely and make the best of it."

The speaker was a woman. The words came slowly, and her eyes filled with tears that did not fall before they were wiped away. The woman was Lizzie Borden, who had been accused of the murder of her father, and personally has been made to appear in the eyes of the public as a monster, lacking any respect for the law, and stolid in her demeanor to such an extent that she has never showed emotion at any stage of the tragedy, inquest or trial, and, as far as the government would allow they knew, had never shown any womanly or human emotion of any sort since the public first crossed the threshold of the Borden house.

I was anxious to see if this girl, with whom I was associated several years ago in the work of the Fall River Fruit and Flower Mission, had changed her character and become a monster since the days when she used to load up the plates of vigorous young newsboys and poor children at the annual turkey dinner provided during the holidays for them and take delight in their healthy appetites.

I sought her in the Taunton jail and found her unchanged, except that she showed traces of the great trial she has just been put through. Her face was thinner, her mouth had a patient look, as if she had been schooling herself to expect and to bear any treatment, however unpleasant, and her eyes were red from the long nights of weeping. A dark shade now protects them from the glaring white light reflected from the walls of the cell.

"How do you get along here, Miss Borden?" I asked.

"To tell the truth, I am afraid that it is beginning to tell on my health. This lack of fresh air and exercise is hard for me. I have always been out of doors a great deal, and that makes it harder. I cannot sleep nights now, and nothing they give me will produce sleep. If it were not for my friends, I should break down, but as long as they stand by me, I can bear it. They have been, with few exceptions, true to me all through it, and I appreciate it. If they had not, I don't know how I could have gone through it all. I certainly should have broken down. Some things have been very unpleasant, but while everyone has been so kind to me I ought not to think of those. Marshal Hilliard has been very gentlemanly and kind to me in every way possible.

"The hardest thing for me to stand here is the night, when there is no light. They will not allow me to have a candle to read by, and to sit in the dark all evening is very hard; but I do not want any favors that are against the rules. Mr. Wright and his wife are very kind to me and try to make it easier to bear, but of course, they must do their duty.

"There is one thing which hurts me very much. They say I don't show any grief. Certainly I don't in public. I never did reveal my feelings and I cannot change my nature now. They say I don't cry. They should see me when I am alone, or sometimes with my friends. It hurts me to think people say so about me. I have tried very hard to be brave and womanly through it all...

"It is a little thing, I suppose, but it hurt me when they said I was not willing to have my room searched. Why, I had seen so many different men that day and had been questioned about everything till my head was confused and in such a whirl that I could not think. I was lying down and Dr. Bowen was just preparing some medicine for me when a man came to my room and began to question me. I knew he was a policeman because he had brass buttons on his clothes. I asked the doctor:

'Must I see all these people now? It seems as if I cannot think a moment longer, my head pains me so.'

"He went out. When he returned he said I must see them, and then the policeman came back with another man. They spoke about my mother, and that was the time I said, 'She is not my mother, but my stepmother.' I supposed, if it was necessary that I must talk to them just then, I must tell as near as I could what was right...

"If people would only do me justice, that is all I ask, but it seems as if every word I have uttered has been distorted and such a false construction placed on it that I am bewildered. I can't understand it."

There was not a trace of anger in her tones – simply a pitiful expression. She recovered herself with an effort and we said "goodbye."

For the first time in print, a different side of Lizzie had been shown to readers. This was not the callous, hardened, bitter spinster that so many reporters had already painted. Instead, the public was shown a sad, gentle woman who was bearing up as best she could under terrible, grievous circumstances.

This was certainly not the Lizzie Borden who had been portrayed in the *Globe*, and they responded to the interview in their own pages the following day:

The flap-doodle, gush, idiotic drivel, misrepresentations, and in some instances, anarchic nonsense, which is being promulgated by women newspaper correspondents, WCTU conventions, and other female agencies in connection with the Borden murder just now, may originate in good intentions but do not strengthen Lizzie Borden's case much in the opinion of the public. The Commonwealth of

Massachusetts will, for the present, adhere to the forms of law in conducting cases, regardless of the clamor or criticism of any petticoat propaganda.

Along with this attack on women in general, the *Globe* (probably Edwin H. Porter), in the same edition, totally manufactured – and printed as fact – a story that claimed that Lizzie, six months before the murders, consulted with a Providence attorney about the disposal of property in case of death. The next day, the police denied all knowledge of any such consultation or attorney. Reporters from other newspapers canvassed every attorney in Providence and found that none of them had been contacted. The more honest papers branded the story a hoax, and it was never mentioned in the *Globe* again. However, it did prove that the editors of that questionable rag knew quite a lot about "flap-doodle and misrepresentations" themselves.

On Monday, August 22, Judge Blaisdell, who had presided at the inquest and the arraignment, was prepared to sit as well for the preliminary hearing in Fall River. Just as she had gone to the Taunton jail, wearing blue and escorted by Marshall Hilliard and Reverend Buck, Lizzie returned, wearing the same dress and with the same two escorts. She arrived on the 11:00 a.m. train, and by noon, the crowds had once again filled every available space around the courthouse. Once again, they were disappointed. Knowlton explained to the judge that the Commonwealth was not yet prepared for the hearing and asked for three more days. Jennings raised no objection and the postponement was granted. Lizzie was again placed in charge of the jail matron and remained in Fall River for the three days.

The preliminary hearing lasted for six days and there were 23 people – all from the usual cast of characters – on the witness list. The whole thing was merely a dress rehearsal for the real trial in superior court, and since the cases presented by both sides were almost identical to those to come, they will appear in detail in later chapters.

At the conclusion of the witness testimony, both Knowlton and Jennings argued their viewpoints with great intensity. Jennings was first:

I must say that I close this case with feelings entirely different from those I have ever experienced at the conclusion of any case. This man was not merely my client, he was my friend. I had known him from boyhood days, and if three short weeks ago anyone had told me that I should stand here defending his youngest daughter from the charge of murdering him, I should have pronounced it beyond the realm of human credibility...

I suggest that even the learned district attorney himself cannot imagine that any person could have committed that crime unless his heart was as black with hatred as hell itself.

In Edwin H. Porter's book, he stated repeatedly that Lizzie never showed any kind of emotion from the moment the murders were discovered. However, he did acknowledge that her tears flowed freely during Jennings' closing speech at the preliminary hearing. In a later paragraph, though, he returned to his usual form and said that she showed no emotion.

Jennings continued to speak and attacked the prosecution's failure to show motive or means in their case. It was almost impossible, he said, "for a person to commit these crimes without being almost covered with blood, from the waist upward in the case of Mr. Borden, and from the feet upward in the case of Mrs. Borden."

He added that the police had developed a theory that the murders had been committed by someone in the house and then set about "proving" it, one way or another. The persecution of Lizzie had been an outrage. He said, "Here was a girl they had been suspecting for days. She was virtually under arrest and, yet, for the purpose of extracting a confession from her to support their theory, they brought her here and put her to the rack, a thing they knew they would have no right to do if they placed her under arrest." Jennings was referring to the inquest, which had been hastily arranged to keep Lizzie from having an attorney present when she was being questioned.

Jennings continued, "Day after day the same questions were repeated to her in the hope to elicit some information that would criminate her. Is it a wonder there are conflicting statements? They haven't proved that this girl had anything to do with the murder. They can't find any blood on her dress, on her hair, on her shoes. They can't find any motive. They can't find the axes and so I say I demand the woman's release."

He begged the court, "Don't put the stigma of guilt upon this woman, reared as she has been and with a past character beyond reproach. Don't let it go out into the world as the decision of a just judge that she is probably guilty."

As Jennings returned to his place at the defense table, there was a moment of silence in the courtroom, and then it was followed by a ripple of applause that swelled until it became almost deafening. No effort was made to silence it. As it faded, tears could be seen in the eyes of the spectators. Lizzie, no matter what Edwin Porter claimed, openly wept and the court adjourned for a two-hour recess.

Knowlton was undoubtedly grateful for the break. This allowed the passion stirred by Jennings' argument to subside. No prosecutor, no matter how skilled, would have wanted to immediately follow such an appeal. He opened by agreeing with Jennings that, "There crime of murder touches the deepest sensibilities of feeling. There is the deepest feeling of horror about it, and above all, in the unnaturalness that brings the thrill of horror to every mind."

The murder of one's parents was a crime that went beyond mere tragedy, he said. "There was not a man, woman, or child in the world of whom we could not have said, they would have done it. But it was done. There is no motive for murder. There is reason for it, but no motive."

He explained that the police had directed their inquiries toward Lizzie simply because she was the one who benefitted from her parents' deaths. They had found, he said, the only person in the world with whom Abby did not get along. Since Jennings had chastised the police for not looking more diligently for the murderer outside the home, Knowlton protested that they had done that; they had followed every lead no matter how inconsequential it seemed, no matter where it went. They had chased tips, rumors, and reports, always ending up back at the Borden home in their search for the killer.

Knowlton had not alluded to the demeanor of the defendant, he said, and would not do so now. But then he promptly did, in his very next sentence: "While everybody is dazed, there is but one person who, throughout the whole business, has not seen to express emotion." He also added that he was relieved that, "these facts do not point to a woman who expressed any feminine feeling." Knowlton, like so many other men of the era could not understand a woman who did not faint, sob, and fall apart as stereotypes of the time demanded that they do. Even so, Lizzie's sensitivity to the events had brought her to tears and near collapse on numerous occasions – just apparently not often enough for law enforcement officials not to suspect her of murder.

He concluded his speech: "We are constrained to find that she has been dealing with poisonous things, that her story is absurd and that hers and hers alone has been the opportunity for the commission of the crime." And, to take the edge off the applause that had greeted Jennings' remarks, he added, "Yielding to clamor is not to be compared to that only and greatest satisfaction, that of a duty well done."

There was no applause when he sat down; only deathly silence.

Judge Blaisdell ended the proceedings: "The long examination is concluded and there remains but for the magistrate to perform what he believes to be his duty. It would be a pleasure for him, and he would doubtless receive much sympathy if he could say, 'Lizzie, I judge you probably not guilty. You may go home.' But upon the character of the evidence presented through witnesses who have been so closely and thoroughly examined, there is but one thing to be done – painful as it may be. The judgment of the court is that you are probably guilty and you are ordered committed to await the action of the superior court."

Blaisdell was later to say that he was satisfied the government had not produced enough evidence to warrant a conviction, nor perhaps the finding of an indictment, but he felt satisfied that enough had been shown to warrant holding the defendant for the grand jury, which could consider the entire case against her and report on the evidence.

Lizzie stood and listened to the clerk read the decision ordering her back to Taunton jail to await the action of the grand jury, which was scheduled to meet on November 7.

At this point in the narrative, many readers, especially those with anything more than a mild interest in crime and legal proceedings, are undoubtedly asking just what in the world could have happened in the case that Lizzie Borden would be judged "probably guilty" in the preliminary hearing. Unless the reader has come to this volume with the belief that Lizzie was indeed guilty of the murder of her father and stepmother, then it's likely that they are as baffled by all of this as I am. It's true that many legal standards have changed over the last century or so, but as far as I can tell, there seems to be no solid evidence at all that Lizzie could have committed the murders. I can assure the reader that I am holding nothing back for the purposes of suspense or to further any hidden agenda. What has been revealed in the book so far is what was revealed to the public at the same point in the case in 1892.

The police certainly believed that Lizzie committed the murders. They stated that she was the only person involved with the motive, means, and opportunity. Such things are useful as sort of a "directional arrow" way, meaning that they are used in the early part of a case to focus the investigation. Motive, means, and opportunity are useful in telling the investigators where they should look for evidence at the beginning of the case. But if a prosecutor is arguing at the end of the investigation that the accused had the motive, means, and opportunity to commit the crime, he is essentially saying that he has no clue about what actually happened.

We will explore all of the problems with the prosecutor's case in a later chapter, but suffice it to say, it never should have gone as far as it did. A few things were true – Lizzie and her stepmother may not have gotten along; Lizzie stood to inherit a large sum of money when her father died; many of her statements about the events of the morning were untrue, or at least confused – but did those things make her guilty of murder? No, they don't and, in fact, there was more working against Lizzie's guilt than for it. It's impossible that she could have committed the murders in the short window of time that she had. She would have been covered in blood after brutally slaying two people and, yet, according to eyewitness testimony, she had never changed her dress or had time to wash up that morning.

In my opinion, the fact that Lizzie was ever brought to trial at all is almost as puzzling as to who really committed the murders. But forensic science and DNA evidence did not exist in 1892 like it does today and Lizzie Borden was brought to trial. And that story, and what happened after, has yet to be told.

On November 15, a grand jury was seated for Lizzie Borden's case. During the two months between the preliminary hearing and the grand jury session, Knowlton was in almost daily contact with Attorney General Pillsbury. There were meetings, telephone calls, and letters dealing with every facet of the case. The content of their private conversations is unknown, but it is apparent from the letters that were preserved that Knowlton had no confidence in the prosecution's case and was debating with the attorney general over some method by which they would be justified in not taking it to the grand jury. Even Knowlton had come to realize that no real evidence existed against Lizzie, however, his hands were tied by the decision that Judge Blaisdell had reached in the preliminary hearing. There was nothing he could do but present the case to the grand jury.

On that afternoon in November, the jury listened to the Commonwealth's case, as outlined by the unenthusiastic Knowlton. Pillsbury had written: "I still favor holding back all that can be prudently held back especially as I now think that what you have absolutely determined to put in will make the case as strong to the public as if everything went in." It was bad advice. The grand jury adjourned six days later without taking any action.

In the meantime, Lizzie and Emma's friend, Alice Russell, had wrestled with her conscience and had come to the conclusion that Lizzie was guilty of the murders. She met with Knowlton and agreed to be a witness for the prosecution. In a flurry of activity, Knowlton called the grand jury into session again and presented Alice's story. The incident happened on the Sunday morning after the murders when Alice said she was at the Borden house and observed Lizzie burning a dress in the kitchen stove. She told Lizzie, "If I were you, I wouldn't let anybody see me do that." Lizzie said it was a dress stained with paint and was of no use.

Whatever else was said during this session is unknown, but on December 1, the grand jury voted 20 to 1 to return three indictments against Lizzie: one for the murder of Andrew, one for the murder of Abby, and third charging her with the murder of both. They had deliberated for only 10 minutes.

Soon after, Knowlton received a letter from Pillsbury, congratulating him for his continued work on "this accursed case."

Lizzie was returned at once to the Taunton Jail, and Jennings renewed his plea to Pillsbury that she be allowed to furnish bail; that there was no threat that she might flee the country. Pillsbury dismissed the request and wrote Knowlton: "Jennings spent the afternoon with me on Friday on the question of bail, but I think I have quieted him."

Pillsbury also received a letter asking for bail for Lizzie from the president of the Women's Christian Temperance Union (WCTU), and he sent back a sharp reply: "I have received your request to have Lizzie A. Borden admitted to bail with full appreciation of your feelings and of all the suggestions which you make in support of the request, all of which, however, with many other circumstances, have already been carefully considered. I cannot properly make any further reply than to ask that you give the prosecuting officers credit for some knowledge of the circumstances of the case, and of their own duty; and that you will extend to them the consideration which is due to public servants who are trying faithfully and conscientiously to discharge their duty without fear or favor."

Attorney General Pillsbury

Pillsbury's condescending reply to a women's organization was another example of the overall tenor of the case, dismissing the idea that women could have any knowledge of such lofty pursuits as the law. Lizzie did not behave in the way that women were expected to behave, so she must be guilty. Women who sent pleas for her to be allowed to post bail, even under the strictest conditions, were dismissed as not having any idea of what they were talking about.

Pillsbury may have been a misogynist, but he was also a bit of a coward when it came to his political ambitions. When Knowlton had balked about trying to take Lizzie's case to trial, Pillsbury could have stepped in as the principal attorney for the prosecution. However, as pressure began to build from Lizzie's supporters, particularly women's groups and religious organizations, he began worrying about the next election. He left Knowlton in place and later assigned William Moody, District Attorney of Essex County, to assist him.

As the months wore on and no date was set for Lizzie's trial, Jennings repeatedly wrote Pillsbury asking that it be done. The best he received was a curt "I am not at present able to give you any information upon that subject."

In December, Jennings asked if the trial could be set in Taunton, where Lizzie was being held. He wrote, "She is very urgent in this desire, and I trust that it can be brought about without seriously interfering with the arrangements of the government."

Pillsbury sent a one-sentence response: "I don't suppose anybody on the part of the government has so much as thought about it and of course it will be for the court to determine."

Finally, on May 8, 1893, six months after the grand jury's decision to indict, Lizzie was taken to New Bedford and arraigned before Judge J.W. Hammond of the superior court. She entered a plea of "not guilty" to each of the three indictments, and her trial was set for June 5 in New Bedford.

By this time, the entire town of Fall River had divided into two camps – those convinced of Lizzie's guilt and those convinced of her innocence. The murders and Lizzie's upcoming trial were still the subject of nightly supper conversation. Murder had always been a topic of both horror and fascination, but the Borden murders were something different. They did not involve sordid criminal offenders, drunks, or street brawlers. Murders of that type were common, almost expected. Had Andrew and Abby been murdered by a vagrant or a man that Andrew had cheated in business, the case would have vanished from the public eye in a matter of weeks. What kept interest in the case so high was the conflict between the two competing convictions: Lizzie must have done it – yet couldn't have done it. The public had six months in which to compare notes with their neighbors, argue their theories, and complain about or praise the officials in charge of the case.

Meanwhile, Knowlton and Pillsbury, even with the addition of Alice Russell's dress burning story, were still worried about their case. Left with all of the evidence that the police had managed to unearth – which didn't amount to much – they knew it was still highly doubtful that they could convict their prisoner. But then Knowlton came up with a new idea, which he took to Pillsbury: what if Lizzie could be examined by outstanding medical authorities and found to be insane? Jennings could then plead her incompetent and the Commonwealth could plea bargain with her and avoid a trial. Pillsbury agreed, and Knowlton and Hilliard dispatched officers throughout the city to see if anyone could be found who would say they had thought the Bordens were crazy.

District policeman Moulton Batchelder reported back to Knowlton with his findings:

Captain James C. Stafford of New Bedford said he knew Lizzie's mother well and she was a peculiar person but he had never heard of any of the Bordens or Morses being insane.

A Mrs. Holland said the same, though she had always thought them peculiar.

Abraham G. Hart of the Fall River Savings Bank said he didn't know much about Lizzie but didn't think either the Bordens or the Morses were insane.

Southard H. Miller, longtime friend of Andrew, who had commented to a newspaperman on the day of the murders, told of his lifetime friendship with the family and his opinion that, though somewhat peculiar, none of them was insane.

* *Rescome Case said he had never heard that any one of them was insane, but he thought some of them were worse than insane, whatever that meant.*

* *John S. Brayton knew of no streak of insanity, and neither did Mrs. William Almy, widow of one of Andrew's former partners. David Sewell Brigham, ex-city marshal of Fall River, didn't know of insanity in the family but offered the comment that Lizzie had a bad disposition. George A. Patty went further: "Lizzie is known to be ugly." Mrs. George Whitehead agreed with this opinion.*

Pillsbury was not finding what he was looking for, so he worked on his own, attempting to enlist the help of Dr. George F. Jelly, a Boston psychiatrist, and Dr. Edward Cowles of the McLean Asylum in Somerville, Massachusetts. Dr. Jelly turned him down with two sentences: "I have received your letter of today. I do not think the indications of insanity which you mention, are sufficiently strong or tangible enough to enable me to express any opinion."

Dr. Cowles response was just as negative: "I will say that my inferences are against any theory of insanity in the person charged with the crime, from anything I have so far read concerning her conduct before or after the event."

Knowlton reported his less that helpful findings to Pillsbury. Undaunted by the negative reports, they invited Jennings to Pillsbury's office in Boston to see if he could be talked into allowing Lizzie to undergo a sanity examination. Pillsbury wrote to Knowlton: "Jennings was here today, evidently indisposed to consent at first, but more inclined before he left, I think. He went away saying that he must see Adams [Jennings' associate, Melvin Adams] and that he would let us hear from him as soon as possible."

But Jennings did not fall for the ruse. He wrote to Pillsbury the next day: "Since my talk with you, I have been seriously considering your proposition and have come to the conclusion that I cannot consent to unite with you in the examination proposed. I asked Adams's opinion on the advisability of the course proposed, without expressing an opinion of my own, and also on my return hence, that of Mr. Holmes who, to a certain extent, represents the Borden girls, without informing him that I had consulted Adams. Both came to the same conclusion: that, in view of all the circumstances, we could not do anything which suggested a doubt about her innocence and that the course proposed would not be wise or expedient on our part."

In December, Pillsbury became gravely ill and was confined, first in the hospital and later, at home. He wrote to Knowlton that this turn of events almost insured his inability to take charge of the case at trial. In Massachusetts, the attorney general was charged to lead the team of prosecutors in cases of such importance, but Pillsbury had already balked at the glare of such a spotlight. His illness guaranteed that he would not be present. Knowlton would have no choice but to be in charge. This was depressing news for Knowlton and in a letter dated April 24, he wrote of his despair:

Personally, I would like very much to get rid of the trial of the case and fear that my feelings in that direction may have influenced by better judgment. I feel this all the more upon your not unexpected announcement that the burden of the trial would come upon me.

There is no way of knowing what had been discussed between the two men about the case, but it is apparent from Knowlton's letter that it was his opinion that they should have quashed the indictment. However, his fear of public sentiment caused him to wait too long. At this point, he could only pass the buck back to another jury and let them decide what to do.

His letter continued:

I confess, however, I cannot see my way clear to any disposition of the case other than a trial. Should it result in disagreement of the jury, there should be no difficulty in disposing of the case by admitting the defendant to bail; but a verdict either way would render such a course unnecessary. The case has proceeded so far and an indictment has been found by the grand inquest of the county, that it does not seem to me that we ought to take the responsibility of discharging her without a trail, even though there is every reasonable expectation of a verdict of not guilty.

At this point, even the prosecutors had realized that they had no real case against Lizzie. But the words of the letter speak volumes about the callousness exhibited by these two men that they would allow Lizzie to be stigmatized forever by bringing her to trial even though they had every reasonable expectation of an acquittal. This was what Reverend Jubb had prayed they would not do in his sermon after the murders, and what Jennings had pleaded with Judge Blaisdell not to do when he addressed the court at the preliminary hearing.

We can only wonder if they would have taken the same approach if it had been a man on trial for murder in a questionable case that would probably end in acquittal – a man with a family name or a reputable business that could be ruined if his name was slandered in such a way. Lizzie was simply a woman and thus, expendable, by the standards of the day.

What it amounted to was that, although they couldn't prove Lizzie guilty, she can't prove she is innocent, therefore she must be brought to trial. It was an incredible interpretation of the presumption of innocence. Even Knowlton, at this point, does not accuse her of murder, only that she has "had some knowledge" of the occurrence.

Nor does he now accept any of the responsibility for the grand jury's indictment. Reaffirming his reluctance in presenting the case, he continued:

She has presented for a trial by jury which, to say the least, was not influenced by anything said by the government in the favor of the indictment.
Without discussing the matter more fully in this letter, I will only say as above indicated that I cannot see how any other course than setting the case down for trial, and trying it, will satisfy that portion of public sentiment, whether favorable to her or not, which is worthy of being respected.
June seems to be the most satisfactory month, all things considered. I will write more fully as to the admission of her confession after I have looked the matter up.

What Knowlton was referring to when he wrote of her "confession" is yet another mystery in this case. Certainly, Lizzie had not confessed to anything. It could have been a typographical error or an error in dictation. If it was some reference to her testimony at the inquest, it had been anything but a confession.

Had a copy of this letter fallen into the hands of Andrew Jennings, there would never have been a Lizzie Borden trial --- or, if it was indeed unavoidable, it would only have lasted as long as it would have taken to read the letter to the jury. It is a revealing look at what was taking place behind the prosecution's closed doors, and a reprehensible one at that.

But, of course, that letter was not made public until many decades later, and there was a Lizzie Borden trial, which was set by the court for June 5 in the town of New Bedford.

7. LUNATICS, CONFESSIONS & MESSAGES FROM THE SPIRIT WORLD

As with any other case that captures the public imagination, it was not only curiosity-seekers and amateur detectives who found themselves drawn to the Borden murders. Letter after letter came pouring into the offices of Marshal Hilliard and Prosecutor Knowlton, offering confessions, bizarre clues, and a wealth of ghostly information that had been gleaned from the world beyond.

Several people confessed to Knowlton. "Whiskey done the deed, not me," one anonymous letter-writer said. Another confession, dated eight days after the murders, was written from an Albany, New York hotel:

The killing of old man Bordon [sic] and his wife was not perpetrated by any member of his family as is generally supposed. But they were put out of the way by an illegitimate son whom Bordon refused to recognize after the mother of his offspring died a number of years ago in a certain Massachusetts insane asylum of a broken heart.

That son is now 25 years of age. He was not known to any member of the family save the old man and woman.

The letter went on to say that the writer was that illegitimate son, and that Andrew had been bribed into paying him each year for the past 25 years and was supposed to have made a final payment of $5,000, but Abby had convinced him to renege on the deal. Angry, the writer claimed that he had killed Andrew and Abby with a hatchet, which he dropped overboard from a Fall River steamer. "There is no use in tracking me," the letter concluded, "for it will be an utter impossibility to do so. At the hour this letter is mailed, I shall take a train for hundreds of miles away."

If Knowlton investigated the existence of such a son, he left no written record of it but, oddly, the story rings very close to one of the "solutions" to the murders that emerged in the 1990s, but it was largely dismissed at the time. Marshal Hilliard had also received the same letter and he commented to Knowlton that it was strange that the illegitimate son hadn't known how to spell the Borden name. He had spelled it "Bordon" throughout both letters.

Another letter arrived from Boston:

You are fooling your time away trying to place the deed of the Borden family upon the young lady Miss Lizzie Borden as I can satisfy you if you could only get hold of me that she is not guilty.

No power will ever hang me for the deed for I shall blow my brains out. But, before I do, I shall clear Miss Borden in some way without showing the Fall River police that they are in any way smart. I had a motive and swore that I should kill the Bordens and kill I have, but I hope no innocent person will suffer for my crime. I could tell you all the particulars if I could have my revolver at my head to not give you a chance to hang me. I slept in the barn the night before. After the deed, I jumped the fence, flew down to the pond, and washed my face and hands. The police will find my coat and pants buried about ten feet out in the pond, and my old black slouch hat, all covered with three large stones.

Alfred A. Smith, a 16-year-old resident of the Massachusetts Reformatory, where he was serving a term for breaking and entering and larceny, wrote to say that he had been passing by the Borden home on the morning of the murders and had seen a woman looking out an upstairs window and she had hastily backed away at the sight of him. He had passed back by on the street a little while later and the same thing had happened again. On a third trip, he claimed, he had found a hatchet and a pair of blood-stained gloves just inside of the fence. He had sold the hatchet for 10-cents and had thrown away one of the gloves, but thought the other was home in a bureau drawer. Believe it or not, the police checked out his story. The glove was nowhere to be found.

Letters poured in, flooding Knowlton and Hilliard with criticism, advice, theories, even fan mail. The letters came from attorneys, society matrons, learned thinkers, farmers, housewives, and meat packers. "I am a woman away up in Vermont, but I am also an invalid and have much time for thought and reading," Elvira Daggett wrote. " . . . From the first I have been convinced of her guilt."

One "theorist" concluded that Lizzie Borden avoided splattering her clothes with blood by disrobing before she committed the murders. Another said she dressed like a man, an attempt to explain sightings of a stranger. "Can it be possible that you are not going to put Emma Borden on the stand? She KNOWS whether her sister committed that murder or not," wrote "a woman who wonders if there is such a thing as Justice."

And speaking of "justice," in the file that Knowlton kept marked as "cranks" were a number of letters from a correspondent who called himself by that very name. In the letters, "Justice" alternately berated the police, who "deserve knocking on the head for their stupidity," and advised Knowlton how the investigation should be conducted. He stated that Dr. Bowen should be taken by the neck and flung into a cell (although he did not say why); the murderer had hidden himself under a bed; the murder weapon was buried in the garden among the flowers and vegetables. And on and on.

A dentist from Toledo, Ohio, wrote to say that he believed the murderer had chloroformed his victims before he killed them. A former warden at the New York Pasematta Convict Prison said that Lizzie had worn a dress or wrap and used gloves that would "take but a moment to destroy." More than a dozen people claimed that the murder weapon was not an axe, but the iron that Lizzie had used to press her handkerchiefs. Letters arrived that urged Marshal Hilliard to look for the missing weapon in the well, the stove flue, in the piano, under the floor, in the walls, in the oven, and every other conceivable place in the house that had already been searched. A Dedham, Massachusetts, letter writer wanted to know if there was an old-fashioned privy where the murder weapon might have been "deposited." There wasn't. Another writer suggested that the axe might be found in the chimney. It wasn't.

Religion and racism figured prominently in the letters to Knowlton. One letter stated, "Your chances will not be hurt for the attorney generalship by doing your duty, even if it does hang an Irishman." A Vermont writer warned "Beware of Jesuits," which became a common theme in many letters. One writer helpfully explained that "True Americans will learn in time to never employ a foreigner," and noted that Bridget was the villain in the saga. A man from Newport, Rhode Island, agreed: "I have seen enough Roman Catterlicks to believe they can do some poisonous, murderous deeds against Protestants!" A New York man wrote that the "Portugee" the police had been looking for was actually Mr. C. Norlander, a Swedish newspaperman who lived around the corner on Third Avenue.

Many wrote to congratulate the police on the job they had done, and at least half of them stated that Knowlton and Hilliard were heroes. But one post card writer, signed "Voter," said that one thing was certain: Knowlton would never be district attorney again. "The people of Bristol County will tend to that next November after the mean, underhanded part you have taken in the Borden case."

For every crank letter that Knowlton received, Hilliard could count three. Within a week, "confessions" had come from Minneapolis, Boston, New York, Circleville, Ohio, Chicago, Rochester, New York, and Springfield, Massachusetts. One writer said that he murdered them for $60; another wanted "the old man's money"; an Ohio man did it with his "Indian tomahawk;" another wrote, "I taken them by my own hand. Spare the fair maiden"; a man from Chicago claimed, "I took revenge for the harm done to me nearly hav a score years ago by the old perjurer and outrager"; and a

Massachusetts writer dared the police, "Catch me if you can old boy! I'm too sharp for you!"

One letter from Brockton, Massachusetts, said that he did not commit the crime, but offered to tell the police who did if they simply responded to his letter – which was unsigned and had no return address. A writer from Providence, Rhode Island, offered to "place in your hands the circumstances and actors in this fearful drama," for the mere sum of $85,000. Mrs. S.A. Douglas of River Point, Rhode Island wanted much less for her crime-solving services. She would come to Fall River and obtain a confession for just $8 or $10 a day, whichever the police department wanted to offer.

Hilliard received a number of letters urging him to blame the "Anarchists," just on general principles, or on a "secret alien order" the writer knew about. Another wrote from New York saying that Lizzie had contacted him several years ago, offering a large sum of money if Andrew and Abby could be electrocuted. A man named John S. Adams from Boston tried to convince the police to find a man named Dominick Flynn and "keep a red eye on him."

Three writers said that the solution to the murders was simple. All Hilliard had to do was look in the eyes of Andrew and Abby. Everyone knew that the last image seen before death was frozen on the victim's retina!

If all earthly methods of detection continued to fail, then perhaps it was time to turn to the spirit world. Scores of Spiritualists contacted Knowlton and Hilliard, claiming to be in contact with Andrew and Abby on the other side, or to pass along messages from spirits who knew the true identity of the killer. One psychic medium wrote from Lynn, Massachusetts, to say that she was in communication with the dead and had been told there was a closest at the end of the "sopha" where Andrew had been resting (there wasn't) and that a man had hidden there until he had the opportunity to commit the murder. The weapon had been a broad blade claw hammer and he had "thrown it in the cellar."

Another medium from Boston wrote to say that she had experienced a vision that told her that the bloodstained "effects" of the Bordens were hidden under the floor in a lower room covered by a carpet. She assured Knowlton that her visions were "inspirational," and he would do well to listen to her.

The owner of a Ouija board penned an 8-page transcript of a conversation that he had with the board in which every question about the murders was clearly answered. There was also "assistance" received from astrologers who needed to know the birth dates of Andrew, Abby, and Lizzie to determine of the planet Saturn had been on a spot in the sky occupied by the sun or the moon at the time of the murders. Mrs. Alexander of Rochester, New York, wrote to say that she "had the charm" and could make Andrew and Abby speak the name of the person who murdered them.

M.T. Richardson, publisher of the *Boots and Shoes Weekly*, was a well-known phrenologist (a "science" of the late nineteenth century that studied the human mind by way of the bumps on the skull) and claimed that he only needed a good photograph of Lizzie's head to determine if she would murder anyone under the right circumstances. A man named Theo VanWyck of Mount Vernon, New York, asked for a photograph of Lizzie's hand. He was an expert at palmistry, he said, and could read the lines in her hand to see if she was capable of murder.

But it would not be Spiritualists, palm readers, cranks, kooks, or crazed confessors that would provide the weirdest chapter of the Borden case – that would come from the otherwise illustrious newspaper, the *Boston Globe*, the largest paper in New England. The *Boston Globe* was in the midst of celebrating its twentieth anniversary. Just a month before the trial, it had printed a special commemorative edition that celebrated the date, and it had contained an unprecedented 183 columns of advertising, trumpeting the fact that it had the largest circulation in the region.

Their leading crime reporter, Henry Trickey, had been in Fall River since the day after the murders. Working for a great Massachusetts paper, rather than an out-of-state one, gave Trickey an inside track with the local police. He was especially tight with officers Medley and Mullaly, Assistant Marshal Fleet, and E.D. McHenry, a private investigator with questionable credentials. McHenry was probably hired by the Fall River police in some capacity, but after what became known as the "Trickey Affair," there was no one who admit to knowing him.

According to the story in the *Boston Globe*, McHenry had approached Trickey and told him that Marshal Hilliard had given him the task of copying the affidavits of 25 witnesses who were going to testify against Lizzie. It was the Commonwealth's entire case, and, for $1,000, Trickey could have an exclusive look at the statements.

Sensing that he could scoop all of the competition, Trickey gave him $30, which was all that he had on him at the moment, and took the next train to Boston to get the rest of the money from his editors. The newspaper put up the remaining $970, and Trickey was on his way back to Fall River the next afternoon.

For a week, McHenry stalled and dodged him, but finally handed over a collection of papers, accepting another $400 from Trickey.

Jumping back on the train, Trickey took his scoop back to Boston. Without ever bothering to verify McHenry's claims, the *Boston Globe* stunned the nation the following day with a story that occupied the entire center of their front page. The headline flashed:

LIZZIE BORDEN'S SECRET
MR. BORDEN DISCOVERED IT AND HOT WORDS FOLLOWED
STARTLING TESTIMONY OF 25 NEW WITNESSES
EMMA WAS KICKED DURING THAT QUARREL
FAMILY DISCORD AND MURDER

It turned out to be a wild, ludicrous story, but the *Boston Globe* assured their readers the information "here published for the first time, is corroborated in a most convincing manner":

The Globe *is enabled to lay before its readers not only every facet of importance and now in the government's possession, but as well to describe how and by whom the information was secured by the patient and unceasing toil of the police. The evidence is forthcoming from 25 people, all of whom stand high in the community and have no motive for speaking maliciously about the defendant.*

Column after column exposed the details of the 25 "affidavits"; each one of them quoted in full.

John H. Murphy, Bedford Street, for instance, planned to testify that he was standing on the sidewalk close to the Borden house and had seen Lizzie open the window of the room in which Abby had been killed. The time was such that, at that very moment, "she must have been standing over the mutilated remains of her stepmother."

Mrs. Gustave Ronald and Mr. Peter Mahaney were also standing in front of the Borden house at 9:40 that morning and they both heard a "terrible cry or groan." Looking up at the open guest room window of the Borden house, they had both seen Lizzie in plain view, her head covered with a rubber hood. Augustus Gunning, described as a lodger at Mrs. Churchill's home, planned to testify that he, too, saw Lizzie at the window in a hood.

According to the *Boston Globe*, "These witnesses fix Miss Borden at her mother's side almost at the minute when she was probably killed."

This testimony was bad enough, but worse would come from Mr. and Mrs. Frederick Chace and their daughter, Abigail, who had been guests of the Bordens on the night before the murders. They had overheard a terrible quarrel between Lizzie and Andrew. Andrew had screamed at his daughter, "You can make your own choice and do it tonight! Either let us know what his name is or take the door on Saturday and when you go fishing, fish for some other place to live, as I will never listen to you again. I will know the name of the man who got you into trouble!"

Lizzie replied, "If I marry this man, will you be satisfied that everything will be kept from the outside world?"

"I would rather see her dead than have it come out," Andrew had said to his guests. When asked if he knew the name of the man who had gotten Lizzie into trouble, he said, "No; but I have my suspicions and have had all along. If I am right, I will never recognize this man in the world. She has made her own bed, so let her lie upon it."

It was a shocking story, but a Mr. G. Romaine Pittson would also swear that Andrew had discussed Lizzie's "condition" with him just a few days earlier.

Almost as condemning as all of the testimony about Lizzie's "condition" was that of Mrs. George Sisson, who planned to speak about a conversation that she had overheard at the funeral between Lizzie and Bridget Sullivan. Lizzie snapped at the maid, "Are you a fool or a knave? Why don't you say how much money you want and keep quiet?" Even though, in truth, Bridget had not attended the funeral, Mrs. Sisson would testify that Andrew had told her that he had made out a will leaving $25,000 to be shared by Emma and Lizzie and all else to Abby. She also would state in court that Lizzie had offered to sell her a watch that had been stolen in the earlier daylight robbery of the Borden home for $10. And Bridget, she said, would swear that Lizzie called her aside on the afternoon of the murders and had whispered to her, "Keep your tongue still and don't talk to these officers and you can have all the money you want."

McHenry himself would take the stand and testify that, for days, he had hidden under Lizzie's bed in the jail quarters and had listened to conversations between Lizzie, Reverend Buck, Andrew Jennings, police matron Reagan, Emma, and all of her other visitors. To make his vigilance more comfortable, he had removed a portion of the wall in the adjoining bathroom, replaced the wall with muslin cloth, and had himself a clear view of Lizzie's cell at all times. From behind this curtain (and the story did not address the obvious issues of privacy and impropriety subjected on a woman of the Victorian era), he had heard an overheated argument between Lizzie and Emma in which Lizzie cried that Emma wanted to see her hanged and would not keep her secret. The argument culminated with Lizzie viciously kicking Emma three times, throwing biscuits at her, and called her a "damned bitch."

The evening edition of the *Boston Globe* added more lurid details. Even though by this time, the story had gotten so ridiculous that it was hard to believe the newspaper's editors were even reading the articles before they were being printed, in the evening edition, they actually boasted about their "scoop":

ASTOUNDED!
ALL NEW ENGLAND READ THE STORY
GLOBES WERE BOUGHT BY THE THOUSANDS
LIZZIE BORDEN APPEARS IN A NEW LIGHT
BELIEF IN HER INNOCENCE SHAKEN
EXCITEMENT RUNS HIGH IN FALL RIVER
POLICE THINK THE SCOOP A CORKER

In addition to everything else the articles had gotten wrong, the police in Fall River certainly did not think the "scoop a corker." One of the main points of

McHenry's story was that the Fall River police were baffled by the crime and had admitted defeat. In fact, they had basically given up on the investigation, and turned it all over to McHenry, who had experienced little difficulty in coming up with 25 witnesses and had single-handedly solved the case.

But as the *Boston Globe's* evening edition was hitting the newsstands, blaring the triumph of their "corker," the story was already starting to unravel. Inspector Harrington of the Fall River police was the first to fire off a telegram to the newspaper saying that the entire testimony attributed to him in the piece was a lie.

Andrew Jennings issued an immediate statement calling the story a tissue of lies, citing the fact that many of the addresses of the "witnesses" were vacant lots or did not exist at all. Many of the witnesses could not be found in the city directory – they had been made up completely – and others reported that they had never been questioned and had certainly not made a statement. Dr. Bowen, Lizzie's physician, telegraphed the paper to say that she had no secret "condition." By nightfall, responsible parties at the *Boston Globe* began to realize that they had been taken in by a gigantic hoax.

In the next edition of the paper, they began to backtrack, but they were still not yet willing to admit that they had been duped in a way that few newspapers ever had. Admitting no responsibility for publishing the story without verifying any part of it, they pointed the finger at McHenry:

DETECTIVE MCHENRY TALKS
HE FURNISHED THE GLOBE WITH THE BORDEN STORY
IT HAS BEEN PROVED WRONG IN SOME PARTICULARS

Some particulars? There was hardly any part of the story that was true, and the newspaper knew it. And so did McHenry, even though he stuck to his guns, claiming, "the names of the witnesses were given wrong for obvious reasons," but not saying what those obvious reasons were. The facts, he said, were all correct. They weren't, of course, and, by now, the *Boston Globe's* attorneys had convinced management that they needed to admit that they had been tricked. At this point, it was unlikely that the newspaper could withstand the lawsuits that were definitely coming.

The center section of Tuesday's front page carried a retraction and apology in boldface type:

THE LIZZIE BORDEN CASE

The Globe feels it its duty as an honest newspaper to state that it has been grievously misled in the Lizzie Borden case. It published on Monday a communication that it believed to be true evidence. Some of this remarkably ingenious and cunningly contrived story was undoubtedly based on facts. The Globe believes however that much of it is false and never should have been published. The Globe being misled has innocently added to the terrible burdens of Miss Lizzie Borden. We hereby tender our heartfelt apology for the inhuman reflection on her honor as a woman and for any injustice the publication reflected on her.

It was a well–written and tactful retraction and apology, but had Lizzie filed libel action against the paper, as Andrew Jennings urged, in all probability she would have been the owner of the *Boston Globe* when all had been said and done. Perhaps with that fact in mind, the paper continued to apologize the next day:

HONEST AMEND
GLOBE APOLOGY PLEASED ITS READERS
REGRETS SPREAD BROADCAST AT FALL RIVER
MCHENRY'S ACTS CONDEMNED BY FAIR–MINDED CITIZENS

The editorial page went on to offer additional apologies, but this was not the end of the affair.

In addition to paying McHenry, Henry Trickey had also offered Bridget $1,000 to leave the country. Bridget reported it to Knowlton, and the same grand jury that had indicted Lizzie also handed down an indictment of Trickey for tampering with a government witness. The indictment was kept secret for some time because Trickey had fled the region, but word leaked on December 3. Attorney General Pillsbury was incensed over the tampering charge and ordered Knowlton to have Trickey hunted down. Two days later, though, it was the *Boston Globe* that found him:

HENRY G. TRICKEY DEAD
TRIED TO BOARD A MOVING TRAIN AND FELL

Not satisfied with this quick and easy solution, Pillsbury told Knowlton that he needed to send someone to examine the corpse and make sure that it was Trickey – it was.

In the meantime, E.D. McHenry was fired from the detective agency that he had been working for in Providence and fled to New York. He mailed off incoherent letters to Hilliard, Knowlton, and Pillsbury, blaming everyone connected with the investigation, claiming that Trickey had committed suicide, and begging that he be paid for his services in Fall River. A short time later, he vanished from history and his part in a scam that colors the Lizzie Borden case to this day remained unpunished.

8. THE TRIAL OF LIZZIE BORDEN BEGINS

On the morning of June 5, 1893, just as they had in Fall River, crowds began to gather outside of the courthouse in New Bedford. They shuffled in early, filling up the sidewalks along County Street, jostling onto the pavement and trampling on the grass. Many of the curiosity-seekers remained all day in hope of spotting someone associated with the case. By the next day, it would be necessary to put up a temporary fence around the trim, columned brick building to hold them back. Every hotel and boarding house was filled to capacity. The passing of ten months since the murders of Andrew and Abby Borden had done nothing to cool the public's interest in the drama.

At exactly 11:28 a.m., Andrew Wright, sheriff of Bristol County, now acting as bailiff, silenced the crowd that was packed shoulder to shoulder in the second floor courtroom. With flourish, he swung open the door to the chambers of the justices and escorted to the bench, one at a time, the three judges who would preside over the trial – Associate Justice Caleb Blodgett, Associate Justice Justin Dewey, and Chief Justice Albert Mason.

At separate facing tables were the counsels for the defendant and the Commonwealth. Andrew Jennings and Melvin O. Adams represented Lizzie. A third attorney, former Governor George D. Robinson, would not be present until later in the week. Hosea M. Knowlton, district attorney for the second district, and William H. Moody, district attorney for the eastern district, were seated for the prosecution.

Lizzie was the next to enter the courtroom. She was dressed in black except for a blue plume of feathers in her hat, two blue velvet rosettes in her hair, and an enameled pansy pin at her throat. Her brown hair was pulled back into a soft, long roll behind her head. In her gloved hands, she held a tiny spray of flowers and a silk fan to try and keep cool in the oppressively hot courtroom. One reporter, who had heard nothing but horrible things about Lizzie but was just now seeing her for the first time, wrote: "She is no Medusa or Gorgon. There is nothing wicked, criminal, or hard in her features. She was modest, calm, quiet, and it was plain to see that she had complete mastery of herself and could make her sensations and emotions invisible to an impertinent public."

With the suffocating courtroom filled with 145 prospective jurors (three had been excused by death or illness), 40 or more newsmen, a handful of Lizzie's supporters, and the officers of the court, no spectators were admitted on the first day. Seating capacity had been increased by 50 chairs, and 25 had been set aside for reporters, but even that was not enough to accommodate the crowd. Another 15 seats were hastily added but, even after that, reporters found themselves scribbling their notes on tablets resting on their knees, while other reporters were forced to stand along the walls.

The prospective jurors were farmers and merchants. All of them were bearded and at least middle-aged. Both sides had agreed there would be no young men on the jury, and none from Fall River. There were, of course, no women considered for jury duty in those days.

Jury selection was much quicker in 1893 than it is today. Deciding on the jurors for Lizzie's trial was strictly in the hands of Judge Mason. Tradition was that if the judge considered a prospective juror to be sane and solid, then he was. Each counsel was permitted to challenge 22 of them peremptorily, with or without cause. Jennings challenged 15, and each time, Lizzie was required to stand at her place in the dock and say the single word, "challenge." Moody challenged 12 for the prosecution.

By 5:00 p.m., 108 of the jurors had been questioned by Judge Mason and 12 were chosen for the trial. They were William F. Dean, Louis B. Hodges, and John C. Finn of Taunton, Frank G. Cole of Attleboro, Charles I. Richards of North Attleboro, George Potter of Westport, John Wilbur of Somerset, Frederick C. Wilbar of Raynham, Lemuel K. Wilber of Easton, William Westcot of Seekonk, Augustus Swift of New Bedford, and Allen H. Wordell of Dartmouth. Judge Mason appointed Charles Richards to act as the jury's foreman.

Someone on Knowlton's staff had prepared short descriptions of the men who would hear the case. Whoever this staff person was, his handwritten comments offer an interesting look at the trial from the prosecution's side of the courtroom:

Frank G. Cole, Republican and unmarried, but all these jewelers are intelligent men and read papers. A good straight man. Grand Army.

John C. Finn, Irishman, but very intelligent.

Augustus Swift, Protestant and a deep believer in circumstantial evidence. Good man. With us.

Charles I. Richards, string-straight man no matter what anyone said.

George Potter, American and Universalist, but a Mason. Limited education but has common sense.

The jury at the Lizzie Borden trial.

Lemuel K. Wilber, didn't believe in capital punishment but wife thinks Lizzie is guilty.

Judge Mason advised the jury that their pay would be $3 per day, plus board and lodging, for the duration of the trial. At some time the next day, he told them, they would take the short train ride to Fall River to familiarize themselves with the Borden home and property. After that, court was adjourned for the day.

In the time between Christmas -- when Attorney General Pillsbury decided that he was not going to take the lead prosecution chair in Lizzie's trial -- and the start of the proceedings, District Attorney Knowlton had made the interesting decision that he was going to take as little part in the trial as he reasonably could. As noted from his letters to Pillsbury, his heart was not in it. He had no faith in the case and after failing to find a way out of going to trial, he was forced to continue with it. But Knowlton had no intention of taking the blame for what was going to happen. His associate, William Moody, was neither as experienced nor as familiar with the details of the case, but he was a competent, energetic man. He would carry the bulk of the presentation. For the first seven days, Knowlton handed the entire case to Moody.

At 9:00 a.m. on day two, Moody was the first to address the jury. The Essex county district attorney walked to the railing and spoke to the assembled men in a low, quiet manner, which fit the melancholy mood of the moment. He was obviously ill at ease, but was determined to present the evidence in such a way that the jury would have no choice but to find Lizzie guilty. He had a grim task ahead of him.

He leaned forward toward the jury members:

Upon the fourth day of August of the last year, an old man and woman, husband and wife, each without a known enemy in the world, in their own home, upon a frequented street in the most populous city in this county, under the light of day and in the midst of its activities were, first one, then, after an interval of an hour, another, killed by an unlawful human agency.

Today, a woman of good social position, of hitherto unquestioned character, a member of a Christian church and active in its good works, the own daughter of one of the victims is at the bar of this court accused by the grand jury of this county of these crimes.

There is no language, gentlemen, at my command which can better measure the solemn importance of the inquiry which you are about to begin than this simple statement of facts.

He then spent the next two hours describing that "simple statement of facts."

An opening statement made by an attorney on either side is not, of course, actual evidence. They are really recitations of what each hopes to prove. Exaggerations as to the strength of those positions are commonplace, and the worthiness of the evidence to come is accented by what is said and what is not said. Each side works hard to convince the jury that theirs is the true version of events, hoping that what their case lacks in hard evidence can be made up for in histrionics and sleight of hand. The opening minutes of any trial are often the most important. Setting the tone, winning the trust of the jury, and appearing sincere are almost of greater importance than the details of the evidence to come.

Moody talked the jury through the minutes of that fateful August day, pausing along the way to put special emphasis on things that were important to the prosecution's case. He spoke at length about the animosity and hatred that the Commonwealth would maintain filled the house on Second Street, and pointed out that Lizzie refused to call Abby her mother. He told of the sickness that the family had suffered the days before and the day of the murders and promised that they would prove that Lizzie tried to purchase prussic acid the very day before. He described the house and property in great detail, though the jury had come to the courtroom that day prepared to travel there in the afternoon for their own inspection of the scene. Minute by minute, he timed the day of the murder as the prosecution believed that it had taken place. The doors with locks on every one were described, as were the details of Bridget's window washing, and the gruesome state of Andrew and Abby's mutilated bodies.

Moody said: "There was blood spattered in every direction and it is probably spatters would be impressed on the clothing of the assassin." This was a statement that he would later twist into one of the focal points of the trial.

After listing all of the things that the prosecution was prepared to prove, Moody concluded his opening, "We shall ask you to say whether any other reasonable hypothesis except that of the guilt of the prisoner can account for the said occurrences which happened upon the morning of August 4. The time for idle rumor, for partial, insufficient information, for hasty and inexact reasoning, is past."

From the opening minutes of the trial that morning, Lizzie had sat erect and almost motionless in her seat, her eyes fixed on Moody, attentive to his every word as he spoke to the jury. She held her tightly folded fan in her hand, lightly touching it to her cheek. During Moody's graphic description of the multiple wounds and the contents of the victims' stomachs, she became visibly pale and she covered her eyes with a handkerchief. All eyes in the room were on her as Moody stepped away from the rail.

A reporter that was sitting a few feet away from her detailed the scene:

Two or three minutes had passed and Lizzie had not moved. The fan and arm that held it up dropped into the prisoner's lap. The head was back against the rail, her eyes were shut, her mouth was open and her breath heaved with very long breaths.

"Lizzie Borden is asleep!" was the whisper that galloped through the courtroom. Deputy Sheriff Kirby, who sat beside her, took friendly alarm at such disrespectful behavior and tried to waken her before the court should see her. He shook her arm. Her heard rolled over so that her cheek rested on the rail at right angles to the line of her body. A purple cast came over her face. City Missionary Jubb of Fall River sprang to his feet and began to fan her.

A deputy sheriff came quickly with a glass of water. After a little, she regained partial consciousness. Mr. Jubb ordered somewhat sharply to find her smelling salts. Then she put both hands on the arms of the chair and fell back against the railing, not half over her faint. Mr. Jubb was applying the smelling salts and was so much in earnest that her breath went from her and she put up her hand to push the bottle away. In another minute her eyes opened. Sheriff Wright, in the meantime, began rapping on the desk for order. The people crept back into their seats and the episode ended with Miss Borden leaning her head against the rail, with her eyes shut.

In short, Lizzie fainted, likely from a combination of the heat in the courtroom, her heavy dress, and the vivid descriptions of her father and stepmother's slaughtered corpses. The headlines in the papers the next day made much of her fainting spell, but, since such a public display of distress and emotion did not match up with his carefully constructed image of Lizzie, Edwin Porter did not mention it in the newspaper or in his history of the Borden murders.

Lizzie's fainting spell did appear in the *New York Times*, however, and the editors added their own commentary on the trial and the case against her:

The trial of Lizzie Borden on a charge of murdering her father and stepmother opened at New Bedford yesterday with the process of selecting jurors. This trial is likely to be followed with peculiar interest on account of the extraordinary character of the case and the mystery in which the murder has been enveloped from the moment of its discovery. The probability would seem to be overwhelmingly against the young woman who is charged with it unless she was insane, but the crime itself affords the only evidence of her insanity and that plea was repelled by her counsel. On the other hand, not the slightest evidence has been found so far as has yet appeared to the public of the perpetration of the crime by anyone else, and circumstances have seemed to point to the guilt of the accused. The development of the evidence before the court will be watched with unusual interest.

The editors at the *New York Times* had managed, with a single paragraph, to sum up the entire mystery of the Lizzie Borden case: she couldn't have murdered Andrew and Abby unless she was insane, which she wasn't; but there was no evidence that anyone else could have done it! It was on this proposition that the prosecution had built its case. The fatal flaw of it was not on shoddy work by the police or the prosecutors, but their arrogant belief that the uneducated public would never perceive the difference between what *might* have been and what *must* have been.

A brief recess was called to allow Lizzie to recover herself, and when all were again settled, Moody called the trial's first witness, civil engineer Thomas Kieran. He gave a drawn-out description of the Borden house and detailed the size and location of the rooms, as well as the relationship between the house, the barn, and the neighboring homes.

Civil engineer Thomas Kiernan testified that Abby's body could not have been seen from the hall, angering the prosecution.

Andrew Jennings was aware that the prosecution would attempt to make something of the fact that, during the morning hours, Lizzie had gone upstairs to her room and had passed the guest room where Abby's body was found when she was both coming and going. Since the door was known to be open, it seemed odd that she did not see Abby. She was lying "in plain view from the hall," Moody had said.

When cross-examined by Jennings, Kieran admitted that he had conducted a series of tests while measuring the Borden house to determine what could be seen when opposite the guest room door as a person walked up and down the stairs. He had even had one of his assistants lie in the same spot where Abby had died. "Then I went downstairs and came up the stairs in the middle of the stairs, as I would if I had been trying to see this man," the engineer said.

Moody immediately jumped to his feet, protesting the evidence given by his own witness, but his objection was overruled.

Kieran continued, stating that when he climbed the steps as a person ordinarily would, he could not see his assistant, even though he knew he was lying there. Only by pausing on one certain step and gazing along the floor line, could he see the man's feet protruding – a man who was much taller than Abby. From the hallway – and the door to Lizzie's room – he could see nothing.

Jennings had made a small point, but an important one. On this victorious note for the defense, court was adjourned for the field trip to Fall River.

On day three, the trial moved ahead with its deadly business. Photographer James A. Walsh identified the official photographs he had taken of the crime scene, including the mutilated bodies, and they were introduced into the record.

The second witness on the stand was the still mysterious uncle, John Vinnicum Morse. He told how he arrived the day before the murders, had a midday meal with Andrew and Abby, and then visited their Swansea farm, returning at 8:30 that evening. He had not seen Lizzie during the noon meal, during the evening, or the following morning. He had left soon after the mutton breakfast and before Lizzie had come downstairs. He offered no explanation for arriving for a several-day visit with no luggage.

He had left the Borden house at about 8:45 in the morning, he testified. He first stopped at the post office and then went along to Weybosset Street, about a mile away, to visit his niece. She would later provide him with an unshakable alibi when questioned by the police.

When he returned to the house about 45 minutes after the first cry of murder was raised, he said that he didn't notice the huge crowd of curiosity-seekers gathered in front of the home. Nor had he noticed burly Charles Sawyer in a red plaid shirt guarding the side door. He had strolled around to the backyard, eaten some pears that he picked up from the ground, and only then went into the house where "someone informed me that something had happened." Of course, that "something" was only the murders of Andrew and Abby Borden.

John Morse may have had a solid alibi on the day of the murders, but there was something very strange going on with him, as was noted earlier. It is almost as if, even though he was not directly involved in carrying out the killings, he had some knowledge of what was about to happen – and knew more about what had taken place than he was willing to admit.

Morse was followed to the stand by a series of witnesses: Abraham G. Hart, treasurer of the National Union Bank; Everett M. Cook, cashier of the First National Bank; Jonathan Clegg, a hat maker; and Joseph Shortsleeves and James Mather, carpenters, who traced Andrew's trip downtown on the morning of the murders. They were able to place him downtown at 9:30 and then back home again at 10:45.

In his opening statement to the jury, Moody had said that Lizzie's motive for the murders had been to prevent Andrew from changing his will in favor of Abby. This presupposed that he actually had a will. As an officer of the court, Andrew Jennings advised the judges and jury that he had been Andrews's lawyer for many years and had never been asked to write a will for him, and none existed. Hart, Andrew's advisor at the Union Savings Bank, confirmed that he had never heard of a will either. Knowlton sat silent during this exchange and offered no challenge to this vital testimony, but neither did he allow it to change his prosecution plans. He continued to maintain that this was Lizzie's motive.

After lunch, Bridget Sullivan took the stand for the prosecution, but as the newspapers stated the next day, her testimony was really more helpful to the defense.

Bridget had worked for the Bordens for more than three years and her duties, she explained, included cooking, washing, ironing, and cleaning the downstairs rooms and her own. Abby, Lizzie, and Emma each took care of their own bedrooms. She was on the stand for four hours, describing every detail of the morning of August 4.

She woke that morning, at 6:15, with a sick headache. After going downstairs, she took in the daily milk can from the back stoop and put out the clean one, along with a pan to receive the iceman's daily 25-pound block of ice. By 6:30, she was working on a fire of wood and coal and preparing the breakfast of mutton stew, reheated mutton, johnnycakes, cookies, bananas, and coffee. It seemed an odd choice of meals for the hottest day of the year and for a household that had been sick for two days.

When she came down, John Morse was already sitting in the dining room reading a newspaper. Abby was next down the backstairs, followed by Andrew about five minutes later. He had his chamber pot with him, which he emptied in the backyard, and returned with a basket of pears picked up from the ground around the trees. After he had washed his hands in the kitchen sink, the three had sat down for breakfast.

After eating heartily, Morse left by the back door and Andrew had invited him back for dinner, which was customarily served at 12:00 noon. Andrew brushed his teeth in the kitchen sink, drew a basin of water, and went up the back stairs to his room.

About five minutes later, Lizzie came down and Bridget testified that she sat down for a breakfast of black coffee and a cookie. Bridget herself went out to the back yard, where she was sick to her stomach. After about ten minutes, she returned to the kitchen, locked the screen door, and was met by Abby, who told her that she wanted all the downstairs windows washed, inside and out. From the cellar, Bridget retrieved a pail and took a brush from the kitchen closet. The handle was out in the barn and she went out to get it. She had told Lizzie that she would be working outside and the screen door could be locked after her because there was water in the barn for her to use.

Meanwhile, Lizzie had taken down the ironing board and put irons on the stove to heat. She asked Bridget if she planned to go out that afternoon, explaining about the sale of dress goods at Sargent's, but Bridget told her that she wasn't feeling well and probably wouldn't be going.

When asked, she stated that she had not seen anyone outside while she was going to and from the barn, making six or seven trips for water. She couldn't see the side door or the front door most of the time and someone could have entered either one of them without her knowing it. And no, she had not seen anyone delivering a note to Mrs. Borden.

And Lizzie's dress that morning had been a blue dress with a sprig in it.

The window washing had taken about an hour-and-a-half, and then Bridget had come into the house to rest for a bit. The morning was already becoming hot. Andrew had returned from downtown and she had been lying down for just a few minutes when the City Hall bell rang 11 times. The next thing was Lizzie's cry, "Maggie, come down!" She then told of trying to get Dr. Bowen from across the street and of running to Alice Russell's house.

Bridget's description of the morning and its events revealed nothing new during the trial – if you failed to note the time discrepancy, as both Knowlton and Lizzie's third attorney George D. Robinson did.

Robinson stood for the cross-examination, and it can be said that, from this point, he would remain a dominant figure of the trial. He had a commanding presence, but he was never described as being arrogant or domineering. He was always impeccably dressed and had a neatly trimmed mustache. He had graduated from Harvard at the age of 22. He had been elected to the state legislature three times, three times to the U.S. House of Representatives, and three times as governor of Massachusetts. Robinson was a skilled politician, which translated to his skill with juries. When he was riding the circuit looking for votes in the old days, he instinctively knew that his choice of horses was just as important as what his voting record would be in the next assembly. If his horse was too fine, a hardworking farmer would see him as putting on airs, but at the same time, an inferior nag would suggest that he had no knowledge of good horses, which could be worse. As he

Former Governor George Robinson

visited in barnyards or chatted in parlors, Robinson, at some point, would always inquire about the time. No matter what his constituent's timepiece showed, Robinson would adjust his own watch to agree. He was an amiable man with a good family, money, and a Harvard education, and he had the unique gift of being able to fit into any kind of company, from wealthy mansions to hardscrabble farms. It's no surprise that Lizzie put great trust in him to lead the defense team during her trial.

For the moment, his principal task when cross-examining Bridget was to destroy the prosecution's description of 92 Second Street as a place of hatred and anger. He knew that there were no family secrets that the servants didn't know.

Bridget had been an impressive and solid witness. For three hours, she had stood in the witness box and after two hours of being grilled by Moody, Justice Dewey had motioned for the bailiff to bring her a chair, but she had waved it away. Her replies to Moody's questions had been crisp, courteous, and to the point. She had stood erect and seldom even rested her hands on the railing.

Now, it was George Robinson's turn to ask the questions:

Q. You were called Maggie?
A. Yes sir.
Q. By Miss Emma and Miss Lizzie?
A. Yes sir.
Q. But that was not unpleasant to you?
A. No sir, it was not.
Q. Not at all offensive?
A. No sir.
Q. Did not cause any ill-feeling or trouble?
A. No sir.
Q. Do you have any trouble there in the family?
A. No sir.
Q. A pleasant place to live?
A. Yes sir, I liked the place.
Q. And for aught you know, they liked you?
A. As far as I know, yes.
Q. It was a pleasant family to be in?
A. I don't know how the family was. I got along all right.
Q. You never saw anything out of the way?
A. No sir.
Q. You never saw any conflict in the family?
A. No sir.
Q. Never saw the least – any quarreling or anything of that kind?
A. No sir, I did not.

Bridget added that Lizzie and Abby always spoke civilly to each other and that meals were always taken together, though not always, since Lizzie and Emma did not get up in the morning until 9:00, long after their father and stepmother.

Q. How was it [the family's conversation] this Thursday morning after they came downstairs?

A. I don't remember.

Q. Didn't they talk in the sitting room?

A. I heard her talk as she [Lizzie] came along.

Q. Who spoke?

A. Miss Lizzie and Mrs. Borden.

Q. Talking in the sitting room?

A. Mrs. Borden asked some question and she answered very civilly.

Q. When you heard them talking, they were talking calmly, the same as anybody else?

A. Yes sir.

Q. There was not so far as you knew, any trouble that morning?

A. No sir, I did not see any trouble with the family.

She was reminded that at the preliminary hearing, she said they had discussed some Christmas plans and that, when asked if she knew of any trouble between Miss Lizzie and her stepmother, she had replied, "No sir, never a word in my presence." Robinson had clearly made his point but pressed Bridget once more time:

Q. Now if nothing had happened that morning, Miss Sullivan, nothing unusual had happened that day, would there be any reason why you should remember that Thursday more than any other day?

A. Why no, there was no reason that I should remember that day any more than any other day...

If there had been some sort of murderous hatred between Lizzie and Abby, it had been totally hidden from their only servant for the entire three years of her employment. Bridget had said nothing damaging about Lizzie, and her calm manner on the stand must have been sympathetically viewed by the jurors.

The third day of the trial ended on that quiet note.

The *Boston Advertiser* noted:

Up to this point the government has distinctly failed to convict Lizzie Borden. The opinion deepens that it will not fasten the guilt upon her. The duty of the

*government is to prove absolutely that Lizzie Borden committed these murders or
she ought to, and will, go free.*

Day four of the trial began much as the previous day had, although if it had been
a prizefight, the referees would have undoubtedly scored this day as a draw. The
prosecution put their two star witnesses on the stand and gained points with each,
but counterpunches from the defense kept the damage to a minimum, and even
landed a few punches of their own.

The prosecutors led off on the morning of June 8 with Dr. Seabury Bowen, a
physician for 26 years, who had lived across the street from the Bordens for 22 of
those years and had been their family doctor for 12 of them. He took the stand and
told how he had been sent over to the Bordens by his wife on the morning of August
4. He made a cursory examination of the two bodies of his old acquaintances and it
was apparent that both victims were beyond medical help. Mr. Borden's face was so
terribly mutilated, he said, that he could hardly be recognized, even by a man who
knew him as well as the doctor did.

Lizzie had asked him to send a telegram to Emma, who was away in Fairhaven,
and he had gone a few blocks to the telegraph office, sent the message, and returned,
only to be told by Mrs. Churchill that Mrs. Borden's body had been discovered
upstairs.

District Attorney Moody continued his obsession with Lizzie's clothing and asked
the doctor what she had been wearing when he first went into the house. At the
inquest, he had said, "It is pretty hard work for me. Probably if I could see a dress
something like it, I could guess, but I could not describe it. It was sort of drab, not
much color to attract my attention. A sort of morning calico dress, I should judge."

At trial, Moody tried desperately to move Bowen to answer what "drab" was, but
the doctor refused to add to the description. He knew nothing about women's dresses
and even less about feminine colors and designs.

On cross-examination, defense attorney Melvin O. Adams asked about Lizzie's
emotional state. The ladies present, Dr. Bowen said, his wife, Mrs. Churchill, and Miss
Russell, had been "fanning and working over her. I don't know exactly what – rubbing
her wrists and rubbing her head." She had, he added, thrown herself on a lounge in
the dining room, and he had finally told the ladies to take her to her room. He had
given her a preparation called Bromo-Caffeine to quiet her "nervous excitement" and
another dose to take an hour later.

*Q. Did you have occasion to prescribe for her on account of this mental distress
and nervous excitement, after that?*
A. Yes sir.
Q. When was it?

A. Friday.

Q. Was the prescription or medicine the same as the other?

A. It was different.

Q. What was it?

A. Sulphate of morphine.

Q. In what doses?

A. One eighth of a grain.

Q. When?

A. Friday night at bedtime.

Q. The next day you changed that?

A. I did not change the medicine but doubled the dose.

Q. That was on Saturday.

A. On Saturday.

Q. Did you continue the dose on Sunday?

A. Yes sir.

Q. Did you continue it on Monday?

A. Yes sir.

Q. And on Tuesday?

A. Yes sir.

Q. How long did she continue to have that?

A. She continued to have that all the time she was in the station house.

Q. After her arrest, was it not?

A. And before.

Q. In other words, she had it all the time up to the time of her arrest, the hearing and while in the station house?

A. Yes sir.

Q. Does not morphine, given in double doses to allay mental distress and nervous excitement, somewhat affect the memory and change and alter the view of things and give people hallucinations?

A. Yes sir.

There was an audible stirring in the courtroom at this information and later, the jury would be reminded during Robinson's summation that Lizzie had been heavily sedated by an opium derivative during the time she had been questioned by the police and when she had been interrogated at the inquest. The suggestion was that this could have had a great effect on whatever she told the authorities.

The questions continued for Dr. Bowen. No, he had not seen any bloodstains on Lizzie's person and he had ample opportunity to notice if there had been.

Adelaide Churchill was next on the stand. She was returning from the grocers when she saw Bridget, "white and going rapidly" across the street to Dr. Bowen's house. She had put down her groceries and looked out her kitchen window to see what was happening.

She saw Lizzie outside the back door, looking excited and agitated. Adelaide had called out, "What is the matter?"

Lizzie cried, "Oh, Mrs. Churchill, do come over. Someone has killed father!"

After her report of the morning's happenings, the prosecution's questions turned to what Lizzie had been wearing:

Q. Will you describe the dress that she had on while you were there?

A. It looked like a light blue-and-white groundwork. It seemed like calico or cambric and it had a light blue-and-white groundwork with a dark, navy-blue diamond printed on it.

Q. Was that the dress she had on this morning? [showing her the dark blue dress that Lizzie had given to the police]

A. It does not look like it.

Q. Was it?

A. That is not the dress I have described.

This was a victory for the prosecution and, as far as Moody was concerned, justified his belief that Lizzie had changed out of her bloody dress after the murders.

Alice Russell, a long-time friend of the Borden sisters, was next on the stand. Her friendship with Lizzie had ended in wake of the murders and now she was present to testify against her. She had volunteered to the police that she had seen Lizzie burn a skirt on the Sunday afternoon following the murders, and Knowlton had promptly told news reporters that her testimony at the trial would assure Lizzie's conviction. Moody called her to the stand to make good on that promise.

Joe Howard, one of those reporters, described her as "very tall, angular, and thin, with a lofty forehead and pale blue eyes and holds her mouth as though 'prism' and 'prunes' were its most frequent utterances. With crossed arms, she emphasizes her replies with little taps with a bombazine fan."

Alice spoke first of Lizzie's visit to her home on the evening before the murders; how she appeared to be agitated and depressed, saying that she feared for her father's life, as well as her own.

Could she give a description of the dress Lizzie had been wearing the following morning? Her answer was a curt, "None whatever."

The important subject of the dress burning was next – what exactly had she seen? Alice replied, "I went into the kitchen and I saw Miss Lizzie at the other end of the stove. I saw Miss Emma at the sink. Miss Lizzie was at the stove and she had a skirt in her hand, and her sister turned and said, 'What are you going to do?' and Lizzie said, 'I am going to burn this old thing up. It is covered with paint.' Miss Emma left the kitchen, saying, 'I wouldn't let anyone see me do that, Lizzie.'"

It seemed another score for the prosecution, however, as every lawyer knows – or should know – it can be fatal to ask a question of a witness when you don't already know what the answer will be. Moody blundered badly when he interrupted Robinson's cross-examination to ask:

Q. Miss Russell, will you tell us what kind of dress – give us a description of the dress that was burned, that you testified about, on Sunday morning?
A. It was a cheap cotton Bedford cord.
Q. What was its color?
A. Light-blue ground with a dark figure – small figure.
Q. Do you know when she got it?
A. I am not positive.
Q. Well, about when she got it?
A. In the early spring.
Q. Was your attention called to it at the time she got it, in any way?
A. She told me that she had got her Bedford cord and she had a dressmaker there and I went over there one evening and she had it on, in the very early part of the dressmaker's visit, and she called my attention to it, and I said, "Oh, you have got your Bedford cord." This is the only time I saw it until this time.
Q. Until the time it was burned?
A. Yes sir.
Q. To make it clear, between the time you saw it on Miss Lizzie Borden and had the talk about it in the spring, you did not see it again until the Sunday morning after the homicide?
A. I never remember ever seeing it and I am quite sure I did not – that I never did.

Moody sat down, completely unaware that he had just discredited his own witness. By asking these additional questions, he had unwittingly wiped out one of the prosecution's principal claims – that on Sunday morning, Lizzie had burned the dress she had worn on Thursday morning.

Alice had said that she could give no description whatsoever of the dress Lizzie had worn on the morning of the murders. Her description of the dress burned in the kitchen stove was, on the other hand, quite detailed. It was the Bedford cord, and she emphatically stated four times that she had not seen that particular dress from the day in the spring when it was first worn until the Sunday morning that it was burned. Therefore, she testified that she had *not* seen the dress on the morning of the murders and it was *not* the dress Lizzie had worn.

It was not even necessary for Robinson to call the jury's attention to the fact that Alice had said Lizzie burned a "skirt," not a dress. The defense had snatched the "victory" of Alice Russell's testimony right out of their hands.

The next witness that was outwardly hostile toward Lizzie to take the stand was Assistant Marshal John Fleet. A reading of the courtroom transcript, mixed with the comments of many reporters, shows Fleet to have been both belligerent and arrogant on the stand. He was the only witness to actually engage Robinson in verbal combat. That he won is extremely doubtful, since the truth and accuracy of his testimony was itself doubtful. Fleet was very full of himself. He had directed the efforts of the Fall River police in the numerous searches of the Borden house, barn, and grounds on Thursday, Friday, and Saturday. They had, so they said, done everything short of stripping the wallpaper and taking up the carpet. He was now going to explain to the jury why no bloodstained dress had ever been found and why it had taken them five days to decide on what the murder weapon had been.

It was, however, a known fact that Lizzie had not left the house after the murders, and there had been a very few minutes from the time of Borden's death until the police received the first telephone call, so where were the clothes and hatchet if she was the murderer? When had there been time for a murder and all the events that must have taken place before that call was received at headquarters?

Assistant Marshall Fleet had all of the answers.

But he met his match in former governor Robinson, who adroitly handled both witnesses – Fleet and Alice Russell. Both of the witnesses were hostile, but they had different temperaments. The rule for most lawyers is to never provoke a hostile witness for fear of what they might blurt out. Robinson followed this plan when questioning Lizzie's former friend, but masterfully defied it when dealing with Fleet. He was aware that some time after the murders, Alice had come to the conclusion that Lizzie was guilty, and he dealt with her gently. His approach suggested that what she had to say was of no importance, when, to her, this was the high point of her life.

Fleet was a different kind of opponent, a professional with professional motives that had somehow become personal. Robinson deliberately badgered Fleet so that he could get him flustered and show the jury his hostility and prejudice.

Although Fleet had arrived on the scene at 11:45, he had not spoken to Lizzie until she retired to her room. She had told him the now–familiar story of her father returning from downtown, going to the sitting room and, ultimately, at her suggestion, lying down on the sofa because he didn't appear to be feeling well. She had told him of her trip to the barn and that Morse had been a houseguest the night before. She did not think that he had anything to do with the murders, nor did she believe that Bridget was involved. The fact that Lizzie had absolved them of any suspicion, when it would have been to her advantage to encourage that thought if she

The hatchet with no handle that police claimed had been the murder weapon – despite the lack of blood, fingerprints or any other relevant evidence.

herself was the killer, seems to have made no impression on him. He had been struck, though, by Lizzie saying that Abby was not her mother, but her stepmother. That remark, innocent or abusive, seemed to convince Fleet of her guilt and directed his every action from that point. He had no time for Lizzie's mourning. He had asked her for an immediate search of her room.

Fleet and Officers Minnehan and Wilson had found nothing in her bedroom. He had then gone to the cellar to take part in the search there. Officer Mullaly had shown him two axes and the hatchets that Bridget had led him to. In addition to those four weapons, Fleet testified that he had discovered a box on a shelf and in it had found the hatchet head they would later claim to be the murder instrument. This, in direct contradiction to testimony that Bridget had taken down the box and showed it to Mullaly. This would not be the only time that Fleet's description of events would be in conflict with the stories of others – always putting himself at the center of the action.

He described the hatchet as "covered with a heavy dust or ashes." Moments later, he said it was not dust, but ashes, probably since it could not have just been used as a murder weapon if it was covered with dust. The handle of it had been broken and it appeared to be a recent break. At the time, he apparently had not thought it was the murder weapon (that came later), since he left it in the box and put it back on the shelf. The two axes and both hatchets had been sent to Harvard for laboratory examinations. No bloodstains were found on any of them. The only other possible weapon then, was the hatchet head, so the police had then seized upon it as the instrument of death.

Then came the embarrassing questions about the searches of the house.

Most of Thursday afternoon had been consumed with searches of the house, barns, and property. Five men had conducted the search on Friday: Fleet, Marshall Hilliard, Captain Desmond, Medical Examiner Dolan, and State Detective Seaver. Jennings had insisted on being present to be sure that nothing untoward went on. The Borden house was a small one, and places to hide bundles of bloody clothing and murder weapons were few. The Friday search had taken more than four hours, and on Saturday the same team had spent an additional five hours on the property.

Apparently in an effort to lessen the appearance of incompetence, Fleet did not even mention the searches that had taken place on Thursday and Friday. He indicated at the trial that the first search had been on Saturday.

He admitted that they had found a basket in the barn loft containing "lead and iron" that could be used as sinkers, as Lizzie claimed. He paid little attention to it, even though Lizzie had described just such a container in her inquest testimony. He was obviously not looking for anything that could be construed as favorable to Lizzie.

At first, he indicated that the search on Saturday had been a cursory one, even though by saying that, he only accentuated the incompetence of the police. After all, finding the weapon and bloodstained clothing was an absolute necessity before accusing anyone of the crime. Robinson doggedly pursued this line of questioning, forcing Fleet to change his original testimony and admit the searches – which turned up nothing – had been meticulous and detailed.

He also initially told Robinson that he had not really examined Lizzie's various dresses very closely. But Robinson refused to let that stand. He forced him into giving a description of each room–by–room search. Fleet finally had to admit that he had taken each garment out, examined the outside, and turned each one inside out. He found no bloodstains of any kind.

Robinson was also relentless when it came to the hatchet with no handle. At the inquest and again in his direct testimony, he had maintained that the hatchet was covered with ashes, that they had been put there after it had been washed, for the purpose of making it appear unused for a long period of time. Robinson forced him to admit that there was an ash heap in the cellar big enough to fill 50 baskets, and that the dust on the other items in the box might have come from ashes as well.

How clear it was to the jury that Fleet's only concern in the investigation had been to build a case against Lizzie Borden – and not consider any other suspect – will never be known. That he "managed" his testimony to fit his convictions must have been transparent.

Robinson finally finished with Fleet at 5:15 in the afternoon and court was adjourned.

The New London, Connecticut *Day* commented:

Although the Lizzie Borden case is yet in its early stages, it is already apparent that the prisoner stands in no danger of conviction. The web of circumstantial evidence which the state has been weaving for ten months, has been rent in various places by ex-governor Robinson.

The Worcester, Massachusetts *Spy* agreed and added:

Lizzie Borden has not yet been acquitted, but it certainly looks as if the Fall River police were going to be disappointed in their hunger for a "pound of flesh." That warrant for her arrest was a stroke of forehandedness that quite overreached itself.

And the *Worcester Telegram*, warned:

If the government can show that it was justified in arresting this girl, it had better be about it.

9. THE HATCHET

The fifth day of the trial turned out to be the most dramatic so far, as evidenced by the headlines that appeared in the *New York Times* on June 10:

BREAK IN THE STATE'S CASE
POLICE WITNESSES IN BORDEN CASE DISAGREE
ONE OF THEM SWEARS THAT HE SAW THE PIECE OF
HATCHET HANDLE ALLEGED TO BE MISSING IN THE VERY BOX
WHERE THE HATCHET WAS FOUND

Or as reporter Joe Howard summed it all up, "The fifth day of the trial of Lizzie Borden for her life was marked by the most dramatic sensation in its record. The tattered web which the legal spiders of the Commonwealth have been weaving around her had one of its strongest threads snapped by a sudden and totally unexpected blow that left it sagging at one side. The government's witnesses did not agree. One stuck to the outline programmed in his testimony and another followed him with a startling disclosure. Then the first witness was called back and made to confirm his apparent insincerity."

Captain Phillip Harrington followed Fleet to the witness stand as day five began. On the day of the murders, he had been a foot patrolman; he had since jumped a number of ranks to be made captain. The *Fall River Globe* found him to be an excellent source of "inside information," particularly because he was leaking his obviously biased stories directly to them.

Harrington's description of events from the time he arrived at the Borden house at 12:15 was detailed and meticulous, even down to describing which hand he used to open each door and where each person had been standing or sitting when he spoke with them. He had been the fourth or fifth person (depending on whose account was accurate) to interrogate Lizzie about what had happened that morning. She had told him of her father's return from the post office and his sitting in the dining room for a moment and then stretching out on the sofa in the sitting room. She recounted her trip to the barn, where she had been for 20 minutes, and said she had seen no one and heard nothing while there.

Downstairs, he had noticed Dr. Bowen with some note paper in his hand, standing near the stove. He had seen the word "Emma" written on

one corner of it, but Bowen had tossed the paper in the grate. He had asked Bowen what the paper was and had been told it was nothing – a personal note he had taken from his pocket – something about his daughter going somewhere.

Defense attorney Robinson, fearing the impression that might be left that Bowen had burned the missing note that summoned Abby from the house, objected, saying, "I cannot let this go in the record unless you [Knowlton] give me an assurance that it has nothing whatsoever to do with the case." Knowlton assured him that it had nothing to do with the case at all.

Needless to say, the most important job for a defense attorney during a trial is to try and discredit the witnesses for the prosecution. By creating a doubt about the accuracy or truthfulness of any portion of the testimony, however insignificant, a doubt can be planted in a juror's mind about the accuracy and truthfulness of all of it. A defense attorney only has to make it so that a reasonable doubt exists in the mind of the juror, and if that doubt exists, he cannot find his client guilty. During Harrington's testimony, Robinson spotted a problem with the police officer's testimony that he knew he could exploit.

On direct questioning, Harrington testified that all the windows in the barn were closed. Robinson, during the cross-examination, read from the testimony that he had given at the district court, in which he said one of the windows had been open. It was a minor point and, of course, meaningless as evidence, but worth making, since it helped establish the fact that not everything said in the trial was entirely accurate.

Since it worked once, Robinson pressed on, leading Harrington to swear he had particularly noted that Andrew's shoes were laced. Robinson produced one of the official crime scene photographs showing that the shoes had no laces; they were congress gaiters with elastic sides. They simply slipped onto the feet. Harrington's response? "The photograph is wrong."

Robinson turned away, shaking his head, and making sure the jury saw his disgust. There would be other, even better opportunities to question witness credibility when the next two officers took the stand. Robinson would figuratively tear the two men apart.

The next witness on the stand was Officer Michael Mullaly. There was nothing that could have predicted that Mullaly was just about to blow a sizable hole in the prosecution's case, but he was. A younger man than most of the other officers, he was lean, trim, and in very good physical condition. His first questions of Lizzie on the morning of the murders had been to determine what valuables Andrew might have been carrying on his person. He was told to look for a silver watch and chain, a wallet with money in it, and a gold ring on his smallest finger. An examination showed that all were accounted for. Robbery, apparently, had not been a motive.

He had then asked about axes and hatchets. Lizzie said there were both in the house and sent Bridget to show him where they were. She led the way to the basement and showed him two claw hatchets and two axes. From a niche in the chimney, she had taken down a box, which contained a hatchet head. Fleet had come down a few minutes later, and Mullaly had also shown him the various tools, which might have been used as weapons. He had then conducted a general search of the house and yard, but found no other axes or hatchets, weapons, or deadly tools, and no signs of any blood.

Officer Michael Mullaly

Since Fleet said that he was the one who had found the box containing the hatchet head, Robinson enjoyed the opportunity to cross-examine Mullaly and get him to repeat that it was Bridget, not Fleet, who had pointed out the box. It was one more occasion to bring attention to the fact that the police witnesses were flawed – and one more chance to tweak Fleet for his brusque manner on the stand. However, it turned out that what he got next from Mullaly was of far greater value than both of those small satisfactions.

When he was asked to describe the contents of the box that Bridget had shown him, Mullaly said that it contained several odd pieces of metal, a doorknob, some hinges, and the handle of the hatchet head.

"Mr. Fleet not only took out the blade but the handle also," Mullaly said.

Robinson was stunned. "What?"

Mullaly replied, "In addition to the bit of wood stuck in the eye of the hatchet, there was another piece as well."

The transcript continued:

Q. Another piece of what?
A. Handle.
Q. Where is it now?
A. I don't know.
Q. Was it a piece of the same handle?
A. It was a piece that corresponded with that. [points to the piece of wood that had been in the hatchet head]
Q. The rest of the handle?
A. It was a piece with a fresh break in it.

Q. The other piece.
A. Yes sir.
Q. Was it a handle to the hatchet?
A. It was what I call a hatchet handle.
Q. Well, did you take it out of the box?
A. I did not.
Q. Did you see it taken out?
A. I did.
Q. Who took it out?
A. Mr. Fleet took it out.
Q. You were there?
A. I was there.
Q. Anybody else?
A. Not that I know of.
Q. Did Mr. Fleet put it back, too?
A. He did.

Journalist Joe Howard recorded this dramatic moment in the courtroom:

The feelings of the counsel for the Commonwealth may be imagined. They sat rigid in their chairs like statues. Governor Robinson ordered the witness to stand where he was until Fleet could be found. He was to have no chance to tell the marshal what he had been saying. Mr. Jennings was all over the room at once. He sent his office assistant to the foot of the courthouse stairs to see that no one spoke to Fleet. He sent a shrewd detective from Cambridge to stand at the head of the stairs and see that Mullaly had no chance to say a word to his chief. At the same instant, a friend of the police seated in the courtroom slipped from a chair within the bar and went unostentatiously out into the hall.

District Attorney Knowlton, leader for the government, felt the glare of the ex-governor's eyes.

"Where is the handle?" the governor asked.

"I don't know," said Mr. Knowlton. After another pointed inquiry, he said, with a voice unlike his own, "I never heard of it before."

Mr. Knowlton, who is best-described as a man of round-headed, vigorous Cromwellian figure, soon found his voice and his feet. He suggested the court detail an officer to go to the Borden house and see if the missing handle is there now and Mr. Robinson protested.

"I only suggest it in the interest of justice," Mr. Knowlton replied.

"I want justice too, but not in that way," said the ex-governor.

Robinson asked the court's permission to recall Fleet immediately to the stand, and the justices agreed. Mullaly was told to stand down while Fleet was returned to the stand. Knowlton wanted to question Fleet first, but the court ruled against him. Robinson immediately went on the offensive.

Q. Will you state again what you found at the time you looked in the box?
A. I found a hatchet head, the handle broken off, together with some tools in there and the iron that was inside there. I don't know just what it was.
Q. You did not find the handle, the broken piece, not at all?
A. No sir.
Q. You did not see it, did you?
A. No sir.
Q. You did not see it?
A. No sir.
Q. Did Mr. Mullaly take it out of the box?
A. Not that I know of.
Q. You looked in so that you could have seen it if it was in there?
A. Yes sir.
Q. You have no doubt about that, have you, at all?
A. What?
Q. That you did not find the other piece of the handle that fit on there?
A. No sir.
Q. You saw no piece of wood with any fresh break in the box, around the box, or near it?
A. No sir, not that I am aware of. I did not see any of it.

There was an audible rustle among the spectators in the courtroom. Whispers broke out, and the jurors exchanged looks with one another. It was obvious to everyone: Fleet was lying under oath.

As any attorney can attest, eyewitness testimony is, and has always been, one of the shakiest method of evidence to present in court. It is always subject to human error, but, in this case, since the hatchet was presented as the prosecution's most important item of physical evidence, any fact about it, no matter how trivial, would not be overlooked or casually forgotten by the police. During the inquest and preliminary hearing, they had maintained that one of the other hatchets or one of the axes had been the murder weapon. When all of them had been ruled by examinations done at Harvard University, only then had they turned to the hatchet without the handle. Now it strained credibility too far to ask the jury to believe that Mullaly had only imagined finding a handle for it.

According to the defense, a handle was vital to the theory. Without one, the head alone could not be seriously regarded as a lethal weapon in the hands of a woman who possessed no unusual strength.

The public, and more importantly, the jury, was left to ponder the significance of the missing handle and the reason that it had been broken at the time of the murder, if indeed it had. The police wanted to create the assumption that it had been broken off and thrown away because it was stained with blood that could not be quickly washed away. That would not, however, explain why there was no blood on the wooden piece that was still stuck in the head. If the handle had been stained, certainly the piece nearest to the bloody wounds in the skulls of the Bordens would also be.

Robinson pressed on with the case. There were more prosecution witnesses to discredit and he was determined to do as much damage as possible.

Earlier, Adelaide Churchill had defiantly maintained that the dress Lizzie had turned over to the police was not the one she had been wearing when Adelaide had first run over to the Borden house on the morning of the murders. Left unchallenged, this statement could do serious damage to Lizzie's defense. She was recalled in the afternoon and questioned again. Robinson asked her to describe what Bridget was wearing that morning, and Adelaide responded, without question, that it was a light-colored calico.

Bridget, though, had said that she was wearing a dark indigo blue dress. Robinson read Bridget's testimony aloud but, like Harrington with Andrew's shoelaces, Adelaide could not be swayed. Bridget, she said, had been wearing a light-colored calico. It didn't matter what Bridget herself insisted that she had been wearing that morning – Adelaide knew better.

Robinson scoffed and the jury got the message: if Adelaide was wrong about what Bridget had worn, she could also easily be mistaken about Lizzie's dress too.

The sixth day of the trial continued the setbacks for the prosecution.

Faced with conflicting testimony about the hatchet handle and the now-confused description of Lizzie's dress, the prosecution hoped to get things back on track with the help of Lieutenant Francis L. Edson. He had been one of six men who ransacked the Borden house on the Monday after the murders, following the news from the Harvard laboratory that none of the hatchets or axes collected from the house had been the murder weapon. It was the defense, however, that benefitted from his description of the events of that Monday.

From the beginning, the police had never believed Lizzie's story about being in the loft of the barn when Andrew was killed. If the prosecution could convince the jury that she had not been there, Lizzie would be placed inside of the house at the time of the murder. It would prove opportunity, one of the three things they believed necessary to convict her – motive, means, and opportunity.

Edison testified that he had been sent to pick up the hatchet head at the house. He had also picked up a basket of odds and ends in the barn and had taken it back to the station for inspection and inventory. On cross-examination, Robinson managed to get him to provide a list of the basket's contents: sheet lead, a doorknob, and an assortment of metal pieces. The basket was exactly as Lizzie had described it at the inquest and lent credence to her story of being up in the loft rummaging in this very basket. This damaged the prosecution's claim that Lizzie had not been in the barn, as she said she had.

But all was not lost for the prosecution, or so it seemed. Officer William Medley was also on the stand that day and he was questioned about the barn. Asked to describe what he had noticed during his examination, he spoke in great detail: "I went upstairs until I reached about three or four steps from the top, and while there, part of my body was above the floor – above the level of the floor – and I looked around the barn to see if there was any evidence of anything having been disturbed and I stooped down low to see if I could discern any marks on the floor of the barn having been made there. I did that by stooping down low and looking across the bottom of the barn floor. I didn't see any and I reached out my hand to see if I could make an impression on the floor of the barn and I did, by putting my hand down – and I found I made an impression on the barn floor."

The following is a transcription of his testimony that followed:

Q. Describe what there was on or about the floor by which you made an impression.
A. Seemed to be accumulated hay dust and other dust.
Q. How distinctly could you see the marks you made with your hand?
A. I could see them quite distinctly when I looked for them.
Q. Go on and describe everything else which you did.
A. Then I stepped up on the top and took four or five steps on the outer edge of the barn floor, the edge nearest the stairs, then I came up to see if I could discern those, and I did.
Q. How did you look to see if you could discern those footsteps which you made?
A. I did it in the first place by stooping down and casting my eye on a level with the barn floor, and I could see them plainly.
Q. Did you see any other footsteps in the dust than those you made yourself?
A. No sir.

Medley's testimony was potentially devastating to the defense and the prosecution must have been delighted by what he had *not* found in the barn. They had suffered heavy losses with both the dress and the hatchet, but may have won the battle of the barn – or did they?

During Medley's testimony, he was referring not to the floor of the barn itself, but rather to the floor of the hayloft. When Edison was being questioned on the stand, he described the same basket that Lizzie had described and stated that he had found it inside of the first floor of the barn, not the hayloft. Lizzie very well could have been inside of the barn during the murders, based on the discovery of the basket. However, her statement had insisted that she had been in the hayloft, a fact that Medley's testimony seemed to refute.

But readers are asked to remember Medley's description and the detail with which he pictured what he had done that day. What seemed like a solid victory for the prosecution took on a different dimension when the defense later presented its case.

While Medley was still on the stand, the subject again came up as to who found the hatchet head and what had been done with it. By now, no one was certain; not the police and certainly not the jury.

Medley confidently said that he had picked it up that Monday, carefully wrapped it in brown paper, and took it to Marshal Hilliard. Egged on by Robinson, he demonstrated exactly how he had wrapped it, using a piece of paper that Robinson had courteously offered him.

Captain Dennis Desmond took the stand next to describe how he had found the hatchet and had carefully wrapped it in newspaper, and then demonstrated exactly how he had wrapped it, using a piece of newspaper that was also courteously furnished by Robinson – who was obviously enjoying the conflicting stories.

Desmond was not able to say whether it was the *Boston Globe* or *Providence Journal* that he had used. It was, however, just about the only humorous moment in the trial with two serious officers, each under oath, solemnly swearing that he had done something that only one of them could have actually done. There is no way to know if the jury considered it deliberately false testimony or a case of two bragging police officers, each wanting to place themselves in a historical moment in time.

Things became heated just as the court was preparing to adjourn until Monday. The prosecution proposed to offer into evidence the testimony that Lizzie had given at the so-called "inquest." Robinson, of course, objected to this. The prosecution argued that Lizzie had given statements under oath in a judicial proceeding and that she was not under arrest at the time. She had been warned that she was a suspect and was not allowed to leave her home, but that was all. Robinson stated that Lizzie had actually been under arrest at the time of the inquest. She had also asked for counsel before testifying at the inquest, but she had been refused. He also said that she had never been cautioned that she was not obligated to testify to anything which might be incriminating. For this reason, Robinson said, anything that she said at the inquest was inadmissible as evidence. When court reconvened on Monday, this would be a compelling issue.

The next day was Sunday, a day of rest for the judges, attorneys, reporters, spectators, and likely most of all, for the jury. Everyone needed an escape from the brutal heat of the cramped, overcrowded courtroom, where temperatures soared to over 100 degrees. The jury members were up every morning at 6:00 and had breakfast at 7:00. They were taken to the courthouse at 9:00, where they sat on a hard oak bench until 1:00, tramped back to their hotel under a hot sun for dinner, returned to courthouse until 5:00, and then were sent back to the hotel for supper when the day was over. At 8:00, they were locked in their rooms, sworn not to discuss the day's events. No refreshments, alcoholic or otherwise, were permitted. Their only recreation was a cribbage board and three worn decks of cards. Without question, these men needed a break.

The reporters filed their stories on Saturday night, anxious to get them into the Sunday papers. That day, the Woonsocket, Rhode Island, *Reporter* noted:

After a week's testimony on the part of the prosecution in the Borden murder trial, the indications are that the accused young woman will never be convicted. The defense, if the layman can judge, has much the best case so far, for there has been no direct evidence fastening the atrocious crime upon the prisoner, and leading witnesses have, in several important instances, been flatly contradictory. As the case now stands, a disagreement is the most the government can expect, while public sentiment already clamors for an acquittal.

10. THE HARVARD MEN

Day seven of the trial opened with the same horrific heat that had plagued the previous days of the proceedings. The prosecution and the defense immediately addressed the inquest testimony problem that had come up at the end of the trial's previous day. It was the contention of the defense that Lizzie's three days of testimony at the "inquest" had been obtained while she was under virtual address, and she had not been told that anything she said could be used against her. It was her basic legal right and Robinson stated that she had been denied it.

Knowlton sat, still silent, at the prosecution's table. William Moody spoke for the prosecution. He argued that the "inquest" had been properly called and held under the public statutes of the Commonwealth. He attacked Robinson's complaint that Lizzie's attorney had not been allowed to be present by citing the provisions of Massachusetts law that stipulated that inquiries "may be private" and "any and all may be excluded." But this evaded the question as to whether or not the "informal examination of witnesses," as it had been called, had been an "inquest" when it had taken place.

The central question now was, he said, "whether there is anything in the circumstances – which would take the declarations there made by her out from the general rule that any act or declaration of the defendant – is competent and admissible."

He argued that what Lizzie had said was not important; that it was not a confession. And besides, there was a difference between a confession and statements that might be evidence of guilt. Yes, Lizzie had the Constitutional right to not give evidence against herself, but since her declarations had been voluntarily given, they were fair game. It was a callous argument. Basically, Moody was saying that if someone was foolish enough to testify against herself when she was told she was under suspicion, then she deserved whatever happened to her.

Robinson, of course, objected to this argument, providing a timeline of events to make his point. The homicides had occurred on August 4. The defendant had been accused of crimes by the mayor on August 6, when she was first placed under police observation and told not to leave her home. A warrant for her arrest was issued on August 8. Her testimony at the inquest did not occur until August 9, when she had

Even the empty courtroom steamed with humid heat during most of the trial.

requested counsel that was denied. She was arrested at the conclusion of her testimony.

"In other words," Robinson said, "the practice that was resorted to was to put her really in the custody of the city marshal, beyond the possibility of any retirement, or any release or any freedom whatsoever, keeping her with the hand upon the shoulder – she, a woman, could not run – covering her at every moment, surrounding her at every instant, empowered to take her at any moment, and under those circumstances, taking her to that inquest to testify.

"She was taken by the city marshal and with no advisor to warn her that she did not have to unless she wanted to, was made to stand for three sweltering days of grilling, unaware of the pregnant fact that all the while, the marshal had a warrant for her arrest in his pocket.

"The police said, 'We will hold the paper in our pockets and get what we can from her and later, if we decide arrest her, we will put away that paper and arrest her on another.'

"And that went on for three days, with no intimation to her from anybody who was authorized to make it – nay, we may say, who was *bound* to make it, that she had any rights at all. Denied counsel, neglected as far as the court acted or the district attorney, to tell her that she ought not to testify to anything that might tend to criminate herself, she stood alone, a defenseless woman, in that attitude.

"If *that* is freedom, God save the Commonwealth of Massachusetts!"

Robinson's presentation was typical for his performance during the trial. It had taken Moody 45 minutes to laboriously present his stance, citing precedents back to and including English law. Robinson had managed to present his argument, with flourish, in less than five minutes. Moody's only reply in rebuttal was that Robinson's argument had been magnificent, but it was not the law.

The chief justice called the noon recess at 11:15 and court resumed at 12:40. The conduct of the inquest, he said, was not this court's concern, only the admissibility of what had been said there. He continued:

The common law regards this species of evidence with distrust. Statements made by one accused of crimes are admissible against him only when it is affirmatively established that they were voluntarily made.

The common law regards substance more than form. The principle involved cannot be evaded by avoiding the form of arrest if the witness at the time of such testimony is practically in custody. From the agreed facts and the facts otherwise in evidence, it is plain that the prisoner at the time of her testimony was, so far as relates to this question, as effectually in custody as if the formal precept had been served; and, without dwelling on other circumstances which distinguish the facts of this case from those of case on which the government relies, we are all of the opinion that this consideration is decisive and the evidence is excluded.

The prosecution was in serious trouble.

The *New York Times* was not the only newspaper to print something along the lines of "the decision will go a great way toward making Lizzie Borden a free woman."

Fall River Medical Examiner William A. Dolan took the stand for the prosecution in the afternoon session of day seven. He used gruesome details to describe the various wounds on the heads of the two victims and the beheading that had taken place at Oak Grove Cemetery on the day of the funeral. He brought along plaster casts of the heads, and they were admitted into evidence.

In the words of one reporter, "It was a hard day for the prisoner." Lizzie learned for the first time what had taken place when the burial service had been halted, and she wept openly. At one point, she had to be helped from the courtroom.

Dolan recounted how he had been passing the Borden home on the day of the murders and had been summoned inside soon after Andrew's body had been discovered. By then, Dr. Bowen had covered the body with a sheet. He had found Andrew's hands still warm and bright red blood still oozing from the wounds on his head and face. Dolan had then gone upstairs and looked at the body of Mrs. Borden, touched her head and hands, and found them much colder than Andrew's.

Because of the talk about possible poisoning, he had removed the stomachs of both bodies and collected samples of the milk delivered that morning and the day before. He had gone with officers to the basement and was shown two axes and two hatchets. All of these items had been sent to the Harvard Medical School for examination. He stated that two hairs had adhered to the head of one of the hatchets, and there were spots on the axes that looked like blood.

He then produced the plaster cast of Andrew's head, each wound outlined in blue ink.

Q. How many wounds did you find on his head?
A. Ten on the fleshy part.
Q. And what was the condition, generally speaking, of the skull of Mr. Borden as to being crushed in?
A. From in front of the ear, commencing about 1 ½ inches in front of the ear, to probably 1 ½ inches behind the ear, the bone was all crushed in.

For almost an hour, Dolan measured each of the wounds in the plaster skulls of Andrew and Abby and described the bloodstains found on the bodies, as to number and size. Taking into account the contents of the stomachs and the color of the blood around the wounds, it was his opinion that Abby died first, from one-and-a-half hours to two hours before Andrew suffered his own grim fate.

Asked if wounds such as he had described on both bodies could have been inflicted by a woman of ordinary strength using a hatchet, his terse answer was yes.

Lizzie's attorney, Melvin Adams, handled the cross-examination. He went on the offensive by reading back to Dr. Dolan his testimony at the preliminary hearing:

Q. In your opinion, would that hatchet that you saw furnish an adequate cause of these incised wounds?
A. Yes sir.
Q. The wounds in both cases?
A. Yes sir.

Adams asked Dolan if he wished to now change that testimony.

A. I do; yes sir.
Q. In what respect?
A. That is, providing the cutting edge of that axe is a certain distance – a certain length.
Q. Hadn't you measured it at that time?
A. No sir, I had not.

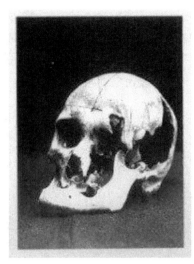

The skull of Andrew Borden

Q. Have you measured it since?
A. No sir.

It was a startling admission. Dr. Dolan had identified the hatchet with no handle as the murder weapon without ever doing one very necessary thing – measuring the blade. The absurdity of it was not lost on the jury, especially when, a few questions later, Dolan admitted that some of the wounds were five inches in length, an inch-and-a-half wider than the blade of the hatchet that had been introduced as the murder weapon.

On the eighth day of the trial, Dr. Dolan returned to the stand to complete his testimony. This time, instead of the plaster cast of Andrew's skull, he brought the real thing. A horrified Lizzie was allowed to sit in the hallway during the time it was on display in the court.

Of all the mysteries connected to the Borden murders, the most profound was revealed in the first few questions that Adams put to Dr. Dolan. Discussing the nature of the blows to the heads of Andrew and Abby, he asked Dolan:

Q. You think the assailant swung the instrument from left to right, don't you?
A. Yes sir.
Q. And all these wounds can be fairly accounted for by blows from left to right?
A. Yes sir.
Q. That is to say, by a left-handed person?
A. Yes, by a left-handed person.

Lizzie Borden was right-handed.

The questioning took another turn at this point, and it was never mentioned again, either in examinations, cross-examinations, or Robinson's summary.

Why was this? It would seem that this would have been an almost certain vindication of Lizzie if it had been pursued. In few accounts of the Borden murders has this point ever been mentioned, or speculated about. And this is in spite of the fact that the trial transcript is a public record and, by repetition of the question, cannot be regarded as an error by the stenographer.

Why this mysterious left-handed killer was not seized upon by the defense, we will never know, although some modern-day theories of the crime have embraced it, as we will see later on in this volume. Even so, the identity of the left-handed murderer is almost as puzzling as why Robinson did not act on this piece of evidence. It's not hard to imagine him attacking the prosecution for ignoring this fact, and perhaps even acting out for the jury how a right-handed person would clumsily swing the hatchet with his left hand. But he never did. He never mentioned it at all – making this one of the most baffling mysteries of the entire case.

On redirect examination, the prosecution made a valiant effort to explain how a three-and-a-half inch hatchet could have possibly have made wounds that were two inches long. The answer was, Dr. Dolan explained, because the whole cutting edge hadn't been used. How, he was asked, could a three-and-a-half inch hatchet make a four-and-a-half inch wound? By sliding and also by crushing its way into the skull. This all seemed to make perfect sense until Adams stood to examine him once again and asked his first question: "From the appearance of an injury having various lengths like one, two, three, four, and five inches, you are hardly able to determine the length of the cutting edge giving them, are you?"

"No sir," Dr. Dolan replied.

Dr. Edward Stickney Wood, the physician and chemist who had headed the forensic team of examiners at Harvard, was called to the stand. It's likely that Dr. Dolan was more than happy to turn the spot in the witness box over to him. Wood was a red-faced, gray-haired stalwart, and handsome man of upright bearing and solid reputation.

Prosecutor Knowlton, from the first day of the trial, had yielded the Commonwealth's case to Moody. He had occupied the head chair at the prosecution's table, but throughout the week's proceedings, he had only occasionally exchanged quiet words with Moody. He had followed the questioning and cross-examinations with interest and attention, but it was obvious that he was not passionate about the case. At this point, though, he now stood to take charge. And he had a very good reason for doing so.

Four days before the trial began, he had received a letter from Dr. Frank W. Draper, who had been involved in the autopsies of the Bordens' bodies at the Oak Grove Cemetery with Dr. Dolan. Draper, educated at the Harvard Medical School, had been in practice for 24 years. He was one of the medical examiners for Boston and Suffolk County. In addition, he was a Professor of Legal Medicine at the Harvard Medical School. Among his duties as Boston's medical examiner, he had been called upon in nearly 3,500 cases of death, when homicide was suspected or charged. He was not a novice when it came to testifying in court.

On May 31, he conferred with Dr. David W. Cheever, and Draper wrote a four-page letter detailing what their testimony would be if they were called to the stand. Dr. Cheever was also a graduate of the Harvard Medical School. He had continued his studies in Paris and then returned to Harvard as an instructor for 23 years. He was also on the staff of the Boston City Hospital. The two men were in complete agreement on the following facts:

1. That the cause and manner of deaths were the same in both cases, namely, fracture of the skull and injury to the brain by blows to the head.

2. That the weapon was an edged tool of some weight, like a hatchet.

3. That the length of the edge of the weapon was about 3 ½ inches.

4. That Mrs. Borden was killed by blows inflicted from behind, the assailant standing astride the body.

5. That Mr. Borden was killed by blows given by the assailant standing at the head of the sofa just within the door.

6. That the assailant was right-handed and used his left hand, or, if using both hands, that the left hand was foremost, or in front of the right hand on the handle.

7. That Mrs. Borden died first, and that the supposition of an hour's interval is not inconsistent with the facts relating to the stage of digestion, the body temperature, and the condition of the blood in the two cases.

8. That the deaths were not instantaneous.

9. That a woman would have sufficient physical strength to inflict the blows, assuming that she was of normal adult vigor.

He continued in his letter, "I write especially to inform you of two important discoveries which I made upon careful examination of the two skulls. On Mr. Borden's skull, I found that the blow just in front of the ear left its mark on the base of the skull within the cavity." That blow, he wrote, cut immediately through the carotid artery and was necessarily and immediately fatal from hemorrhage.

When Knowlton read this summary, he must have thought that it was all well and good and beneficial to his case. There was nothing unexpected in these words, he believed – until he read the rest of it:

The other discovery is still more important. On one of the cuts in Mrs. Borden's skull near the right ear, there is a very small but unmistakable deposit of the gilt metal with which hatchets are ornamented when they leave the factory; this deposit (Dr. Cheever confirmed the observation fully) means that the hatchet used in killing Mrs. Borden was a new hatchet, not long out of the store.

The "shining deposit," he noted, could be seen with the magnifying glass or, for that matter, with the naked eye.

We can never really know what went through Knowlton's mind as he read this letter, but it must have been one of the most disheartening reports of his career. As he had written to Attorney General Pillsbury, the case against Lizzie was fatally weak, and he believed he had no real hope of convicting her. Now, at the last minute before the trial was to begin, he receives a letter from two unimpeachable authorities – his own expert witnesses – saying that the old, dull, and rusty hatchet on which the police and prosecution had built their case was not the murder weapon at all.

If Draper and Cheever were allowed to state their findings from the witness box, there would be no point in even continuing the trial. The prosecution had surely lost the dress as physical evidence. They had created a motive for murder out of a five-year-old quarrel over an insignificant piece of property, and now, with the hatchet discredited, about the other thing left was the fact that at some point over the years, Lizzie had stopped calling Abby "Mother."

It seems likely that all of this was running through Knowlton's mind as he walked up to the railing to question Dr. Edward S. Wood. Since the subject would not center around the Harvard examinations of the bodies, clothing, and suspected instruments, he certainly wanted no testimony from Wood about the discovery made by Draper and Cheever.

Wood acknowledged that he had been Professor of Chemistry at Harvard for the past 16 years. His specialty was poisons and bloodstains, and he had previously been called to testify in several hundred trials just like this one. He had, he said, examined the two containers of milk and found no evidence of poison in either of them. In his opinion, Abby had preceded Andrew in death by approximately three hours, two times the 90 minutes that Dr. Dolan had estimated. The claw-hammer hatchet had several stains on the handle, the side, and the edge, all of which appeared to be bloodstains, but chemical and microscopic tests gave absolutely negative results. Both axes had stains on them that appeared to be blood, but the tests turned out negative with them also.

Knowlton hoped for a positive answer with his next question: "Did you make an examination to be able to determine whether it was reasonably possible that that hatchet could have been used in inflicting the wounds that you have described and then washed soon afterwards, so that traces of blood might or might not be found on it?"

Once again, an attorney should never ask a question to which he does not already know the answer. Wood replied that it could not have been washed quickly enough to remove all traces of blood. In addition, small amounts of blood would have remained in the spaces between the head and the handle. This put a crimp in the prosecution's picture of Lizzie hastily rinsing blood from the hatchet and dipping it into ashes to make it look dusty. Unless she had spent 10 or 15 minutes scrubbing it – for which no time had been left in the schedule of events – this idea would not hold up.

And Dr. Wood continued dashing Knowlton's hopes. The hair, labeled as "taken from the hatchet," was, without question, animal hair, and probably that of a cow. There was a brown "smooch" that looked like blood on the skirt Lizzie wore, but it wasn't. There was another spot, lower down, but it was also not blood. There was one stain of blood, though, about the size of a small pinhead, eight inches from the hem of the back of her slip, that was consistent with the characteristics of human blood. Nothing had been found on her shoes or stockings.

During cross-examination, Adams asked Dr. Wood if he was able to say that the pinhead spot on Lizzie's petticoat did not come from her menstrual flow and Wood replied that he could not; it might have. Adams then asked if the character of the blood was satisfactory for the determination that it was even human blood. The doctor's reply was an enigmatic, "If it is satisfactory at all, it is."

In reality, that tiny speck of blood was totally insignificant. The prosecution's suggestion that this tiny spot coming as a result of the slayings was ridiculous because any splatter would have been on the front of Lizzie's garments, not the back. The prosecution had not attempted to show that the blood speck was the blood type of either of the victims and did not go beyond the phrase "consistent with human blood." As to whether it had penetrated the garment from the outside rather than the inside, their own answer was that it was "more distinct" on the outside, which really gave no information. It was a waste of time over a speck that measured one three-thousandth of an inch.

Finally, the question turned to the important matter of the spatterings of blood on the walls and furniture near each body. It was important to the defense to establish the volume, distance, and variety of these spatters, since it had been established by the state's own expert that Lizzie had no blood on her person or clothing. Knowlton, in redirect examination, tried to dismiss the importance of the spatter by asking Wood:

Q. Have you had occasion to consider the subject of the spattering of blood when blows are struck in the manner in which you have heard these blows described?

A. Yes sir.

Q. What can you say to that generally?

A. It might spatter in any direction and might not spatter in every direction.

Q. That is, there is no rule at all.

A. No sir.

Q. What happens? Does it spatter or spurt?

A. Spatters. When any blunt surface strikes a pool of blood, of course it will spatter in that direction, varying according to accidental circumstances.

Q. Would there be any way in which you could determine whether any given surface near the wounds would receive the spattering or not, or how much?

A. No.

It must be remembered that Dr. Wood was a prosecution witness and, as such, framed his testimony in a way that would help the Commonwealth's case. His answers to Knowlton's questions were technically correct, but fell far short of what any objective testimony would have offered.

As a medical professional, familiar with bloodstains and human anatomy, Dr. Wood knew that, in both cases, the aortic artery of the victim had been severed. There is a great pressure in the main trunk artery and, when severed, blood does not flow from it – it spurts, gushes, and sprays. It is almost certain that anyone standing nearby would be showered with it.

When Adams took over the questioning, he was well aware that Wood was faltering in his replies and he pressed him for better and more accurate answers:

Q. Assuming that the assailant stood behind Mr. Borden when these injuries were given and received, have you formed an opinion whether he would be spattered by blood to an extent?

A. I have thought that he must be spattered with blood, but I don't think it is absolutely necessary that he should.

Q. You have expressed that opinion, have you not?

A. Yes.

Q. And you give that opinion, taking into mind the bloody spots on the wall and parlor door?

A. I beg your pardon. I will correct what I just said. Your question was if the assailant stood behind him, at his head. I don't see how he could avoid being spattered.

Q. What part of the body would receive these spatters?

A. Above the position of the head, or from this level up. [Pointing with his hands]

Q. From the waist up?

A. Yes sir.

Q. Assuming that the assailant of Mrs. Borden stood over her when she was lying down on the floor, face downward, and taking into account the spatters of blood which you saw, have you formed an opinion as to whether her assailant would be spattered with blood?

A. I don't see how the assailant could avoid being spattered in that place.

Q. What portion of the body would receive spatters in your opinion?

A. From the lower portion of the body and upward.

Adams had made his point: the assailant would have been covered with blood spray from the waist up after killing Andrew and from the waist down after Abby was slain. In other words, whoever had killed them would have been drenched in blood. There would have been no way to hide it. The prosecution's own forensic witness had described an assailant that was covered with blood, yet every witness who had seen Lizzie that morning saw no blood on her dress, her face, her hands, or in her "immaculate" hair.

Adams and Robinson both looked very pleased when they went back to their seats at the defense table.

Dr. Draper was called to the stand next. At first, he used plaster casts of the two skulls and verified the marks that showed the wounds on them. In the dock, Lizzie put her head down almost on the back of George Robinson, the former governor and her staunch defender. Not satisfied with the plaster casts, Knowlton apologized to the court, but insisted that the skull itself be brought in for the witness to use. The always reliable Joe Howard described the macabre scene:

It was Mr. Borden's skull. It was done up in a white handkerchief and looked like a bouquet such as a man carries to his sweetheart. A pile of law books was arranged high on the table in front of the jury and made a stand for the skull to rest upon. The professor uncovered the skull and put it on this heap of learning, but the jaw came separately in his hand. When the doctor put it in its place by lifting the rest of the skull, he moved the two parts so that the mouth opened and shut like the silent jaws of a ghost. To see the jaw wag made the spectators wonder what it would say if it could talk.

Sentence by sentence, Knowlton walked Dr. Draper through a detailed description of each gash in the skull, what damage it had done, its width and length. Mercifully, Lizzie, near the point of collapse, was escorted from the courtroom and allowed to sit where she could hear the proceedings, but would not have to look at the leering skull of her father.

There is no way to know what arguments Knowlton used to get Dr. Draper to change his testimony in court from what he had written to him in his letter. Somehow, though, he managed to convince him to forget that he believed the murder weapon had been a new hatchet with gilt metal that had come off when the first blow had been struck. That his contradictory testimony was a cover-up is obvious and shameful. Knowlton put it squarely to him:

Q. [Showing him the hatchet head without the handle] Are you about to say whether that hatchet head is capable of making those wounds?
A. I believe it is.

And later, in re-direct examination, Knowlton pressed the point as to "whether in your opinion those wounds that you found could have been inflicted by that hatchet?" Draper responded, "In my opinion, they could."

Dr. Cheever, who followed Draper to the stand, was asked the same question. He also lied, "This hatchet [holding the hatchet head without the handle] could have caused those wounds."

It might be argued that neither doctor had, technically, perjured himself. In response to Knowlton's two questions, Draper had said it "could" have made the wounds in the skull. He had not said definitively that it had done so. The same is true of Dr. Cheever's testimony. Knowlton may have found a way to frame his questions so that neither respondent would have to perjure himself when replying. If that was, indeed, Knowlton's solution to his dilemma, it did nothing to protect the Harvard men from an equally serious charge, a sin of omission rather than commission, that of withholding evidence that was known to them. In either event, it was a manipulation of the truth – and of the entire case – that brought no credit to Harvard University or to the Commonwealth that Knowlton represented.

It was nearing 5:00 p.m. when Dr. Cheever left the stand. Overall, the eighth day of the trial had been an almost complete loss for the prosecution. Even though the prosecutor in charge knew the case was unwinnable, he continued to stumble on.

12. SMELLING SALTS, POISONS AND THE END OF THE PROSECUTION'S CASE

June 14 was the ninth day of the trial and the temperature outside had soared to 98 degrees. It was even warmer in the courtroom but, regardless, every seat was filled. And something intriguing was happening at the New Bedford courthouse: women occupied most of the seats, a phenomenon never before witnessed in the staid courts of New England. These were not idle housewives or shop girls seeking drama or titillation either. They were, for the most part, well-dressed matrons from the upper level of society, dressed in silks and soft cottons from the finest Boston shops. They had come to bear witness to what they saw as the persecution of one of their own. And in many ways, they were right.

And the presence of a courtroom filled with women was not the only odd thing occurring. Two extraneous matters had suddenly become important during the trial.

First, it was Lizzie's condition. After her fainting spell on opening day, brought about by the graphic descriptions of the wounds on the heads of the victims, she, on two other occasions had to be led from the courtroom; once at the sight of her father's grinning skull and once from the oppressive heat. There was speculation as to whether, if there was more of the blood and horror show to come, she would be able to remain in the stifling courtroom and witness it. If not, could the trial continue in her absence?

The second item had occurred on the previous day when the grisly photographs of Andrew's battered and mutilated face had been distributed to the jury members

again. Perhaps because of the heat and perhaps he was simply sickened by what he saw, juror Louis B. Hodges had swayed in his seat and was only saved from collapse by a fellow juror. He was vigorously fanned by one of his comrades, while another fetched a glass of water and gave it to him to drink. Judge Mason called a five minute recess while Hodges was taken out into the (slightly cooler) hallway and given

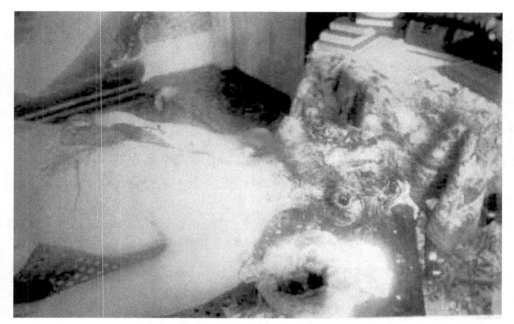

When the grisly autopsy photo of Andrew's savaged face was passed to the jury members, one of them, Louis B. Hodges, nearly fainted. He had to be revived with cool water, smelling salts and fresh air.

smelling salts and fresh air by the other jurors. He returned to his seat after the recess and sat, visibly weak and shaken, for the remaining six hours of testimony that day. Many wondered if the trial would end up in an appeal if only 11 jurors could make it through the rest of the grim ordeal.

The court came to order with the 9:00 a.m. chime of the clock. City Marshal Rufus Hilliard took the oath and stood in the witness box. He described how he had received a call telling him of some trouble at the Borden House on the morning of August 4, and how he had dispatched first, Office Allen and, soon after, Officers Doherty, Mullaly, Medley, and Wilson, and Assistant Marshal Fleet. He had gone to the house himself in the middle of the afternoon. He had participated in the day–long search on Saturday, and it had been a thorough one, from attic to basement. No, he had not spoken to Lizzie, but he had picked up the dress she had worn on the day of the murders.

Mayor John W. Coughlin was next on the stand. He had accompanied the marshal to the Borden house on Saturday evening. He described the crowds collected around the house, pushing on the sidewalks and milling in the streets. It had been difficult, he explained, to reach the house in their carriage without running over someone. They had made their way through, however, and had assembled the family in the parlor for a meeting. Lizzie had been there, along with Emma and John Morse. He recalled it as a somber occasion.

"I have a request to make of the family," he had said, "and that is that you remain in the house for a few days, as I believe it would be better for all concerned if you did so."

Lizzie had spoken up immediately. "Why? Is there anybody in this house suspected?"

The mayor had replied, referring to John Morse's rescue from the mob the night before, "Well, perhaps Mr. Morse can answer that question better than I, as his experience last night, perhaps, would justify him in the inference that somebody in this house was suspected."

Lizzie, recognizing this as a weasel-like answer, had said, "I want to know the truth." The mayor had not responded, and Lizzie had said again, "I want to know the truth." Obviously, what she had wanted to know was whether she was the suspect or whether it was John Morse.

The mayor then handed Robinson his prime line of defense. He had replied, "Well, Miss Borden, I regret to answer, but I must answer yes. You are suspected."

Lizzie's reply: "I am ready to go now or any time." Emma's parting remark had been, "I want you to do everything you can to find out this murder."

On cross-examination, Robinson questions the reluctant mayor for all the details. His answers were defensive and evasive, but that did not daunt the former governor. He was very comfortable ferreting out the details from witnesses who tried to avoid explicit answers to his questions. He pushed ahead with the mayor:

Q. You had said, as I understand it, you did the talking in the parlor?
A. I believe I did.
Q. The marshal did not participate in that?
A. I would not swear he did not.
Q. Do you recall that he did?
A. He may have re-affirmed what I said about the request to remain in the house. I don't recall that he entered into any lengthy conversation.
Q. You had advised them to remain in the house and on the premises?
A. Yes sir, I did.
Q. And thereupon Miss Lizzie said, "Why? Is there anybody in this house suspected?"
A. To the best of my knowledge.
Q. Spoke right up to you earnestly and promptly, did she?
A. She made that statement.
Q. Will you answer my question?

At that point, the Chief Justice chimed in and instructed the mayor to answer the question.

Q. You understand it?
A. Yes sir.
Q. Will you give me an answer?
A. She spoke up somewhat excitedly, I should say.
Q. She did?
A. Yes sir.
Q. What did you say to her?
A. When she asked me if there was somebody in the house suspected, I replied by stating that Mr. Morse could best answer that question, as the experience of last night would justify him in drawing the inference that there was.
Q. What was the next thing?
A. Lizzie said, "I want to know the truth."
Q. Lizzie said so?
A. Yes sir, and she repeated it if I remember rightly.
Q. Before you answered?
A. Yes sir.
Q. What did you say?
A. I said, "I regret, Miss Borden, but I must answer yes. You are suspected."
Q. And what did she say?
A. She said, as I now recall it, "I am ready to go now."
Q. "Or any time," didn't she?
A. I cannot recall that; she may have said it.
Q. Spoke up earnestly and promptly then, didn't she?
A. It would depend altogether by what you mean by "earnestly" and "promptly."
Q. I mean what you know the words mean.
A. She replied in a manner you can call earnestly and promptly. There was no hesitation about it.
Q. That is, promptly; no hesitation, isn't it? You understand that, don't you?
A. I do, yes sir.
Q. Now, did she speak earnestly?
A. Well, I would not say that she did not speak earnestly.
Q. What's that?
A. I should say I would not say that she did not speak earnestly.
Q. I know you say so. Did she speak earnestly?
A. Well, I should say yes. She spoke earnestly so far as the promptness of the question goes.

Q. Do you know the difference between promptness and earnestness?
A. There is a difference between promptness and earnestness.
Q. Keeping that distinction in mind, you say she answered you, did she, earnestly?
A. She did as far as I am ---
Q. What's that?
A. As far as I would be able to determine by her action, she was earnest.
Q. That is what I asked you, prompt and earnest.

And around and around it went. Perhaps Robinson's frustration with the mayor caused him to forget to ask Coughlin why it was he, not Marshal Hilliard, who had taken charge of the meeting. As mayor, he had no authority in what was, unquestionably, a police matter, most particularly when the town's top law enforcement officer was standing in the room. The answer to that question will never be known.

Hannah Reagan was the matron at the Fall River police station where Lizzie had been kept for 10 days. Mrs. Reagan, an Irish immigrant who was married to a stonecutter named Quinlan Reagan, was the first matron of the Fall River police station. She had been appointed in 1887, and served until she retired in 1909. She was called to the stand by the prosecution to tell a story that they hoped would cast some doubt on Lizzie's innocence.

On August 24, Emma had gone to the station to visit her sister, as she had done many times since Lizzie's arrest. She had been admitted to her cell while Mrs. Reagan retired to the toilet room, which was about four feet away. She could hear what she described as "very loud talk" between the sisters, and she had returned to the doorway just in time to hear Lizzie say, "Emma, you have gave me away, haven't you?" Emma had replied, "No, Lizzie, I have not. "You have," Lizzie said, "and I will let you see I won't give in one inch." Lizzie had turned away, and they did not speak again during the short visit.

Emma, in the days between the murders and that morning, had neither done nor said anything that questioned Lizzie's innocence, nor did she at any time before her death more than 30 years later. It is questionable that Lizzie, educated and even lyrical in her speech and writing, would have said, "you have gave me away." Her alleged retort, "I will let you see I won't give in one inch," is equally a grammatically poor statement with a hazy meaning.

This supposed interaction was leaked to the press within minutes and, with equal speed, denied by Mrs. Reagan as being untrue. Just to be on the safe side, Lizzie's attorney Jennings drew up a statement confirming that the story was made up by *Globe* reporter Edwin H. Porter, and Reverend Buck asked the matron to sign it. The statement read:

This is to certify that my attention has been called to a report said to have been made by me in regard to a quarrel between Lizzie and her sister, Emma, in which Lizzie said to Emma, "You have given me away," etc., and that I expressly and positively deny that any such conversation took place and I further deny that I ever heard anything that could be construed as a quarrel between the two sisters.

She was willing to sign it, but, by then, Marshal Hilliard had heard about the situation and had stepped in. The story had been printed in the *Globe*, and if it was hurtful to Lizzie, then, so be it. He was not going to have it retracted. When Reverend Buck showed him the statement, he had said to the matron, "You go to your room and I will attend to this business; and you, Reverend Buck, attend to yours."

That was his last word on the affair. If it had any effect on the jury, no one could tell. It is unlikely that it did, since the quarrel – that probably never took place – was a murky one, and, when coupled with Mrs. Reagan's denial, signed or not, it was impossible to know what had really taken place and what it meant.

Poison was the next subject on the prosecution's agenda. They hoped to establish that Lizzie had, on the day before the murders, attempted to purchase 10-cents worth of prussic acid and to imply that this showed she had murderous intentions toward Andrew and Abby.

They hoped to use druggist Eli Bence to illustrate this. He was called to the stand to tell what he knew about the incident, and Robinson was instantly on his feet to object. The chief justice excused the jury and Eli Bence to hear what he knew would be a protracted argument from both sides.

Moody spoke first: "I perhaps ought first to state what the testimony is that we offer," he said. Moody told the court that Bence had 13 years of experience as a druggist, but had never had a request for prussic acid before, which was hard to believe since he carried it in stock. But on August 3, he claimed, Lizzie had come into the drugstore and asked for 10-cents worth of it, stating that she planned to clean the sealskin cape that she carried. Bence had informed her that prussic acid could not be bought without a doctor's prescription and she had left.

It's no wonder that prussic acid required a doctor's prescription, but oddly, there seems to be no medical use for it. Prussic acid was another name for hydrogen cyanide and it was a deadly poison that could kill a man or woman in less than a minute. It was normally used as a pesticide and in this case, it was alleged that moths or insects had infested Lizzie's cape and she wanted the poison to kill them with. This form of cyanide was obtained from fruits that had a pit, such as cherries, apricots, apples, and bitter almonds, and during the nineteenth century, it was popularly used in murders and suicides – which is how it became linked to this case. Lizzie had tried to poison her family, it was suggested, and when that failed, she had hacked them to death with "40 whacks" from a hatchet.

Robinson rose to give us his objections to the testimony from Bence: "It appears upon the testimony of Professor Wood that an examination of the stomachs of the deceased persons showed no traces of any poison whatsoever, or anything but a normal condition. Certainly not any prussic acid. That was directly and fully negatived. So, there is no shown connection, as assailing the lives of these two persons. In fact, this evidence only goes as far as to show, assuming that they may show it for the time being in this discussion, that she asked to buy prussic acid under precisely the circumstances that the offer is now made. She is charged in this indictment with slaying or killing these two people with a sharp instrument; committing the murder with an axe, for instance. Nothing else. Now here, if it has any force at all, suppose it were carried away up to its legitimate result, it is an attempt to charge her with an act causing death by a wholly different means, for which she is not now on trial."

Besides, he continued, it had to be shown that any act on the part of the defendant must have some natural tendency to show that she committed the act for which she stood charged. The fact, even if it were proved, that Lizzie had attempted to purchase prussic acid, a legal product that could be purchased, did not show that she had committed some other act which might be a crime. Does it, Robinson demanded, have a tendency at all to show that this defendant killed two persons with an axe? That was what this trial was about – it was not about a questionable identification by a man who claimed she tried to buy poison.

In rebuttal, Moody began by initially agreeing with Robinson. If Lizzie had, indeed, attempted to purchase prussic acid, it didn't have any direct link to murders by hatchet or axe. It did, however, support the prosecution's charge that the slayings had been premeditated. It was the Commonwealth's position that the illness that struck the Borden family on Monday had suggested to Lizzie that poison might be a good way to do away with Andrew and Abby. She had then, on Wednesday, tried to purchase the poison. She failed and then had resorted to the hatchet.

As he had done during the argument over the admissibility of Lizzie's inquest testimony, the prosecution spent the next two hours tediously recalling legal precedents, all the while admitting that none of them really fit this particular case. Moody closed his argument by saying, "I can conceive of no more significant act, nothing which tends to show more purpose of doing mischief to someone, than the attempt to obtain one of the most deadly poisons that is known to humankind."

Robinson also addressed the judges again, and said there had been nothing placed on records to indicate murderous intent prior to August 4, on the part of Lizzie other than her comment that Abby was not her mother – which was a fact.

He continued, "It is not as if she had said, 'I intend to kill someone before the end of the week,' or 'I have murder in my heart.'" The Commonwealth admitted that there was nothing in the evidence to show that Lizzie planned to commit murder.

Robinson went on, "I grant you that if a man goes to work upon a criminal act, meaning violence in a particular direction, you may draw the logical inference from that. But, if he does an innocent act – we cannot reach forward and say, 'You intended to do that which at that time you had no sort of intention to commit, so far as proof goes.' Would this court sit here for a moment and listen to a proposition that she undertook on a former day to shoot Dr. Bowen, for instance, to show that she had a murderous intent toward Mr. and Mrs. Borden? No, not if she had done it one hour before. That would be setting up a distinct and separate crime."

When Robinson had finished his final argument, the judges withdrew to consider the situation and returned at 4:30. The chief justice addressed the attorneys, "The court are of the opinion, provided the preliminary evidence comes up to the proffer, the evidence is competent." In translation, the judges would listen to the Commonwealth's presentation and then decided whether or not the jury should hear it.

On that upbeat note for the prosecution, court adjourned for the day.

When court convened on June 15 – day 10 of the trial – Charles H. Lawton, Nathaniel Hathaway, and Henry H. Tillson took the stand. Lawton was a pharmacist, Hathaway an analytic chemist, and Tillson was a retailer of ladies furs. They told of the use of prussic acid to clean furs, its properties as an insecticide, and of its risks to humans.

When they had finished, there was a conference at the bench between the attorneys and the judges. It was off the record and no transcript of the whispered conversation exists, but the decision handed down by the three justices made newspaper headlines the next day – the Commonwealth had not been able to keep the proof within the limits they had agreed on with the defense counsel, and all of the poison evidence was excluded.

A *Boston Globe* reporter wrote of Lizzie's reaction to the news: "At the conclusion, she burst into tears – into a convulsion of pleasure, gratitude, and sudden relief that wracked her body. She had learned to brace herself against adversity and unkindness, but mercy and active friendliness were so new to her that she broke down then."

It was yet another stunning blow for the prosecution and Knowlton undoubtedly was thinking of the letter that he had written to Attorney General Pillsbury, bemoaning the fact that it was an unwinnable case. He slowly rose to his feet. "The Commonwealth rests," he said quietly.

This announcement took everyone by surprise. Only the three men on the judge's bench remained impassive. There was a frenzied stir among the spectators in the courtroom, brought on at least partially, one might suppose, by their anticipation that the defense might immediately move for a dismissal of all charges and the trial might come to an abrupt end. The men of the jury stiffened in their seats, wondering if their days of boredom and imprisonment might actually be over. Lizzie smiled, the only evidence of her excitement being the rapid movement of her fan.

A rumor had been going around the courthouse for days that defense would not present a rebuttal to what the prosecution had put forth. Among the spectators at the trial, at least, the feeling was that the government's case could not possibly convince anyone that Lizzie was guilty beyond a reasonable doubt. The general feeling among the reporters covering the case was that the trial would do one of two things: fail for a lack of proof or become the most complete vindication of the potency of circumstantial evidence in American history. A conviction of Lizzie Borden would give hope to every poorly prepared prosecutor in the country. The reporters bolted from the courtroom at Knowlton's announcement to flash the news to their respective papers.

Meanwhile, the stenographers and typists continued the official transcript. The trial required a virtual assembly line of stenographers and typists. The on-duty stenographer, one of a troop of men, sat at a desk in front of the witnesses in the courtroom, working a five-minute shift. As soon as he approached his time limit, another man moved in beside him, nudged, and took over like a hand-off in a running race. At that, the on-duty stenographer hurried out of the room, raced down the stairs, and delivered his steno pad to one of a battery of young female typists. In the meantime, a third stenographer was making his way up the stairs. The system was so efficient that one hour after a witness had testified, both counsels and judges had a typed transcript neatly bound and stitched in front of them.

13. THE CASE FOR THE DEFENSE

Soon after Sheriff Wright had restored order and silence in the second-floor courtroom, Andrew Jennings opened the case for the defense. He was a quick, nervous-acting man with a small, slender build and an excitable face that often seemed filled with anxiety. He opened things with a personal note:

One of the victims of the murder charged in this indictment was for many years my client and my personal friend. I have known him since boyhood. I had known his oldest daughter for the same length of time, and I want to say right here and now, if I manifest more feeling that perhaps you think necessary in making an opening statement for the defense in this case, you will ascribe it to that cause. The counsel, Mr. Foreman and gentlemen, does not cease to be a man when he becomes a lawyer.

Fact and fiction have furnished many extraordinary examples of crime that have shocked the feelings and staggered the reason of men, but I think no one has ever surpassed in its mystery the case you are now considering.

Jennings went on to say that the crime had shocked the whole civilized world. The brutality of the wounds, the audacity of the time and place chosen, and the accusation of the victim's youngest daughter, he said, made this the act "of an insane person or fiend." There is an outcry of human hearts, he continued, to have somebody punished for the crime. "But, Mr. Foreman and gentlemen, no matter how much you want someone punished for the crime, it is the guilty and not the innocent you want." He went on to add that the law of Massachusetts "draws about every person accused of this crime or any other, the circle of the presumption of his or her innocence, and allows no juryman or jury to cross it until they have fulfilled the conditions required. Until they show that the accused has been proved guilty beyond a reasonable doubt, they are not allowed to cross the line and take the life of the party who is accused.

Jennings continued, "There is not one particle of direct evidence in this case, from beginning to end, against Lizzie Andrew Borden. There is not a spot of blood – there is not a weapon that they have connected with her in any way, shape or fashion. They have not had her hand touch it or her eye see it or her ear hear of it. There is not, I say, a particle of direct testimony in the case connecting her with this crime. It is wholly and absolutely circumstantial."

Jennings then listed the three fabled necessities to prove guilt in circumstantial evidence cases: motive, means, and opportunity.

As he reminded the jury of Bridget's testimony about the quietness of the house and the politeness of the family, he stated, "There is absolutely no motive whatsoever for the commission of this crime by the defendant. Though they furnish you with a motive on her part to kill the stepmother, they have shown you absolutely none to kill the father. Absolutely none; unless they advance what seems to be the ridiculous proposition that she, instead of leaving the house after killing the mother, waits there for an hour or an hour and a half for the express purpose of killing her own father, between whom and herself there is shown not the slightest trouble or disagreement whatsoever."

As for means, "The blood that was shown upon the axes, which were so carefully guarded at first in this case, has disappeared like mist in the morning sun. The claw-headed hatchet that Dr. Dolan was so sure committed this deed at the Fall River hearing – so sure that he could even see the print which the claw head of the hatchet made in the head of Mr. Borden, has disappeared from the case. I contend that, as to the weapon, they have either got to produce the weapon which did the deed, and, having produced it, connect it in some way directly with the prisoner, or else they have got to account in some reasonable way for its disappearance."

And as for opportunity: "I want to call to your attention right here that, in all this search and investigation that has been made about the whereabouts and doings of Mr. Andrew J, Borden upon that morning, there has not been a living soul put on the stand here to testify that they saw Andrew J. Borden come downstreet from his house. From his house to the Union Savings Bank, he has been absolutely invisible. Was it any easier for him to be unseen than it would be for somebody escaping from the house if they walked quietly away?"

He promised, in addition, that the defense would prove that Lizzie had been in the barn just as she said she was, and that the burned dress would be put into perspective as their case was presented.

The first witness called to the stand was Sarah Hart. At about 9:50 on the morning of the murders, she had been passing the Borden house with her sister-in-law and had observed a young man standing by the gate, resting his head on his left hand, with his elbow on the gatepost. As she was walking, her nephew passed by and they spent about five minutes chatting with him. The stranger was still there when she walked away.

Dr. Benjamin Hardy followed Mrs. Hart to the stand and confirmed what she had seen. He, too, had also spotted a young man acting strangely in front of the house – so strangely that he had stopped his carriage and turned to watch him. He seemed to be mentally agitated; he stopped at times and then walked on. His actions were different, Dr. Hardy said, from those of anyone he had ever seen on the street in his life.

Mark Chace was called and told of seeing a strange man in a buggy parked in front of the Borden house at the time of the murder.

According to Charles N. Gifford, he also described a strange man, weighing from 180 to 190 pounds, sitting on the side steps of the Borden house the night before the murders took place. He had a straw hat pulled down over his eyes.

Charles Sawyer, who had been recruited into service as a door guard by Officer Allen when the alarm had first been given, testified that Lizzie had been sitting in a rocking chair being cared for by Miss Russell, Mrs. Churchill, and Bridget. He had been close to her at the time and had seen no bloodstains on her head, hair, face, hands, or dress.

When Walter P. Stevens took the stand, it soon became clear for the first time why Robinson had not panicked when Officer Medley had testified in detail how he had gone into the barn loft, sighted along the floor, and found no footprints in the dust. The conclusion was that Lizzie had not been up there that morning.

Mr. Stevens was a reporter for the *Fall River News*. He had been at the police station when Officer Allen had rushed back from the Borden house for reinforcements. Stevens had double-timed it back to the house. As he poked around the property, he had gone out to the barn at the same time Officer Medley arrived at the house. He had not gone up to the loft, but while he was on the ground floor, he heard three people go up the steps and walk around the loft – before Medley made his inspection.

Alfred C. Clarkson, a steam engineer, was called, and he identified himself as being one of the three men who went into the loft. He added that he had also seen two other men go up – before Medley.

The next witness was not only the last nail in Medley's coffin, but it provided one of the lightest moments of the trial. Thomas E. Barlow, age 12, and his friend, Everett Brown, also 12 and nicknamed "Brownie," were also at the Borden house on the day of the murders. Tommy, referring over and over to "me and Brownie," told how they were playing on the sidewalk and had arrived at the Borden home just as the first cry of alarm had been sounded. Having thoughts of a great adventure, "me and Brownie," after being refused admission to the house by Charles Sawyer, went to the barn with the idea of capturing the murderer hiding in the straw. "Me and Brownie" had gone up to the loft and hunted around and played awhile, but, of course, found no killer hiding there. That had all taken place before Officer Medley arrived on the scene. In cross-examination, Knowlton tried very hard to shake the boy as to what time "Me and Brownie" had been in the loft, but "Me and Brownie" knew what time they had started playing. It was always 11:00 a.m. Who could challenge a 12-year-old as to what time he had finished his chores so that he could go out and play on a fine summer day?

The defense had made their point. There were either five or seven people who had been up in the loft before Medley claimed that he had been there and had seen nothing. Attorney Jennings, in his opening statement, had said Medley's trip to the loft had been a "cakewalk – a figment of his imagination."

But really, it was more than that. It was essential for the prosecution to strip Lizzie of her alibi of being in the barn when Andrew was killed. It was obvious that Medley was not merely mistaken; his description had been too detailed and meticulous. He had outright lied. He had perjured himself, just as Fleet had done earlier in the trial. And this was not the first time, it was discovered, that Medley had fiddled with evidence. During the investigation, he had reported to Fleet that Charles O. Cook, one of Andrew's property managers, had told him that Andrew had said two days before the murders that he needed to get around to making a will. Cook vehemently swore at the preliminary hearing that he had never given the police officer any such statement.

Thomas F. Hickey, a reporter for the *Boston Globe*, was called by Robinson to add his knowledge of Hanna Reagan's story of the Lizzie–Emma quarrel. He had seen Hannah just after the story had appeared in the *Fall River Globe*. He had teased her, saying "I see you're getting yourself in the paper." "Yes," Hannah had replied, "but they have got to take it all back."

Hickey told the court, "I asked her about the quarrel and she said there had been no quarrel. I asked her if she had repeated any of the words of the sisters; asked her if there was any truth in the report, and she said, 'Absolutely none.'"

The defense brought in another startling witness with Hyman Lubinsky. He was a Russian immigrant and spoke only basic words of English. On that fateful Thursday, he had picked up his ice cream wagon and horse just a few minutes before 11:00 a.m. Using a complicated explanation of this timetable, he could prove that he left the stable between 11:05 and 11:10 and passed the Borden house just minutes later. He said, "I saw a lady come out of the way from the barn right to the stairs at the back of the house. She was wearing a dark-colored dress."

He had delivered ice cream to the Borden house many times before and the lady that he saw was not Bridget; he knew her. His testimony fit to the minute with the time that Lizzie had said she had returned to the house from the barn. He had told Officer Medley, among others, but apparently the police were not interested in his story. Jennings' staff had sought him out, however, and brought him to court to testify about events that the police did not want to hear. It didn't fit their version of events.

During the cross-examination, Knowlton was cruel and impatient, irritated with Lubinsky's poor grasp of the English language. Several times during the questioning, Lubinsky protested, "You ask me too fast!" A reporter for the *New York Sun* wrote:

"Never did a lawyer try harder to confuse a witness than did Mr. Knowlton on this occasion. He walked up and down between the witness and his desk, prodding him with rapid questions. He was nervous, agitated, and scolding in his tone."

But, the reporter added, he never made a dent in Lubinsky's story.

One of the most welcome coincidences of the trial was the end of the prosecution's case coinciding with the end of the brutal heat that had scorched participants and spectators alike. Overnight, the temperature dropped 37 degrees, from 92 on Thursday evening to a crisp 55 on Friday morning. It was a much more welcome start to the eleventh day of the trial, which saw a continuation of witnesses to denounce Hannah Reagan's apparently false story of a quarrel between Emma and Lizzie.

Mrs. Marianna Holmes, wife of banker Charles Holmes, testified that she had questioned Mrs. Regan about the story soon after it was published. Mrs. Reagan had told him that it was not true; she had not heard any argument between the sisters. She would be willing to sign a statement to that effect if Marshal Hilliard would let her. However, Hilliard had told her that if she signed it, it would be against his orders. Obviously fearing for her job if she crossed the marshal, she had not signed the paper drawn up by Jennings and presented by Reverend Buck.

Her husband, Charles, also took the stand and said the same thing – the story of the quarrel was a lie. Newspaper reporter John R. Caldwell and Mrs. Mary E. Bingham agreed that there was no truth to the story.

How much of the whole "quarrel" story was the product of *Globe* reporter Edwin H. Porter's active imagination and how was the work of the police will never be known, but, as far as the jury was concerned, it had been watered down by the testimony of reliable witnesses and was believable now only by the anti–Lizzie faction, who were willing to believe anything bad that was said about her.

The most important witness on day eleven of the trial was undoubtedly Emma Borden.

Emma, now 42 years of age, looked worn and tired. Dressed like a spinster New England schoolteacher in plain black, she stood ramrod straight in the witness box. There was no swaying of her slender form, no hesitation in her piercing eyes, and no tremor to her pursed lips. She stood with perfect self-possession, answered every question deliberately and with assurance, and met the skillful cross–examination of Knowlton without defiance, but with determination that her words be clearly understood.

Little was known about Emma Borden, then or now. During his lifetime, Andrew Borden had been a well–known man in Fall River, either respected, feared, hated, or all of the combined. Abby had been little more than a recluse. Her trips to the market,

town shops, and sporadic church attendance had been her only outings. She had never been involved in either the social or civic activities of Fall River. Lizzie was the outgoing member of the family. Significantly, there are dozens of photographs of Lizzie, many of them taken in professional studios, but only a handful exist of Emma. It was almost as if she worked hard to be inconspicuous. She was overshadowed, all of her life, by her sister.

But her evidence at the trial in support of Lizzie was forceful and positive. She spoke clearly and without hesitation. The trial, as it turned out, was her finest hour.

Jennings immediately went to work establishing that murder for inheritance was not the motive. Emma produced records to show that Lizzie had $170 on deposit at the B.M.C. Durfee Bank, $2,000 in the Massasoit Bank, $500 in the Union Savings, and $141 in the Fall River Five Cent Savings. This, in addition to numerous shares of stock was, by 1892 standards, a formidable amount of money for a young woman to have in her own name.

Emma Borden... Unlike her younger sister, Emma was rarely photographed.

Jennings then highlighted the fond relationship that existed between father and daughter. Andrew was not known for his warm personality, or even his tolerance of many people, but he did, reportedly, have a soft place in his heart for his daughters, especially Lizzie, the little girl who had been given a middle name that was also his own.

Q. Did your father wear a ring, Miss Emma, upon his finger?
A. Yes sir.
Q. Was or was not that the only article of jewelry that he wore?
A. The only article.
Q. Do you know from whom he received the ring?
A. My sister, Lizzie.
Q. How long before his death?
A. I should think 10 to 15 years.
Q. Do you know whether previously to his wearing it she had worn it?
A. Yes sir.
Q. Did he wear it constantly after it was given to him?
A. Do you know whether or not it was upon his finger at the time he was buried?

A. It was.

Jennings then turned his attention to the elusive dress that Lizzie was supposed by the prosecution to have been wearing, which would have been stained with blood. He asked her how many dresses were in the various closets searched by the police.

A. Somewhere about 18 or 19.
Q. And whose were those dresses?
A. All of them belonged to my sister and I except one that belonged to Mrs. Borden.
Q. How many of those dresses were blue dresses or dresses in which blue was a marked color?
A. Ten.
Q. To whom did those belong?
A. Two of them to me and eight to my sister.
Q. Were you there on the afternoon of Saturday while the search was going on?
A. Yes sir.
Q. What, if anything, did Dr. Dolan say to you as to the character of the search that had been done?
A. He told me the search had been as thorough as the search could be made unless the paper was torn from the walls and the carpets taken from the floor.
Q. Did you or Miss Lizzie, so far as you know, at any time make any objection to the searching of any part of that house?
A. Not the slightest.
Q. Did you assist them in any way you could?
A. By telling them to come as often as they pleased and search as thorough as they could.

Emma described the blue cotton Bedford cord dress that Lizzie had burned. It had, she said, a very light blue ground with a dark figure measuring about an inch by three-quarters of an inch. It had been an insignificant dress of cheap material, costing about 12 ½ cents a yard or, perhaps, 15-cents.

The dressmaking, as was common in that era, had gone on in the guest room – the room where Abby had been killed. Soon after the dress was made, painters had been at the Borden house, painting the outside and trimming the inside.

Q. Do you know anything about her getting any paint on it at that time?
A. Yes, she did.
Q. Where was the paint upon it?

A. I should say along the front and on one side toward the bottom and some on the wrong side of the skirt.

Q. How soon after it was made?

A. Well, I think within 2 weeks; perhaps less time than that.

Q. Now where was that dress, if you know, on Saturday, the last day of the search?

A. I saw it hanging in the clothes press over the front entry.

Q. How come you to see it at that time?

A. I went in to hang up the dress I had been wearing during the day and there was no vacant nail and I searched around to find a nail and I noticed this dress.

Q. Did you say anything to your sister about that dress in consequence of your not finding a nail to hang your dress on?

A. I did.

Q. What did you say to her?

A. I said, "You have not destroyed that old dress yet? Why don't you?"

Q. What was the condition of that dress at that time?

A. It was very dirty, very much soiled, and badly faded.

Q. When did you next see that Bedford cord dress?

A. Sunday morning, I think, about nine o'clock.

Q. Now will you tell the court and the jury all that you saw or heard that morning in the kitchen?

A. I was washing dishes and I heard my sister's voice and I turned around and saw that she was standing at the foot of the stove, between the foot of the stove and the dining room door. This dress was hanging on her arm and she says, "I think I shall burn this old dress up." I said, "Why don't you?" or "You had better," or "I would if I were you," or something like that. I can't tell the exact words, but I meant, do it. And I turned back and continued washing dishes and did not see her burn it and did not pay any more attention to her at that time.

Q. What was the condition of the kitchen doors and windows at that time?

A. They were all wide open, screens in and blinds open.

Q. Were the officers all about at that time?

A. They were all about in the yard.

Jennings tried to establish that, in the Borden house, they didn't keep a rag bag for such material as the old dress. It is doubtful, however, that he wanted her to tell that the reason they didn't was because Andrew was too cheap to pay to have trash hauled away when it could be burned for free.

Knowlton objected to the question and was sustained.

Alice Russell, Emma's friend, had been present at the time of the dress burning. The following day, Monday, she had told Emma that Detective Hanscom had asked her if all the dresses were there that had been there on the day of the murder and she had told him "yes." Emma had asked her why she had told him that.

"The burning of the dress was the worst thing that Lizzie could have done," Alice had said.

Lizzie was flustered by this. "Why didn't you tell me before I burned the dress? Why did you let me do it?"

Emma had told Alice that she should tell Hanscom about the burned dress and also that she and Lizzie had told her to do so.

Jennings then asked her about the alleged quarrel she was supposed to have had with Lizzie at the jail:

Q. Now, Miss Emma, do you recall a story that was told by Mrs. Reagan about a quarrel between yourself and your sister?

A. Yes sir.

Q. Was your attention called to the fact by me?

A. It was.

Q. How soon after it, do you know?

A. The morning following.

Q. Now, Miss Emma, on that morning, did you have any conversation with Miss Lizzie, in which she said, "Emma, you have given me away, haven't you?"

A. I did not.

Q. And did you say in reply, "No, Lizzie, I haven't." "You have," she says, "and I will let you see I won't give in one inch." Was there any such talk as that?

A. There was not.

Q. Anything like that?

A. Nothing.

Q. That morning or any morning?

A. No time. Not any time.

Q. Was there ever any trouble in the matron's room between you and your sister while she was there?

A. There was not.

Knowlton harshly cross-examined Emma, querying her about the transaction that was supposed to have started the animosity between the elder Bordens and the younger, which was the purchase of the house for Abby's half-sister. Mrs. Whitehead had owned half of the house in which she lived and Abby owned the other half. Fearing that her half-sister might find herself homeless in her old age, Abby had convinced Andrew to buy Mrs. Whitehead's half and give it to her. The price had been $1,500.

Knowlton questioned Emma about it:

Q. Did that make some trouble in the family?

A. Yes.

Q. Between whom?

A. Between my father and Mrs. Borden, and my sister and I.

Q. And also between you and your sister and your step-mother?

A. Yes sir.

Q. Did you find fault with it?

A. Yes sir.

Q. Did Lizzie find fault with it?

A. Yes sir.

Q. And in consequence of your faultfinding, did your father also make a purchase for you and give you some money?

A. Not, I don't think, because of our faultfinding.

Q. Did he, after the faultfinding, give you some money?

A. Yes sir.

Q. How much?

A. Grandfather's house on Ferry Street.

Q. And there was some complaint that that was not an equivalent?

A. No, sir. It was more than an equivalent.

Knowlton didn't gain much ground with these questions, but Emma's answer to his next question must have surprised and shaken him. The prosecution had built their case against Lizzie on the bad feelings that they claimed existed between her and Abby. Emma's testimony told a much different story, though. According to what she said, Lizzie had been the forgiving sister. It was Abby and Emma, she admitted, who didn't get along.

Q. Were the relations between you and Lizzie and your stepmother as cordial after that occurrence of the house that you have spoken of, as they were before?

A. Between my sister and Mrs. Borden, they were.

Q. They were entirely the same?

A. I think so.

Q. Were they so on your part?

A. I think not.

For the next hour, Knowlton grilled Emma on this point, reading back to her the testimony that she gave at the inquest and the preliminary investigation. The best that he could do was to establish that her answers during those proceedings had been open to interpretation. There was no doubt about her answers now – Lizzie's relationship with Abby had been much more cordial than hers.

He then tried to show that there was hostility between the sisters, illustrated by the fact that Emma, at one time, had occupied the larger of the two bedrooms, but had later relinquished it to Lizzie. It was a weak line of questioning, terminated when Emma said that she had traded rooms voluntarily – and it had been at her suggestion. Knowlton still hadn't learned not to ask questions to which the answer would be a surprise.

He also made an equally futile attempt to shake her testimony on points where it conflicted with what Alice Russell had said took place when the dress was burned. Alice's testimony had been that Emma had asked Lizzie what she was going to do with the dress she was holding. Emma said that was not how she remembered it. She recalled Lizzie speaking first, stating that she was going to burn the old dress. Knowlton pressed her on this and Emma insisted that she had not spoken first. Finally, she snapped at the prosecutor, saying, "The reason that I say I didn't say it is because I didn't say it."

Knowlton gave up. His cross-examination had deteriorated to haggling and arguing, gaining him nothing.

The dressmaker, Mrs. Mary A. Raymond, took the stand to say that she had made the Bedford cord dress in question during a three-week stay at the Borden home. It had been paint-stained almost immediately; as a matter of fact, when she was still in the house making other dresses. When faded, she said, Bedford cord has a drab appearance.

Mrs. Phoebe Bowen, wife of Dr. Bowen from across the street, told of Lizzie's distraught condition minutes after the murder. She was positive in her identification of the dress Lizzie had given to the police as being the one she was wearing that morning.

The final witness for the defense was Mrs. Annie White, a court stenographer at the inquest and the preliminary hearing. She read from the notes that she had taken at the inquest in which Bridget described how Lizzie had been crying when she learned of Andrew's murder.

The defense rested its case on day twelve.

Most of the newspapers that covered the murders and the trial formed an opinion about Lizzie's guilt or innocence early on and stuck with it. The sensationalism of the *Fall River Globe* and its penchant for manufactured stories was obvious. The *Boston Globe*, with both an air of superiority and the mess with Trickey hanging around its neck, went back and forth and finally watered down its coverage. The Fall River *Herald* and *Evening News* were, for the most part, supportive of Lizzie. The coverage provided by the *Providence Journal*, another prominent area newspaper, was filled with inaccuracies, and never seemed to decide if they believed Lizzie had done it or not.

The *New York Times* reported impartially and with as much accuracy as could be mustered at the time. The editorial that appeared in its pages that day managed to capture the essence of the trial and the predicament faced by the prosecution:

Will it Remain a Mystery?

It is many a year since a criminal case in this country has excited such universal interest and been the subject of so much discussion as that of the Borden murders. It has all the fascination of a mystery about which there may be a thousand theories and upon which opinions may differ as variously as the idiosyncrasies of those who form them. There is so little absolute evidence that everybody can interpret the probabilities and the circumstantial indications to suit himself, and much will depend upon his general view of human nature and its capabilities. There seems to be little prospect that the mystery will be cleared up by the trial that is going on at New Bedford. The verdict, if there shall be a verdict, will make little difference unless there is to be some disclosure of which there is yet no sign.

The whole case is a tangle of probabilities and improbabilities, with little that is certain except that a man and wife were murdered in their own home on a frequented city street in the middle of an August forenoon, with nobody about the premises, so far as he has shown, but the daughter and a servant girl. It was improbably enough that such a crime should be committed at such a time and place at all. That anyone should enter the house from the outside and commit it and get away without being observed or leaving any trace behind was most improbable. But the officers of the law were unable to find any evidence that the crime was perpetrated by anyone outside of the family, and the testimony brought by the defense to show that it might have happened in that way has proved nothing as to the crime.

The utter absence of any other explanation was the sole support of the suspicion against the daughter. In spite of the circumstances that made it look dark for her, there was as complete a lack of direct evidence against her as of any kind of evidence against anybody else. If circumstantial evidence is a chain only as strong as its weakest link, we have presented here, an attempt to make a chain out of wholly disconnected links, which has no continuity or binding strength at all. Almost as strong a case could be made out against anybody who had the misfortune to be in the house where murder was committed and not on the happiest terms with the victim. The utter absence of proof of anything except the fact of murder, and the lack of real evidence against anybody, is likely to leave this as a baffling mystery, unless a revelation should be made of which there is as yet no premonition.

14. CLOSING ARGUMENTS

In contrast with some of his other moments during the trial, Robinson's closing arguments were rather low-key. He felt no need for theatrics, which were usually the device of an attorney who had a poor case to argue and had to resort to smoke and mirrors to hide his predicament. At this point, the former governor must have known that the prosecution had fumbled its case, and perhaps he had considered moving for a dismissal of the charges. While it would have demonstrated the complete confidence the defense felt in Lizzie's innocence, it would have been a daring move fraught with great hazard.

The prosecution had offered no real evidence against Lizzie – no weapon, no hard motive, no bloodstained clothing, only the same opportunity that, conceivably, others shared with her. Robinson's closing was tailored to make these points to an already skeptical jury. He took them step-by-step in an address that lasted the better part of the day.

He began, "One of the most dastardly and diabolical crimes that was ever committed in Massachusetts was perpetrated in August 1892, in Fall River. The enormity and outrage startled everybody, and set all into the most diligent inquiry as to the perpetrator of such terrible acts. The terrors of those scenes no language can portray. The horrors of that moment we can all fail to describe.

" And so we are challenged at once, at the outset, to find somebody that is equal to that enormity, whose heart is blackened with depravity, whose whole life is a tissue of crime, whose past is a prophecy of that present. A maniac or a fiend, we say. Not a man in his senses with his heart right, but one whose abnormal productions that Deity creates or suffers – a lunatic or a devil."

Robinson's point was, of course, that Lizzie was none of these things.

As for the inquest, preliminary hearing, and her indictment, "You have nothing to do with what was done in Fall River any more than you have with what is now proceeding in Australia. The finding of Judge Blaisdell, worthy man as he may be, is of no sort of consequence here. We would not be safe if, in these great crises, our lives hung upon the decision of a single man in a prejudiced and excited community."

This brought him to the question of why Lizzie had been arrested and charged at all.

"Policemen are human, made out of men, and nothing else, and when he undertakes to investigate a crime, he is possessed and saturated with the thoughts and experience he has had with bad people. He is drifting, and turning in the way of finding a criminal, magnifying this, minimizing that, throwing himself on this side in order to catch somebody, standing before a community that demands the detection and punishment of the criminal, blamed if he does not get somebody in the lockup before morning.

"'What are the police doing?' say the newspapers. 'Look here, Mr. City Marshal, these murders were committed yesterday. Haven't you a murderer in the lockup? Get somebody in!'

"They make themselves, as a body of men, ridiculous, insisting that the defendant shall know everything that was done on a particular time, shall account for every movement of that time, shall tell it three or four times alike, shall never waver or quiver, shall have tears or not have tears, shall make no mistake."

At this point, Robinson summed up what the trial was all about. Certainly, the men of the jury, just like the public, had a burning curiosity about what had happened in the house on Second Street, but that was not why they were sitting in the jury box. Robinson naturally feared that they might be so consumed with the mystery that they might feel an obligation, not unlike the public, to solve the puzzle and find someone – anyone – guilty of the murders. Since it was Lizzie in the dock, it would be her. So, he reminded them:

"It is not your business to unravel the mystery. You are not here to find out the solution of the problem. You are here not to find out who committed the murders. You are here to pursue something else. You are simply and solely here to say, is this woman defendant guilty? That is all. Not, who did it? Not, how could it have been done? But did she do it? That is all.

Now, there is no direct evidence against Miss Borden. Nobody saw or heard anything or experienced anything that connects her to the tragedies. No weapon whatsoever, and no knowledge of the use of one, as to her, has been shown. If you found her with some weapon of that kind in her control, or in her room, or with her belongings, that would be direct evidence. But there is nothing of that kind. It is not claimed. It is not shown that she ever used an implement of the character that must have produced these murders. It is not shown that she ever touched one or knew of one or bought or had one. In fact, the evidence is that she didn't know where in the house the ordinary things of that kind were.

"And the murders did not tell any tales on her, either. There was no blood on her, and blood speaks out, although it is voiceless. It speaks out against the criminal. Not a spot on her, from her hair to her feet, on dress or person anywhere. Think of it! Think of it for an instant!"

Robinson ridiculed the police testimony that had been offered concerning the missing hatchet handle. Had there ever been one? And if so, where was it? What reason could the police even offer to say that Lizzie was guilty? Robinson ran through it with the jury to explain why they claimed she did it.

"In the first place, they say she was in the house in the forenoon. Well, that may look to you like a very wrong place for her to be in. But, it is her home! I suspect you have an impression that it would be better for her if she had been out traveling the streets. I don't know where I would want my daughter to be, than to say that she was at home, attending to the ordinary vocations of life, as a dutiful member of the household. So, I don't think there is any criminal look about that.

"Now, a person may say, 'Where is the note?' Well, we would be very glad to see it; very glad. They looked for it and they could not find it. The construction of Miss Russell was that Abby had burned it up. Very likely that was it. The note may have been part of the scheme in regard to Mrs. Borden. It may have got there through foul means and with a criminal purpose. We don't know anything about that. But that a note came there, you cannot question. That Lizzie lied about it is a wrongful aspersion, born out of ignorance of the facts as they were to be developed in this case. It is not true that Lizzie told a lie about it. If she did, Bridget did the same, and I would not say that for a minute.

"Now she told about her visit to the barn, and they undertake to tell you she did not go out to the barn. They say that is another lie. If she did not go out to the yard or the barn, then she was there at the time when the murder of her father was committed. Did she go to the barn? Well, we find that she did – find it by independent, outside witnesses, thanks to somebody who saw her. Possibly this life of hers is saved by the observation of a passer on the street. There comes along a peddler, an ice-cream man, known to everybody in Fall River. He is not a distinguished lawyer, or a great minister, or a successful doctor. He is only an ice-cream peddler, but he knows what an oath is, and he tells the truth about it, and he says he passed down the street that morning, and as he passed right along, he saw a woman – not Bridget Sullivan, whom he knew – coming along, walking slowly around that corner just before she would ascend those side steps. Now there was no other woman alive in that house except Bridget and Lizzie at that time. He knew it was not Bridget because he had sold her ice cream and he knew her.

"Then they tell us about the ill feelings. Well, gentlemen, I am going to consider that in a very few words, because I say to you that the government has made a lamentable failure on that question. They say that it is the motive that so qualified the different acts that are testified to here, that it puts this defendant in close connection with the murder of Mrs. Borden, and then they say Mrs. Borden being murdered, Lizzie murdered Mr. Borden for his property, or, possibly they will say, murdered him to conceal her crime.

"What have they proved? They have proved that from five or six years ago, Lizzie did not call Mrs. Borden 'Mother.'

"Lizzie is now a woman of 32 or 33 years old; 32 when these crimes were committed. Mrs. Borden was her stepmother; she was not her own mother. Mrs. Borden came there when Lizzie was a little child of two or three years and sometimes we see that where a stepmother has come into a family and has brought up a family, the children known no difference and always call her 'Mother' just the same.

"'Now,' says Mr. Fleet in his emphatic police manner, Miss Borden said to him, 'She is not my mother; she is my stepmother.' Perhaps she did. We will assume that she said it, but there is nothing criminal about it or nothing that indicates it, or nothing that savors of a murderous purpose.

"Bridget Sullivan lived in that family for two years and nine months and was nearer to them than anybody else. She told you the condition of the household. She says, though brought in constant contact with them, she never heard anything out of the way. There was no quarreling. Everything seemed cordial among them. And, mark you, that Thursday morning on which they tell you that Lizzie was entertaining that purpose or plan to murder both these people, that Lizzie was talking with Mrs. Borden. Bridget Sullivan says, 'I heard them talking together calmly, without the least trouble; everything was all right.' Was that an angry family? Was that a murderous group?

"Emma Borden comes to the stand to tell you the inside condition of the family and she went on to say that they had trouble five or six years ago in regard to property and there was no resentment. As far as Lizzie was concerned, it was all adjusted.

"Here was an old man with two daughters. He was a man that wore nothing in the way of ornament, of jewelry but one ring – that ring was Lizzie's. It had been put on many years ago when Lizzie was a little girl, and the old man wore it and it lies with him buried in the cemetery. He loved her as his child; and the ring that stands as the pledge of plighted faith and love, that typifies and symbolizes the dearest relation that is ever created in life – that ring was the bond of union between the father and the daughter. No man should be heard to say that she murdered the man that loved her so.

"Then they say she burned a dress. The government stakes its case on that dress. The government says: 'You gave us the blue dress that lies before me. That is not the dress.' The defendant says that is the dress. The government says, 'We want that Bedford cord and if we had that Bedford cord, we should know all about it and you burned the Bedford cord.'

"Now, let us look at it. There is a dispute here among the persons who saw what Lizzie wore that morning, some of them saying she had this dress, or a dark-blue dress, and Mrs. Churchill speaking of it as a lighter blue than that. Now, between the two there is a difference of recollection. But you will remember that, at that time, there were several ladies in there, and Bridget was there with a lighter colored dress so that those who speak of a lighter colored dress may have had in mind what Bridget had on. It was not a time for examining colors, and afterwards, they recollected as well as they could.

"Well, suppose that had this Bedford cord and Lizzie had it on that morning. The witnesses all say, and every single person who testified says, that while she was there and about with them – including Mrs. Churchill, Bridget, Dr. Bowen, and Mrs. Bowen, and others – that there was not a particle or spot of blood on it. They say there was no blood on her hands, her face, or her hair. Policemen were coming in all about there. She was lying on the lounge. They tell you that the dress was covered or had blood spots on it – but not a living person saw or suggested it. Suppose she did burn it up? The time had elapsed for observation would be long enough. They all had it to look at at that time. They had all seen her and everyone says there was not a spot of blood on it.

"Then, in obedience to Emma's injunction, Lizzie walks down into the kitchen with it that Sunday morning, the windows all open, no blinds shut, policemen in the yard looking right in at everything that was going on and – deliberately, and in the presence of Emma, Emma saying to her, 'Well, I think you had better do it' – put it into the fire and burned it up.

"Had not she time enough from Thursday morning down to that time, to burn it up without anybody's knowing it, if it was covered with blood? Had not she time enough to have got it out of the way? And if she had that purpose to cover up this crime, if she had committed it, would she have burned it in the presence of her sister and Miss Russell – and say she was going to do it? That is not humanly probable.

"If Lizzie Borden killed her mother at 9:45 o'clock in that morning, and then was ready to come downstairs and greet her father, having on that blue dress, do you think that it is probable, besmeared and bedaubed as she would have been with the blood of her first victim? Standing astride her and chopping her head into pieces by those murderous blows, blood flying all over the walls and the furniture, on the bed and everywhere, wasn't she touched all over with that testifying blood?

"Then of course they are going to say, 'Oh, but she changed her dress and then, when she killed her father, either she had that back again or she put on another.' Did she have it back again? Then, she had to put that on over her clothes again and over her person, exposing herself to have her underclothing soiled. And then, if she put on another dress, then there were two dresses to burn and dispose of, instead of one! And the government only wants one. They have all the rest.

"Think of it! That she walked right into that sea of blood and stood there, splashing it over herself in the first murder, and then took off that dress and laid it away until her father came in, and then dressed again for the second slaughter. It is horrible to contemplate. I say it was not morally or physically possible.

"Then they say that she murdered these two people because Mrs. Regan – I forbear almost to mention her name – came up here and told you that those sisters had a quarrel and that Lizzie said to Emma, 'You have given me away.' Gentlemen, if there is anybody given away in this case, it is Hannah Regan, and nobody gave her away but herself. And she is gone so completely that the government did not think it worthwhile to call her on the stand again.

"Lizzie did not try to get Bridget out of the house. If she had undertaken to do those deeds, think you not that she would not have sent Bridget downstreet to buy something, to go for the marketing, to go to the store, one thing and another – or send her on some errand – and then have time undisturbed? But, instead of that, everything goes on as usual and Bridget was about her work."

Robinson paced back and forth in front of the jury box, engaging the seated men in a way that only a polished professional could do. He was relaxed and confident and managed to make his arguments in a conversational way, easing them – he hoped – into his way of thinking. He turned them now to the subject of the murder weapon, walking over to the table where the government's items of evidence were on display. He laid a hand on the two axes that had been brought from the house and turned to the jury:

"Now, what was done with it? The government has a theory about it, or at least seems to have a theory about it, and then does not have a theory about it. You have had all the armory of the Borden house brought here. First, these two axes. I put them down because they have the seal of the Commonwealth; they are declared innocent. Then I pick up this one [the plain-head hatchet] and they tell me it is innocent and had nothing to do with it. I put it down in good company. I pick this one up [the claw-hammer hatchet] and they tell me today that this is innocent and I put it down immediately in the same good companionship. Let us see. The claw-hammer hatchet is four and one-half inches wide on the edge. Dr. Dolan says in his testimony that that could be an adequate instrument and a sufficient instrument to produce all the wounds.

"Then comes Dr. Draper who says that the cutting edge of the instrument which caused the wounds was 3 ½ inches, not 4 ½ inches.

"Dr. Cheever says that he puts the cutting edge at 3 ½ inches but it might have been considerably less. It could be done with one 3 inches wide. Possibly by one 2 ¾ inches wide. These are our *experts* that they are talking about. We do not usually hang people upon the testimony of experts. It is not safe. You see that. The doctors themselves do not agree and they cannot agree and they do not know.

"Well, then comes this little innocent-looking fellow called the handleless hatchet – and that is the one on which your first thing the government is going to

162

stand. Now, whether Mr. Mullaly or Mr. Fleet is right about it, there is no handle here now, and we will leave them to explore, and when they find it, I hope they will carry it to the British Museum. And I hope they will be there to deliver a lecture upon it, to tell the astonished multitude which one of them found it and which one did not find it, and which one of them saw the other put it back into the box when he did not put it back into the box.

"Now this hatchet was not referred to at the preliminary examination at all. Their theory, I suppose, is that it was used, and after it was used, washed thoroughly so as to get all the blood off, and then the handle was broken off by the person that used it. And their theory is that the blood was all gotten off. But this piece of wood was inside of the eye, and Professor Wood tells you that blood will flow into a narrow place. And he boiled it with iodide of potassium, and says that he cannot get the slightest trace of blood. There was no blood, as I tell you, and as a last resort they come in here timidly and haltingly at the opening of the case, and say, 'We bring you this handleless hatchet, but we do not tell you whether it is the hatchet or not.'

"They said they would prove to you that there was exclusive opportunity. They said nobody else could have done it. Emma was gone. Morse was gone. Bridget was outdoors and later in her room. They said that the defendant was really shut up in that house with the two victims and that everybody else was actually and absolutely shut out.

"The cellar door was undoubtedly locked. The front door, in the usual course, was bolted up by Lizzie Wednesday night and unbolted by her Thursday morning. It doesn't make any difference whether it was bolted afterwards or not so far as anybody's coming in is concerned, because if he did, he couldn't have bolted the door behind him when he went out; and it doesn't appear anybody else did, and that is all the significance it has. The side screen door was unfastened from about nine o'clock to 10:45 or 11:00. Now, if that door wasn't locked, Lizzie wasn't locked in and everybody else wasn't locked out.

"Suppose the assassin came there and the house was all open on the north side and suppose he came there and passed through. Where could he go? Plenty of places. He could go upstairs into the spare room; he could go into the hall closet; he could go into the sitting room closet; he could go into the pantry. He could go into such places in that house as all common thieves run into if they find a door open. It was easy enough for him to go up into that bedchamber and secrete himself, to stay there, until he finds himself confronting Mrs. Borden.

"Now what is going to be done? He is there for murder; not to murder her, but to murder Mrs. Borden, and he must strike her down. And when he had done his work and Mr. Borden had come in, he made ready to then come down at the first opportunity. Bridget was outdoors, Lizzie was outdoors. And he could do his work quickly and securely and pass out the same door, if you please, that he came in, the side door. We say that nobody saw him go on and nobody saw Mr. Borden go out down the street."

"There was somebody out there. Dr. Handy described to you a man on the sidewalk he saw there just before the murder. And Mrs. Manley and Mrs. Hart came along there at ten minutes before ten and found a man on the outside looking for things. This was not done by one man alone; there was somebody else in it and there was a man standing at the gatepost. You can see then how everything in this idea of "exclusive opportunity" falls to the ground, because there is no exclusive opportunity.

"Take the facts as they are. What is there to prove to you absolutely, as sensible men, the guilt of this defendant? Were she a villain and a rascal, she would have done as villains and rascals do. There was her uncle, John Morse, suspected as you have heard, followed up, inquired about, and she is asked and she said, 'No, he would not do it.' The busy finger pointed at Bridget Sullivan and Lizzie spoke right out determinedly and promptly, 'Why, Bridget did not do it.' Then somebody said, 'Why, the Portuguese on the farm.' 'No,' says Lizzie, 'and my father has not any man that ever worked for him that would do that to him. I cannot believe it or any of them.'

"How do you account for that except in one way? She was virtually putting everybody away from suspicion and leaving herself to stand as the only one whom all would turn their eyes. Gentlemen, as you look upon her, you will pass your judgment that she is not insane.

"To find her guilty you must believe she is a fiend. Does she look it? As she sat here these long weary days and moved in and out before you, have you seen anything that shows the lack of human feeling and womanly bearing?

"With great weariness on your part, but with abundant patience and intelligence and care, you have listened to what I have had to offer. So far as you were concerned, it is the last word of the defendant to you. Take it; take care of her as you have and give us promptly your verdict of 'not guilty,' that she may go home and be Lizzie Andrew Borden of Fall River, in that bloodstained and wrecked home where she has passed her life so many years."

Robinson let out a great breath and, weary after speaking for more than four hours, returned to the defendant's table and sat down next to Lizzie. In his exhaustion, he placed his head in his hands.

Lizzie did not speak, but touched him lightly on his arm.

Hosea Knowlton was next to present a closing argument. Knowlton was what old-timers in New England called a "solid man," a revered term in the region. He had been a successful student, superior lawyer, and a conscientious member of the legislature for two years. In his 14 years as a district attorney, his experience had been varied, but notably successful. But, as he had written to Attorney General Pillsbury two months earlier, he had no hope of obtaining a conviction this time. The police in Fall River had put together a case so weak that it should have never been presented to a grand jury, and they had spent the last few months trying to knit together what little they had. After reviewing all of the material, Knowlton knew all the prosecution had was little more than what they had started with. In other words, all they could say was, "She *must* have done it. Who else could it be?"

But he would do his job, and he would do it to the best of his substantial ability. He began his summation much in the same way that Robinson had started his, by deploring what had taken place on that hot August morning. Then he continued: "The prisoner at the bar is a woman, and a Christian woman, as the expression is used. We are trying a crime that would have been deemed impossible but for the fact that it was, and we are charging with the commission of it, a woman whom we would have believed incapable of doing it but for the evidence that it is my duty, my painful duty, to call to your attention."

But, he argued, no station in life was a guarantee against the commission of crimes. Widows and orphans were routinely swindled by respectable bankers; ministers were known to have been found to be "as foul as hell inside." Sex was no guarantee because women had been killers before, as had youths of tender years. As for this particular crime, the murder of Andrew and Abby Borden, it was a crime that challenged every belief that nothing of the sort could occur.

"That aged man, that aged woman, had gone by the noonday of their lives. They had borne the burden and heat of the day. They had accumulated a competency which they felt would carry them through the waning years of their lives, and, hand in hand, they expected to go down to the sunset of their days in quiet and happiness. But for that crime, they would be enjoying the air of this day."

He defended the Fall River police department (whether he felt they deserved it or not), which had been criticized by the press, the public, and, of course, the defense: "As soon as the crime was discovered, it became the duty of those who are entrusted with the detection of the crime to take such measures as they thought were proper for the discovery of the criminal. They made many mistakes. The crime was beyond the experience of any man in this country or in this world. What wonder that they did? They left many things undone that they might have done. What wonder that they did? It was beyond the scope of any man to grasp in its entirety at that time. But honestly, faithfully, as thoroughly as God had given them ability, they pursued the various avenues by which they thought they might find the criminal.

"I have heard many an honest man say that he could not believe circumstantial evidence. But, gentlemen, the crime we are trying is the crime of an assassin. It is the work of one who does his foul deeds beyond the sight and hearing of man. When one sees the crime committed or one hears the crime committed, then the testimony of him that sees or hears is the testimony of a witness who saw it or heard it and is direct evidence. All other evidence is circumstantial evidence. Did you ever hear of a murderer getting a witness to his work who could see it or hear it? Murder is the work of stealth and craft in which there are not only no witnesses, but the traces are attempted to be obliterated."

It was a logical, fair, and reasonable explanation of what constituted circumstantial evidence, but Knowlton was arguing against a prejudice that had plagued prosecutors since the inception of the legal system – the hesitance of jurors to convict when faced with a lack of direct evidence. This was the fact of life Knowlton was alluding to in his letter to Pillsbury when he said he saw no other course but to proceed with the trial.

But, determined, he pressed on: "Andrew Jackson Borden probably never heard the clock strike 11 as it pealed forth from the tower of City Hall. And all the evidence in the case points to the irresistible conviction that when Andrew Borden was down at his accustomed place in the bank of Mr. Abraham Hart, the faithful wife he had left at home was prone in death in the chamber of the house he had left her in. At half–past nine, the assassin met her in that room and put an end to her innocent old life.

"Gentlemen, that is a tremendous fact. It is a controlling fact in this case because the murderer of this man was the murderer of Mrs. Borden. It was the malice against Mrs. Borden that inspired the assassin. There she lay bleeding, dead, prone by the hand of an assassin. In all this universe, there could not be found a person who could have had any motive to do it.

"It is said there is a skeleton in the household of every man, but the Borden skeleton – if there was one – was fairly well locked up from view. They were a close-mouthed family. They did not parade their difficulties. Last of all would you expect they would tell the domestic in the kitchen, which is the whole tower of strength of the defense, and yet, there was a skeleton in the closet of that house.

"It is useless to tell you that there was peace and harmony in that family.

"That correction of Mr. Fleet, at the very moment the poor woman who had reared that girl lay dead within ten feet of her voice, was not merely accidental. It went down deep into the springs of human nature.

"This girl owed everything to her. Mrs. Borden was the only mother she had ever known and she had given to this girl her mother's love and had given her this love when a child, when it was not her own and she had not gone through the pains of childbirth, because it was her husband's daughter.

"And then there was a quarrel. A man worth more than a quarter of a millions dollars, wants to give his wife, his faithful wife who has served him 30 years for her board and clothes, who had done his work, who has kept his house, who has reared his children, wants to buy and give it to her interest in a little homestead where her sister lives.

"How wicked to have found fault with it.

"She kept her own counsel. Bridget did not know anything about it. She was in the kitchen. This woman never betrayed her feelings except when someone else tried to make her call "Mother," and then her temper broke forth.

"I heard what Miss Emma said Friday, and I could but admire the loyalty and fidelity of that unfortunate girl to her still more unfortunate sister. I could not find it in my heart to ask her many questions. She was in the most desperate strait that any innocent woman could be in: her next of kin, her only sister, stood in peril and she must come to the rescue. She faintly tells us the relations in the family were peaceful, but we sadly know they were not. Lizzie had repudiated the title of mother. She had lived with her in hatred. She had gone on increasing in that hatred until we do not know – we can only guess – how far that sore had festered, how far the blood in that family had been poisoned.

"I come back to that women, lying prone, as has been described, in the parlor. Was anybody in the world to be benefitted by taking her away? There was one. There was one woman in the world who believed that the dead woman stood between her and her father.

"Let us examine the wounds upon that woman. There was nothing in these blows but hatred and a desire to kill. Some struck at an angle, badly aimed; some struck in the neck, badly directed; some pattered on top of the head and didn't go through; some, where the skull was weaker, went through. A great strong man would have taken a blow from that hatchet and made an end of it. The hand that held the weapon was not the hand of masculine strength. It was the hand of a person strong only in the hate and desire to kill."

Knowlton offered a passionate argument, but it was a weak one when it came to forensic proof. He was beginning to echo Robinson with his rhetoric. A comparison of the two closing arguments, each taking about four hours, would sure have been equal, or with a slight edge to Knowlton. He wasn't bothering to argue facts. Why present facts when smoke and mirrors – which was almost the foundation of the prosecution's case – would do?

Robinson had drawn a scenario of how an outsider could have entered the house, committed the crimes, and then slipped out the side door. He had created this *almost* from thin air, but didn't spend too much time with it. As he said, it was not up to him or the jury to solve the mystery. But, in order to convict Lizzie, the theory of an outsider had to be dismantled, which Knowlton attempted to do.

He approached the jury again. "Never mind the impossibility of imagining a person who was so familiar with the habits of the family, who was so familiar with the interior of the house, who could foresee the things that the family themselves could not see, who was so lost to all human reason, who was so utterly criminal as to set out without any motive whatsoever, as to have gone to that house that morning, to have penetrated through the cordon of Bridget and Lizzie, and pursued that poor woman up the stairs to her death, and then waited, weapon in hand, until the house should be filled up with people again that he might complete his work. I won't discuss with you the impossibility of that thing for the present.

"The dead body tells us another thing. It is a circumstance, but it is one of those circumstances that cannot be cross-examined nor made fun of nor talked out of court. The poor woman was standing when she was struck, and fell with all the force of that 200 pounds of flesh, flat and prone on the floor. That jar could not have failed to have been heard all over that house.

"No matter how craftily murder is planned, there is always some point where the skill and cunning of the assassin fails him. It failed her. It failed her at a vital point, a point which my distinguished friend has attempted to answer, if I may be permitted to say so, and has utterly failed. She was alone in that house with that murdered woman. She could not have fallen without her knowledge. She was out of sight, and by and by, there was coming into the house a stern and just man who knew all the bitterness there was between them. He came in; he sat down; she came to him, and she said to him, 'Mrs. Borden has had a note and gone out.'

"No note came; no note was written; nobody brought a note; nobody was sick. Mrs. Borden had not had a note.

"Little did it occur to Lizzie Borden when she told that lie to her father that there would be manifold witnesses to the fatality of it. They have advertised for the writer of the note which was never written and which never came. Ah, but my distinguished friend is pleased to suggest that it was part of the scheme of assassination. How? To write a note to get a woman away when he was going there to assassinate her? What earthly use was there in writing a note to get rid of Mrs. Borden, when there would still be left Lizzie and Bridget in the house? Oh, no, that is too wild and absurd.

"God forbid that anybody should have committed this murder, but somebody did, and when I have found that she was killed, not by the strong hands of a man, but by the weak and ineffectual blows of woman, when I find that those are the blows of hatred rather than strength, when I find that she is left alone at the very moment of the murder, shut up in that house where every sound went from one end to the other, with the only person in God's universe who could say she was not her friend, with the only person in the universe who could be benefitted by her taking away, and when I find, as I found, and as you must find, if you answer your conscience in this case, that the story told about a note coming is as false as the crime itself, I am not responsible, Mr. Foreman, *you* are not responsible for the conclusion to which you are driven.

"There may be that in this case which saves us from the idea that Lizzie Borden planned to kill her father. I hope she did not. But Lizzie Andrew Borden, the daughter of Andrew Jackson Borden, never came down those stairs, but a murderess. She was coming downstairs to face Nemesis.

"There wouldn't be any question of what he would know of the reason why that woman lay in death. He knew who disliked her. He knew who could not tolerate her presence under the roof. He knew the discussion which had led up to the pitch of frenzy which resulted in her death, and she didn't dare let him live, father though he was, and bound to her by every tie of affection."

This was the high point of Knowlton's closing arguments to the jury. His summation, like Robinson's, took more than four hours and, like Robinson's, it was condensed within these pages. In the preceding paragraphs, Knowlton did all that anyone could do to persuade the jury of Lizzie's guilt. Most of his assumptions, while rooted in logic, were not backed up by hard evidence, but then, nothing about the entire case really was. Knowlton was laboring with the material that the Fall River police had given him.

He went on to deal with the alibi that Lizzie had been up in the barn loft when Andrew was murdered, but he had nothing with which to disprove it, especially since the police officers who claimed she had never been there were found to have lied, or at least been ridiculously mistaken. The certainty that others had been up in the loft before Medley claimed he had checked for footprints in the dust revealed a fabrication that could not be defended. Of the alibi, Knowlton could only say, "I assert that the story is simply absurd. I assert that that story is not within the bounds of reasonable possibilities." He denied its truth, but there was no force in the denial.

Of the lack of bloodstains on her dress or her person, his rebuttal was even weaker: "How could she have avoided the spattering of her dress with blood is she was the author of these crimes? As to the first crime, it is scarcely necessary to attempt to answer the question. In the solitude of that house, with ample fire in the stove, with ample wit of women, nobody has suggested that, as to the first crime, there was not an ample opportunity, ample means, and that nothing could be suggested as a reason why all the evidence of that crime could not have been amply and successfully concealed."

This suggested a new theory – that either the dress, petticoat, stockings, and shoes worn by Lizzie had been burned in the kitchen stove or hidden somewhere in the house. Burning abundant garments like a dress and petticoat, like those worn in that era, could not have been done without the notice of Bridget or without a substantial amount of residue of ashes not seen by the police when the stove was emptied and sifted. To suggest that Lizzie could have hidden two bloodstained outfits from the three intensive searches by the police stank of desperation.

Finally, he just sort of gave up and blamed it all on the fact that Lizzie was a woman. "As to the second murder," he admitted, "the question is one of more difficulty. I cannot answer it. You cannot answer it. You are neither murderers nor women. You have neither the craft of the assassin nor the cunning and deftness of the sex."

This tactic had been used by the prosecution throughout the trial. If they could not prove that Lizzie committed murder based on evidence, then they would try and convince the jury that she did so – and expected to get away with it – because she was a woman. Using this as an explanation for how she had caused two bundles of bloodstained clothing to disappear using nothing more than her feminine cunning and wiles was nonsense, but to suggest that she was using them to get away with murder was reprehensible.

Throughout the trial and, most especially, during his summation, Knowlton referred to the dress that Lizzie had worn on the morning of the murders as a "silk" dress. He was quoted as saying, "This dress has been described to you as a silk dress – a dress which is not cheap, a dress which would not be worn in ironing by any prudent woman. Of course not. It is an afternoon dress. Do your wives dress in silk when they go down to the kitchen to work, and in their household duties in the morning before dinner?"

The dress was not silk; it was a cotton dress. The material, then costing about 20-cents a yard, was a blend of 90 percent cotton and 10 percent silk – a very common material for cheap day dresses. It was called "bengaline silk" for the same reason that glass beads were called "faux pearls," because it was a seller's gimmick to make it sound better than it was. Knowlton knew this and yet, he chose to spin it so it sounded like Lizzie was a haughty heiress who thought she was too good to be doing household chores.

Knowlton shook his head at her many deceptions. "What is the defense, Mr. Foreman? What is the answer to this array of impregnable facts? Nothing; nothing. I stop and think and I say again, nothing. The distinguished counsel, with all his eloquence which I can't hope to match or approach, has attempted nothing but to say, 'Not Proven.'

"Are you satisfied that it was done by her? I have attempted – how imperfectly, none but myself can say – to discharge the sad duty which has devolved upon me. I submit these facts to you with the confidence that you are men of courage and truth.

"Rise, gentlemen, rise to the attitude of your duty. Act as you would act when you stand before the great throne at the last day. What shall be your reward? The ineffable consciousness of duty well done."

It was just a few minutes before noon when Knowlton sat down and Justice Dewey declared the court in adjournment until 1:45, when he would charge the jury.

The ordeal – for the jury, the judges, the lawyers, and for Lizzie – was almost over.

15. "I AM INNOCENT"

On the afternoon of Tuesday, June 20, 1893, Chief Justice Albert Mason – one of the three men who had presided over the 12-day trial of Lizzie Borden – gaveled the court to order. His voice rang out in the hushed chamber: "Lizzie Andrew Borden, although you have now been fully heard by the counsel, it is your privilege to add any word which you may desire to say in person to the jury. You now have that opportunity."

During Knowlton's long summation, Lizzie had intensely listened to the prosecutor's words, her eyes following him as he paced back and forth in front of the jury box. She had been assured by Robinson, Jennings, and even Reverend Buck that the jury would not find against her, and yet there was no complacency in her shoulders or in the expression on her face. She had heard herself repeatedly damned in Knowlton's closing words and her tightly drawn features often winced at his harsh words. The small bouquet of flowers lying on the table before her were never touched. The fan that she had carried each day, opening and closing, waving in front of her face, was abandoned next to the flowers. Her hands had gripped the edge of the table next to these items numerous times, but she had never picked them up.

At the judge's words, she rose without assistance, but seemed for a moment to be unable to speak. Finally, she said quietly, "I am innocent. I leave it to my counsel to speak for me."

The jury was then charged by Associate Justice Justin Dewey, III. Born in Alford, Massachusetts, the small, compact man was 57-years-old at the time of the trial. He had graduated from Williams College and practiced law for 26 years. After the trial was over, many of those who believed in Lizzie's guilt were savagely critical of his charge to the jury, calling it a second summation for the defense. But at no time did he question the facts of either presentation. He only urged clear reasoning interpreting the facts, which was well within the purview of what a judge was expected to advise a jury that was not well-lettered in the law.

He reinforced that point in his opening remarks: "Mr. Foreman and gentlemen of the jury, you have listened with attention to the evidence in this case and to the arguments of the defendant's counsel and of the district attorney. It now remains for me, acting on behalf of the court, to give you such aid toward a proper performance of your duty as I may be able to give within the limits for judicial action proscribed by the law. And, to prevent any erroneous impression, it may be well for me to bring

Leslie's Illustrated drawing of Lizzie during the trial. No photographs were allowed to be taken in the courtroom at that time.

to your attention, at the outset, that it is provided by a statute of this state that the court shall not charge juries with respect to matters of fact, but may state the testimony and the law.

"I understand the government to concede that defendant's character has been good; that it has not been merely a negative and natural one that nobody heard anything against, but one of positive, of active benevolence in religious and charitable work. Judging of this subject as reasonable men, you have the right to take into consideration her character such as is admitted or apparent. In some cases it may not be esteemed of much importance. In other it may raise a reasonable doubt of a defendant's guilt even in the face of strongly criminating circumstances."

In short, the judge was suggesting that Lizzie's moral past could be taken into consideration as the jury was considering its verdict, but whether or not it had any bearing on the charges was up to the individual juror. It is easy to see how the anti-Lizzie faction could take offense to the judge's words to the jury. It was almost as if he were appearing on her behalf as a character witness.

During the trial, seamstress Hannah Gifford had testified that, during one of her dressmaking sessions at the Borden house, when Abby's name had come up in conversation, Lizzie had said, "Don't call her mother; she is my stepmother and she is a mean, hateful old thing." Judge Dewey stepped in and tried to put the value of that comment into context: "I understand the counsel for the government to claim that defendant had towards her stepmother a strong feeling of ill will, nearly if not quite, amounting to hatred. And Mrs. Gifford's testimony as to a conversation with defendant in the early spring of 1892 is relied upon largely as a basis for that claim.

"In judging wisely of a case, you need to keep all parts of it in their natural and proper proportion and not put any particular piece of evidence a greater weight than it will reasonably bear, and not to magnify or intensify or depreciate or belittle any piece of evidence to meet an emergency. But take Mrs. Gifford's just as she gave it and consider whether or not it will fairly amount to the significance attached to it.

"What you wish, of course, is a true conception of the state of mind of the defendant towards her stepmother, not years ago, but later and nearer the time of the homicide. To get such a true conception, you must not separate Mrs. Gifford's testimony from all the rest, but consider also the evidence as to how they lived in the family, whether, as Mrs. Raymond, I believe, said, they sewed together, whether they went to church

Associate Justice Justin Dewey, a man who some critics say may have done more to win Lizzie an acquittal than her attorneys did.

together, sat together, returned together – in a word, the general tenor of their life. You will particularly recall the testimony of Bridget Sullivan and of the defendant's sister Emma bearing on the same subject. Weigh carefully all the testimony on the subject and then judge whether or not there is clearly proved such a permanent state of mind on the part of the defendant toward her stepmother as to justify you in drawing against her upon that ground inferences unfavorable to her innocence."

One can only imagine what Prosecutor Knowlton must have been thinking while these statements were being made by the judge. He had been reluctantly forced into taking the case to trial in the first place, and now it seemed as if even the judge was speaking out against the work he had done. There would be many others who would be angered by the judge's charge, yet the cautions that he made to the jury were clearly within the guidelines that he had cited. If we look at his statements by themselves, we see that he was only telling the jury to keep them in perspective and to give them due weight, but not to be inflamed by a single comment. There were those who recalled Lizzie's seeming dislike for her stepmother, he reminded them, but others who spoke of politeness and courtesy between the two women. But in the greater scheme of the trial, it seems as though Justice Dewey was suggesting that the jury put greater weight on the testimony on Lizzie's behalf, rather than the testimony against her. Or at least that's how the critics of the trial would see it after all of the proverbial dust had settled.

Dewey continued: "Now you observe, gentlemen, that the government submits this case to you upon circumstantial evidence. This is a legal and not unusual way of proving a criminal case, and it is clearly competent for a jury to find a person guilty of murder upon circumstantial evidence alone. However, failure to prove a fact essential to the conclusion of guilt, and without which that conclusion would not be reached, is fatal to the government's case. All would admit that the necessity of establishing the presence of the defendant in the house when, for instance, her father was killed, is a necessary fact.

"The question of the relation of this handleless hatchet to the murder – it may have an important bearing on the case, whether the crime was done by that particular hatchet or not – but it cannot be said that it bears the same essential and necessary relation to the case that the matter of her presence in the house does. It is not claimed by the government but what the killing might have been done with some other instrument.

"I understand the government to claim substantially that the alleged fact that the defendant made a false claim in regard to her stepmother's having received a note or letter that morning bears an essential relation to the case.

"Now what are the grounds on which the government claims that that statement is false, knowingly false? First, that the one who wrote it has not been found. Second, that the party who brought it has not been found. Third, that no letter has been found."

Judge Dewey then went from pointing out the reasons behind the prosecution's theories to actually arguing the case on Lizzie's behalf. Was he technically correct in handling the jury's charge in the way that he did? Yes, he was – but one can't help but see the direction in which he seemed to be steering things.

He continued: "What motive had she to invent a story like this? What motive? Would it not have answered every purpose to have her say – and would it not have been more natural for her to say – that her stepmother had gone out on an errand or to make a call? What motive had she to take upon herself the responsibility of giving utterance to this distinct and independent fact of a letter or note received, with which she might be confronted and which she might afterwards find it difficult to explain, if she knew no such thing was true.

"But, it is said, no letter was found.

"Might it not be part of the plan or scheme of such a person by such a document or paper to withdraw Mrs. Borden from the house? If he afterward came in there, came upon her, killed her, might he not have found the letter or note with her? Might he not have a reasonable and natural wish to remove that as one possible link in tracing himself? Taking the suggestions as the one side and the other, judging the matter fairly, not assuming beforehand the defendant is guilty, does the evidence satisfy you as reasonable men, beyond any reasonable doubt, that these statements of the defendant in regard to that note might necessarily be false?"

Dewey was arguing – and let's face it, he was now arguing for the defense, no matter how you look at it – that it was not enough for the prosecution to simply say that there had been no note and that Lizzie had lied. They either had to prove it, which they had not, or inevitably, leave open the possibility that there had been a note, but that no one knew what happened to it. This was, of course, exactly what the situation was.

Dewey continued: "Something has been said to you by counsel as to defendant's not testifying. I must speak to you on this subject. The Constitution of our state, in its bill of rights, provides that no subject shall be compelled to secure or furnish evidence against himself.

"The superior court, speaking of a defendant's right and protection under the Constitution and statutes, uses these words: 'Nor can any inference be drawn against him from his failure to testify.' Therefore I say to you, and I mean all that my words express, any argument, any implication, any suggestion, any consideration in your minds unfavorable to the defendant, based on her failure to testify, is unwarranted in law. Nor is defendant called upon to offer any explanation of her neglect to testify. If she were required to explain, others might think that the explanation insufficient. Then she would lose the protection of the statute.

"If you are convinced beyond reasonable doubt of the defendant's guilt, it will be your plain duty to declare that conviction by your verdict," the judge told them, and then he added, "If the evidence falls short of producing such conviction in your mind, although it may raise a suspicion of guilt, or even a strong probability of guilt, it would be your plain duty to return a verdict of not guilty. If not legally proved to be guilty, the defendant is entitled to a verdict of not guilty.

"Gentlemen, I know not what views you may take of the case, but it is the gravest importance that it should be decided. If decided at all, it must be decided by a jury. The law requires that the jury shall be unanimous in their verdict, and it is their duty to agree if they can conscientiously do so.

"And now, gentlemen, the case is committed to your hands, the tragedy which has given to this investigation such widespread interest and deeply excited public attention and feeling. The press has ministered to this excitement by publishing, without moderation, rumors and reports of all kinds. You must guard, as far as possible, against all impressions derived from having read in the newspapers accounts relating to the question you have now to decide.

"And entering on your deliberations with no pride of opinion, with impartial and thoughtful minds, seeking only the truth. You will lift the case about the range of passion and prejudice and excited feeling, into the clear atmosphere of reason and law."

With the judge's final words still hanging in the air, the jury filed out of the room, their faces solemn and in no way revealing what their private thoughts might be. The trial had been an experience that none of the men would ever forget. As the years passed, each of them would always be known as "one of the jurors in the Lizzie Borden trial," and when each man died, his obituary would make note of those 12 days in each of the men's lives.

The jury remained in deliberation for exactly one hour. Word then came to the justices that a verdict had been reached. In truth, they had come to their verdict just 10 minutes after reaching the jury room, but out of respect for the prosecution, they had waited an additional 50 minutes before sending the word.

The news that the jury had reached a verdict spread like wild fire through the halls of the courthouse and then spread into the streets. Spectators and curiosity-seekers rushed for the courtroom and the available seats filled immediately. The bailiffs were unable to hold back the crowd until the aisles were filled with spectators. The three judges pushed their way to the bench behind Sheriff Wright.

The clerk called the roll and each juror replied to his name when it was called.

"Lizzie Andrew Borden, stand up."

Lizzie rose carefully and faced the jury.

The clerk asked, "Gentlemen of the jury, have you reached a verdict?"

"We have," the foreman replied.

"Please return the papers to the court. Lizzie Andrew Borden, hold up your right hand. Mr. Foreman, look upon the prisoner. Prisoner, look upon the foreman. What say you, Mr. Foreman?"

He paused only for a moment, and then spoke, "Not guilty!"

A shudder went through the courtroom and then the crowd erupted in a cheer that legend has it was heard a half-mile away.

Lizzie's shoulders sagged and she sank down into her seat with tears and sobs wracking her body. Although the transcript of the trial states that the demonstration was instantly stopped, newspaper reports said that it continued for several minutes, and Sheriff Wright made no effort to stop it. His eyes, several reporters wrote, were filled with tears. Whether they were tears of happiness or frustration, it was never said.

Always reliable reporter Joe Howard wrote:

Jennings, overcome as few men are ever seen to be, and trembling like an aspen leaf, cried, "Oh, thank God!" and pushed his way to the rail of the dock. Lizzie held out her hand to him; he grasped it and made it red with squeezing. Robinson dodged under the rail of the bar and pushed by the now useless deputy who had guarded the prisoner. He stooped down and put his face against hers and his left arm slipped around her waist as he lifted her up.

All her old friends crowded around her. Mr. Holmes was the first to press her hand and Reverend Buck who was weeping, was next. She reached out a hand to her counsel, Melvin Adams and in turn, he took both of hers. Emma, meanwhile, was surrounded by a separate crowd and cut off from Lizzie.

The jurors, in Indian file marched by to shake hands with the woman for whom they had done so much, and she gave each of them warm smiles and grateful remarks of thanks.

Reverend Jubb, along with attorneys Robinson and Jennings, surrounded Lizzie and eased her into the corridor and to refuge in the judges' chambers. More than an hour passed before a more composed Lizzie left the court building as a free woman. The crowd waiting outside burst into song, cheers, and applause, and a long string of carriages followed hers to the station and the train back home to Fall River.

It was finally over, or at least that was how it seemed. In truth, the story of the Borden murders would never really come to an end.

16. "THE HAPPIEST WOMAN IN THE WORLD"

Most of the newspapers the following day led off their end-of-the trial coverage with "I told you so" attitudes, declaring that they had seen the verdict coming all along. The *Boston Herald* wrote that the verdict was "simply a confirmation of the opinions entertained by those who followed the evidence submitted by the prosecution and witnessed the effect upon it of vigorous cross-examination. The government was obliged to prove guilt beyond a reasonable doubt and failed to do so… The tragedy remains quite as much a mystery as it was before."

The *New York Times* echoed this opinion, but voiced a much sharper opinion about what had happened:

It will be a certain relief to every right-handed man or woman who has followed the case to learn that the jury in New Bedford has not only acquitted Miss Lizzie Borden of the atrocious crime with which she was charged, but has done so with a promptness that was very significant.

The acquittal of the most unfortunate and cruelly persecuted woman was, but its promptness, in effect, a condemnation of the police authorities of Fall River and of the legal officers who secured the indictment and have conducted the trial.

It was a declaration, not only that the prisoner was guiltless, but that there was never any serious reason to suppose she was guilty.

She has escaped the awful fate with which she was threatened, but the long imprisonment she has undergone, the intolerable suspense and anguish inflicted upon her, the outrageous injury to her feelings as a woman and as a daughter are chargeable directly to the police and legal authorities. That she should have been subjected to these is a shame to Massachusetts which the good sense of the jury in acquitting her in part removes.

The theory of the prosecution seems to have been that, if it were possible that Miss Borden murdered her father and his wife, it must be inferred that she did murder them. It was held, practically, that if she could not be proved innocent, she must be taken to be guilty. We do not remember a case in a long time in which prosecution has so completely broken down, or in which evidence has shown so clearly, not merely that the prisoner should not be convicted, but that there never should have been an indictment.

We are not surprised that the Fall River police should have fastened their suspicions on Miss Borden. The town is not a large one. The police are of the usual inept and stupid and muddle-headed sort that such towns manage to get for themselves. There is nothing more merciless than the vanity of ignorant and untrained men charged with the detection of a crime, in the face of a mystery they cannot solve, and for the solution of which they feel responsible. The Fall River police needed a victim whose sacrifice should purge their force of contempt that they felt they would incur if the murderer of the Bordens were not discovered, and the daughter was the nearest and most helpless. They pounced upon her.

But the responsibility of the law officers was very different. They were trained in the law, accustomed to analyzing and weighing evidence. They knew what justice required in the way of proof of the crime of murder.

It is not easy to believe that they did not know that no such proof, and nothing like it, was in their possession. Indeed, they seemed to have entered upon a trial without it, and groped along afterward in clumsy efforts to develop it.

We cannot resist the feeling that their conduct in this matter was outrageous; that they were guilty of a barbarous wrong to an innocent woman and a gross injury to the community. And we hold it to be a misfortune that their victim has no legal recourse against them and no means of bringing them to account. Her acquittal was only a partial atonement for the wrong she has suffered.

In just a few words, the editors at the *New York Times* had summed up the utter futility of the Borden case. It was a charge that had been brought against a woman with few means to defend herself, merely because the police had been unable to find anyone else who might have committed the crime. Did she do it? They didn't know, but she might have and they couldn't find any other suspects, so it must have been her. Shameful? Yes, of course, but were their suspicions completely unfounded? Well, that's something that bears a closer look.

But to the vast majority of the people of that time and place, the accusation and the trial that followed had been a travesty of justice. The grotesque, small town murder of two prominent, elderly citizens in their own home, in broad daylight, had been a sensation. It would have been one no matter who had committed the crime. But the fact that the police focused their investigation on, and later indicted, their upstanding, Sunday School-teaching daughter only added to the carnival-like atmosphere of it all.

The total irresponsibility of the reporting that was done by the *Fall River Globe*, with its anti-Lizzie agenda, added fuel to the already excitable situation. The Fall

River police were not the bungling idiots that the *New York Times* made them out to be, but it was certainly not a force that was experienced in detection or any kind of forensic science. What the police department was lacking was not dedication, it was competent leadership. Marshal Hilliard was the head of the department, but Assistant Marshal Fleet was responsible for the day–to–day investigation, and he was as hot-headed and stubborn as he was determined. The department had been ridiculed by the newspapers and the citizenry, and they had panicked. They had to arrest someone or face the contempt of the public. And they would do anything – even lie on the witness stand – to make sure the case stuck.

Fleet had been convinced of Lizzie's guilt from the moment that she failed to show him proper respect and had snapped that Abby was not her mother. From that time on, the efforts of the police were bent not toward solving the crime, but toward proving that Lizzie was a killer. There were other leads that had been followed and rumors that had been run to ground, but the general thrust of the investigation was to get the goods on Lizzie Borden, no matter what it took.

It can be said that this procedure was not totally at fault, at least at first. At the time, it accurately portrayed the prevailing sentiment, but, when it became apparent that practical evidence substantiating her guilt could not be found, three options existed: first, indict and try her with the flawed circumstantial evidence they had; second, direct the search toward other suspects; or, third, put the arrest and indictment on hold until conclusive evidence could be found.

Giving in to the taunts of the press and pressure from the public, they chose the wrong option. As the *New York Times* said, the harassed police department might be forgiven for surrendering to the pressure and making the arrest, but the district attorney and the officers of the court could not. Knowlton, having no confidence in her guilt, as noted in his letters, should have delayed the prosecution when the file landed on his desk. He should have told Hilliard and Fleet that they didn't have a solid case and there was nothing that he could do until they did.

The report from Harvard that showed no bloodstains on the handleless hatchet, dress, shoes, and hose should have been in hand before any arrest was made or any "inquest" held. To have proceeded without it was, at least, foolish; at worst, it was prosecutorial misconduct.

For motive, the police had a story or two about disagreements within the family; stories that may well have been true, but they could not be substantiated with any kind of evidence that should have been presented in court. Even Bridget Sullivan, their own witness, testified strongly to the contrary, and few would doubt she knew more about it than any casual acquaintance who only dropped by the house now and then.

Nor was Fleet able to break down Lizzie's alibi of being in the barn at the time Andrew was murdered, not even with the help of Medley's manufactured testimony about the absence of footprints in the dust.

Without a plausible motive – or really, any kind of motive at all – and without a weapon or bloodstained clothing, and without an exclusive opportunity, the case against Lizzie was simply not a case at all. They had obtained an indictment under rather suspicious circumstances, but had nothing to follow it up with during a genuine legal proceeding. They could prove nothing.

There is no question that the legal case against Lizzie was poorly planned, poorly investigated, and poorly prosecuted, but, under different circumstances, could a more carefully prepared case have had a different outcome? If not, then why did a majority of people in Fall River, at that time and for several generations afterward, accept so readily that a woman of Lizzie's Christian upbringing and impeccable social history could savagely murder her parents?

At the time, many came to see her as guilty based on the immediate announcement by Marshal Hilliard that there would be no further investigation; the case was closed. The inference was unavoidable. As far as the police were concerned, they had caught the killer; the jury had turned her loose. It was difficult, if not impossible, for many people to get the image of Lizzie, hatchet in hand, slaughtering her parents, out of their minds.

The passing of time has been just as cruel. We all know the words…

Lizzie Borden took an axe
And gave her mother forty whacks.
And when she saw what she had done,
She gave her father forty-one.

But, did she really? No, she couldn't have. The opening chapters of this volume proved that time would not have allowed her to murder her parents. But just because her hands were not literally stained with blood does not mean that she wasn't at least partially responsible for the cruel and brutal fate of Andrew and Abby Borden.

17. WHO KILLED THE BORDENS?

There can be no doubt that, even after all of these years and after all of the evidence to the contrary, Lizzie Borden still remains the prime suspect in the minds of most people who know anything about the tragic murders of 1892. Nursery rhymes, poems, books, and films have all portrayed her as the killer. But she was not the only person suspected by the general public – or by the legions of writers, journalists, crime buffs, and amateur detectives who have poked and prodded at this case for the last century and a quarter.

A number of suspects emerged in the hours and days after the first cry of "murder!" was sounded.

The first were the Portuguese. Fall River had become home to a number of immigrant groups in the years prior to the murder, all of whom were considered "suspect" by the locals. The French–Canadians had been the first to settle nearby. Although their presence was no longer considered a threat, considerable hostility remained. The Irish arrived next, followed by the Portuguese in the early 1890s. Several witnesses would report that a foul–smelling, "crazy–looking" man was seen in or near the Borden house on the morning of the murders. Since he smelled bad and looked crazed, he must have been a Portuguese – or at least that was the thinking of the time.

And besides that, everyone knew the Portuguese were killers.

Such concerns were created by the murder of Bertha Manchester in May 1893 and the subsequent arrest of the prime suspect, Jose Correa deMello, a Portuguese from the Azores. The murder of Bertha Manchester occurred just five days before the start of Lizzie's trial and another brutal axe murder shocked the town of Fall River. The startling parallels between this case and the Borden murders – the excessive number of wounds, the fact that both incidents occurred in broad daylight, and the lack of any apparent motive – threatened to open a new line of defense in Lizzie's trial. But as it turned out, Robinson and Jennings had little to worry about.

Bertha, age 22, lived with her father, Stephen, and her brother, Frederick, on a dairy farm on New Boston Road in Fall River. On the morning of May 31, 1893, Stephen and Frederick left to make their regular milk deliveries. When they returned that afternoon, they found Bertha's hacked–up body lying in a pool of blood, next to the kitchen stove. She had been massacred with an axe, which was found lying on the woodpile outside. Bertha's watch and a purse containing a small amount of money had been taken. There was nothing else missing from the home.

An autopsy revealed "twenty-three distinct and separate axe wounds on the back of the skull and its base." Defensive wounds and ripped clothing indicated that she had put up a fierce struggle with her assailant before being overpowered.

Early in the investigation, suspicion fell on Stephen Manchester, a man whose second wife had left him because he was so mean and was extremely cheap. He refused to miss a day's work because of his daughter's murder and so he continued with his daily routine as if nothing had happened. But soon, suspicion fell on Manchester's hired men, several of whom were disgruntled about the low pay that they received from him. Manchester didn't care. He hired French and Portuguese immigrants and paid them as little as possible. He didn't even bother to learn most of their names.

The main suspect became a man named Jose Correa deMello, who had recently left the farm on bad terms with his employer. The police feared that if they began investigating him openly, the Portuguese community in Fall River would rally to deMello's defense and they would get no information. Instead, they used subterfuge to get deMello to turn himself in. The authorities contacted deMello's uncle, Jacinto Muniz Machado, and Frank Machado Silva, a leader in the local Portuguese community, and persuaded them to tell deMello that they needed him as a witness to a horse theft, and they would pay him a hefty witness fee. The man went to the police station with no idea that he was a murder suspect and there, deMello was brutally interrogated for four hours.

The main evidence against deMello came from the owner of a shoe store who claimed that deMello bought a new pair of shoes from him after the murder and tried to pay with a "trade dollar" and a "plugged half-dollar." These distinctive coins were known to have been in the purse stolen from Bertha Manchester.

When he went to trial in 1894, deMello received an attorney appointed by the court. Initially, he pled not guilty, but he later changed his plea to guilty of second degree murder. He was sentenced to life in an institution for the criminally insane. He later claimed his innocence and was eventually pardoned when new evidence was brought on his behalf by John C. Santos, a prominent Portuguese resident of Taunton, Massachusetts. He was released in 1901 and returned to the Azores, never to set foot in America again.

With the murder of Bertha Manchester taking place so close to the start of Lizzie's trial, reporters asked her attorney, Andrew Jennings, if he expected it to have an effect on the case. He snarkily replied, "Well, are they going to say that Lizzie Borden did this also?"

Lizzie was, of course, in jail at the time, awaiting the start of her trial. But Bertha's shocking murder, so similar to the Borden murders, did cause some people to consider the possibility that perhaps Lizzie had not murdered her parents after all. The arrest of Jose deMello occurred on the day that Lizzie's trial opened. However, deMello had not arrived in the United States until April 1893, so he could not have murdered the Bordens in August 1892, but this was not learned until after the jury was selected in Lizzie's trial. As it turned out, deMello may have actually been innocent of Bertha's murder anyway, which allowed him to be released from the insane asylum.

The murder of Bertha Manchester may have had an effect on Lizzie's trial, though. The facts of the case cast doubts on a number of assertions made by the prosecution. The Bordens had each died from multiple blows from an axe – Abby 19, Andrew 20 – this, said the prosecution, indicated that the killer was a woman; a man would use only one blow. Bertha, it was believed at the time, was murdered by a man using 23 blows. The prosecution claimed that because the Bordens were killed in broad daylight that a member of the household must have committed the murders and yet, Bertha was killed at the same time of day, also with neighbors at home, just across the road, and no member of the Manchester household was involved.

While the murder of Bertha Manchester did not play a direct role in Lizzie's trial, the two cases were playing out side-by-side in the daily newspapers. It was not lost on anyone, in or out of court, how easy it was for someone to enter the Manchester house, commit a brutal axe murder in broad daylight, and leave without being noticed.

It also reminded everyone that "immigrants" were not meant to be trusted, which was why they were suspected in the Borden murders at the beginning. Many asked if the "mystery man" that was seen around the house was one of these untrustworthy "foreigners."

The "mystery man" played an important role in the affair. About two weeks after the trial ended, many people thought the Borden murders had been solved. A letter was found on the street in Rome, New York, addressed to Joseph Carpenter, Jr. of Albany. The letter was read and the finder of it hurriedly took it to the police. It was dated June 22, 1893 and read:

My Dear Husband:
Lizzie has been acquitted, and I don't think they can do anything with you now. I want you to come home to spend the Fourth. The papers give a description of the man seen over the fence on the morning of the murder. Can you prove where you were on the morning of the murder?

Annie

There was an immediate excitement. The Fall River police had no trouble recognizing Carpenter's name. He was a former Borden & Almy bookkeeper who had stolen $6,000, but had escaped prosecution when he returned the money.

As soon as the story of the letter broke, reporters interview Pete Driscoll, a barber who originally claimed he saw Carpenter in Fall River shortly before the murders in his shop at the Wilber House. Although police had investigated at the time, and Driscoll said he was mistaken, he still insisted that it had been Carpenter that he had shaved.

After Carpenter left Fall River in disgrace, he went to Buffalo and began to manufacture ink. He later moved to Albany. His wife, meanwhile, quietly returned to Fall River and lived with relatives.

Spurred on by the letter, the police again investigated Carpenter's alibi. It was reported that he was on a sales trip at the time and had not been anywhere near Fall River, once more clearing him as a suspect.

But the "mystery man" seen near the fence refused to go away. It may not have been Joseph Carpenter, but it was definitely someone. During Lizzie's trial, Dr. Handy testified that, while riding by the Borden house at about 10:30 a.m. on the day of the murders, he had noticed a "stranger" walking slowly past. His face was "deadly white" and he appeared to be in his early twenties. Officer Joseph Hyde of the Fall River police had noticed a man of this description as well. A neighbor had reported seeing a man clambering over the six-foot-high back fence that separated the Borden's property from a stonemason's yard on Third Street. Ellan Eagen, a young woman walking up the street near the Borden house, saw a man in the Borden yard that morning. Her description was not as precise as Dr. Handy's, but she would recall his awful and weird smell.

Who was this man? No one could say because it seemed every eyewitness believed the man to be someone else – even the devil.

And in some ways, as we will discover later in this chapter, their identification as the "devil" was closer than most would care to admit.

Bridget Sullivan

Most of the suspects in the murders were more tangible than "mysterious foreigners" and supernatural manifestations.

Bridget Sullivan was an immediate suspect in the case. She had been in and around the house at the time of the killings – and besides that, she was Irish. "Maggie," as the Borden sisters insisted on calling her, had come to the United States in 1887. After working for three other families, she came to the Borden home in 1889. Her duties--washing, ironing, cooking and cleaning--were basically confined to the downstairs part of the house. She seldom was in the "family rooms" on the second floor. The fact that she was Irish made her guilty of something: the actual murder or covering up and protecting the killers, according to popular prejudices. By all accounts Bridget was at home during the killings. Most likely she was outside washing windows when Abby was killed, and upstairs in her bedroom when the slaughter of Andrew occurred. Or so she said...

Some historians believe that Bridget had much to hate the Bordens for. She was a virtual slave to them, they claim, and Andrew paid her meager wages. He and Abby allegedly made it quite clear that she worked for the family, but was not part of it. Not only was she not allowed to enter the family's bedrooms, but she was given a room in the stifling heat of the attic when there were empty guest rooms available. A case can be made for the fact that she, given her whereabouts in the Borden house at the time of the murders, had a better opportunity to commit the murders than Lizzie did. And perhaps she had a better motive: revenge for the miserable servitude under which she had labored for so long.

The homicidal history of house servants killing their employers is long and convincing. And in almost all of these scores of killings, the reasons have proved minor, even petty. A sharp command, a degrading comment could be enough to set off a blind rage, stored for years, in a normally tranquil servant, resulting in murder. In this case, it is thought that Bridget, ordered to wash windows on the hottest day of the year, went mad and hacked Mrs. Borden to death. She then murdered Mr. Borden so that he could not report an alleged argument that Bridget had with Abby earlier in the day.

But such accusations are the thing of fancy, not fact. Assigning a motive of rage to Bridget is difficult, since there is no evidence to suggest that she harbored any great hostility toward her employer. When Bridget was initially accused, it was Lizzie who came to her defense and told the police that she would never so such a thing – which, for many modern writers, opened an entirely different can of worms.

Since Lizzie came to Bridget's defense, then she must have been Lizzie's lesbian lover. It's very likely that this theory has its basis in what happened with Lizzie *after* her trial was over and in light of the suggestive relationship that she developed with actress Nance O'Neil (which will be discussed in a later chapter). If Lizzie was a lesbian later in life, then she must have been one at the time of the murders as well, a suggestion that was certainly never raised in 1892. But those who subscribe to this theory believe that Bridget committed the murders in a rage that was fueled by Lizzie's unjust treatment at the hands of her stepmother and father. Of course, there is no evidence to support this idea, but that has not stopped anyone from suggesting it.

Bridget also figures into another variation of this theory in which Lizzie murdered her parents, but could not have done so without the assistance of her lover, Bridget. It was Bridget who spirited away — virtually under the very noses of the police — the murder weapon and the bloodstained dress. The two plotted the murders together, which explains Lizzie's defense of the maid and Bridget's testimony in support of Lizzie. Supporters of this theory point out that only the two of them were in the house when the 200-pound Abby fell heavily to the floor after being struck. They had to have heard it, theorists have stated, so why did they not check to see what had caused the sound? The answer was simple: they had murdered her.

As mentioned, no evidence of any of this has ever existed. It is also supposition from those who still look feverishly for some definitive answers in this case. Most who have written about the case have described Bridget as open and guileless, but we can't ignore the fact that she might have had some guilty knowledge about the crimes. Rumors and legends about Bridget have persisted for many years, most of them dating back to a supposed "almost confession" that she made on her deathbed in 1948.

Even though stories were told in Fall River that Lizzie gave Bridget a fortune for her testimony and that she returned to Ireland to live out the rest of her days, there was no truth to the tale. Bridget never returned to the Borden home and she soon disappeared from the city. As far as real evidence goes, Bridget Sullivan was never heard from again.

But there is version of events that tell about what happened to Bridget. According to some, she may have gone to Ireland, but she did not stay there. They say that this is because she died in a hospital in Butte, Montana, on March 25, 1948, at the age of 82. She was buried in a cemetery in nearby Anaconda, where she had been living since a few years after the murders.

When she came to Montana, she married a man named Sullivan, so there was no change to her last name. She never spoke about her past, and apparently never told anyone in Anaconda about her connection with the Borden case. She lived there for 45 years and then, after a serious illness, moved to Butte, where she remained until her death.

This alleged strange episode occurred during Bridget's serious illness in Anaconda, when she was stricken with pneumonia and believed that she was dying. The story went that when Bridget first came to America, she had come with another girl from her hometown in Ireland. They separated soon after arriving; Bridget settling in New England, and her friend in Montana. They corresponded irregularly over the years. The friend married and became Mrs. Minnie Green. Bridget never wrote to her friend about the Borden murders and Minnie didn't hear about the case when it happened.

In time, Bridget followed to Montana and settled in Anaconda, resuming her friendship with Minnie, who was living in Butte, about 27 miles away. The old friends visited one another, but Bridget never spoke of the murders.

In 1942, when they were both about 75-years-old, Minnie received an urgent telephone call from Bridget, who said she was dying, wanted to see her friend, and reveal a secret to her before she passed away. Minnie made arrangements to go to Anaconda, but it took a day or two for her to get there. By the time that she did, Bridget had passed the crisis in her illness and she recovered soon after.

Several days after visiting Bridget, Minnie went into the Butte Public Library, where she met a librarian named Mollie O'Meara. The librarian approached the elderly woman who was wandering through the stacks and asked her if she needed assistance. Minnie hesitantly asked her for books about real-life murders and when she learned there had been quite a few, asked if anything had been written about Lizzie Borden. She told Mollie how Bridget had sent for her and related what occurred during her visit to Anaconda.

Mollie O'Meara kept her conversation with Minnie secret until 1960, after both Minnie and Bridget had died. According to her account, Bridget had told Minnie for the first time that she had been a witness in the Lizzie Borden case while she was on what she thought was going to be her deathbed. Bridget said that her testimony was favorable to Lizzie who, to show her gratitude, had given her money to visit her parents in Ireland. She added that Lizzie's attorney had advised her to remain in Ireland and not return to the United States. Bridget said that she was given a substantial amount of cash – enough to buy her parents a farm and stock it with horses, cows, pigs, chickens, and sheep. Later, Bridget said, she became restless, obtained a passport under another name, and returned to America. She settled in Montana and got married. Minnie said that Bridget told her that she was fond of Lizzie and frequently took her side in family disagreements. Bridget also said that she had testified only to the truth at the trial.

Minnie, who had known Bridget since they were young girls, was frankly skeptical of her friend's story. She didn't find anything in it to account for Bridget's urgent desire to have her rush to her bedside to confide a secret before she died. Minnie borrowed a few books about the case from the library and returned them several days later. When Mollie O'Meara asked if she had learned anything, the older woman shook her head, looked puzzled, and left. As far as Mollie knew, she never returned to the library again. Bridget recovered and moved to Butte. Whether the two old friends saw each other again after this incident is unknown.

When this story was made public, believers in the guilt of both Lizzie and Bridget seized on this alleged incident to bolster their claim that Bridget withheld information and was paid off by Lizzie.

What was it that Bridget so urgently wanted to tell her old friend before she died? Was it that Lizzie had indeed committed the murders? Or was it, as some believe, that Bridget herself had wielded the hatchet? And had she done so with Lizzie's help?

Or did this story ever really happen at all?

There is no evidence to say that Bridget ever made a call to her friend to divulge some secret from her past. And since the "secret" was never told, we can never know for sure what it might be. This is quite convenient for journalists who are still trying to point the finger at Lizzie – or Bridget Sullivan – as a plausible suspect in the case.

Unfortunately, there is also no evidence to say that the Bridget Sullivan who died in Montana in 1948 was the same Bridget Sullivan who worked for the Borden family!

According to the death certificate, Bridget Sullivan had lived in the city of Butte, Montana, for 22 years when she died. She had moved there, to her final residence, around 1926. She had been born in Ireland. Her parents were Eugene Sullivan and Margaret Leary and the year of her birth was 1875. This would have made her 17-years-old at the time of the Borden murders. The problem is that the Bridget Sullivan of Fall River, Massachusetts, told the court that she was 25-years-old in 1892.

From the preliminary hearing transcript:

Q. How old are you?
A. Twenty-five.

The "other" Bridget Sullivan lived at 112 East Woolman Street in Butte, Montana. Her occupation was listed as a "housewife" and she was a widow when she died at the age of 73. She died of exhaustion, cardiac failure, chronic myocarditis, arterial sclerosis, and senility. She was also blind, for causes unknown. The death certificate required the doctor to underline the cause of death that should be charged statistically, and he underlined "senility."

Despite the "too good to be true" stories of Bridget's "almost confession," evidence suggests that the Bridget Sullivan who lived and died in Montana – and about whom fanciful tales were spun – was not the same young woman that once worked for the Borden family of Fall River.

With this tall tale now stricken from the record, it seems harder than ever for the enigmatic maid to have had a hand in the murders of Andrew and Abby Borden.

John Vinnicum Morse

One of the first suspects in the murders was "Uncle John" Morse, the brother of Andrew's first wife. On the evening after the murders, Morse was even threatened by a lynch mob in town, who also suspected him of having a hand in the murders. The authorities used this as an excuse to place Lizzie under "house arrest" the following day. But after some investigation, the police ruled that Morse's alibi was solid – but was it? Questions have since been raised and his bizarre behavior on the days before – and especially on the day of – the murders has already been described.

Although born and raised in Fall River, John moved west as a young man, first to Illinois, and then Iowa, where he spent 25 years as a horse breeder. He was virtually out of the life of Andrew, Emma and Lizzie until two years before the murders. Then he began showing up at the Borden house for "visits" with his nieces. During one of his earlier visits, the Borden house had been burgled, which was a difficult task for a house that was usually so secure, due to the demands of Andrew.

His sudden unannounced appearance at the Borden house in early August 1892 was strange in that he did not bring any baggage with him, although he clearly intended to stay overnight, or if not longer. And there were strange things happening during this visit.

During the inquest, Lizzie stated that while her father and uncle were in the sitting room the afternoon before the murders, she had been disturbed by their voices and had closed her door, even though it was a very hot day.

But apparently Lizzie did not tell everything she overheard between her father and uncle to the authorities. Arthur S. Phillips, the young law associate of Andrew Jennings, revealed in a newspaper interview before his death that he always suspected that Morse had committed the murders. He said that John Morse and Andrew Borden had quarreled violently in the house that day, information that must have come from Lizzie. It was obviously the sound of this argument that caused Lizzie to close her door.

Long after the trial had ended, the *New Bedford Standard-Times* quoted Prosecutor Knowlton as saying that if he only knew what Borden said during his conversation with Morse, he would have convicted "somebody." He clearly noted that it would have been "somebody," and not necessarily Lizzie Borden.

It was learned that Morse associated with a group of itinerant horse traders who made their headquarters at Westport, a town not far from Fall River. They were a shady and undesirable bunch with numerous ties to lawbreakers. Investigators from the Fall River police department did go to see if they could get any information against Morse and possibly find an accomplice that he might have hired from among these men, but the officers found no incriminating evidence.

Aside from his disreputable compatriots, Morse's alibi was not as solid as it seemed. He said that he returned from the visit to his niece on the 11:20 streetcar. The woman in the house where his niece was living backed up his story and said that she left when he did to shop for her dinner. Fall River was not a fashionable town – the dinner hour there was at 12 noon. If this woman had delayed until after 11:20 to start her shopping, she would have had little time in which to prepare the substantial meal that was eaten at dinner in those days. It is possible that Morse told the woman that it was 11:20, but it could have been earlier, since she did serve dinner on time.

The police did make an attempt to check on Morse's alibi. They interviewed the conductor of the streetcar Morse said that he had taken, but the man didn't remember Morse as a passenger. Questioned further, Morse said that there had been four or five priests riding on the car with him. The conductor did recall having several priests as passengers, and this satisfied the police, despite the fact that the conductor pointed out that Fall River was a heavily Catholic town and there were priests riding on almost every trip the streetcar made. So, in the end, Morse's statement realistically missed nothing.

We do know that Morse left the house before 9:00 a.m. Bridget testified that she saw him leave through the side door. Morse said Borden had let him out and locked the screen door. From that point on, he said he went to the post office and then walked leisurely to where his niece was staying, more than a mile away. He met no one that he knew during this walk. There is no accounting for the long gap of time that covers the earlier hour when Abby was killed.

Morse testified that while he was having breakfast in the dining room, Mrs. Borden told Bridget that she wanted her to wash the windows that day. Bridget's testimony told a different story. She said that it was after she had returned from vomiting in the back yard that Mrs. Borden told her to wash the windows. This was long after Morse had left the house.

Some have suggested that Morse's knowledge of what Abby had told Bridget could indicate that he had returned secretly to the house and was hidden there. He knew the house fairly well; he had been there on two previous visits during the past three or four months alone. And despite Knowlton's attempts to show that the house was always locked up, this was not always the case. The screen door was unlocked for some 10–15 minutes while Bridget was sick in the back yard. It was unlocked all the time when she was washing the windows. Morse could have returned while Bridget was vomiting, some theorists believe, and gone upstairs to the guest room. Abby might not have even been alarmed if she saw Morse with a hatchet in his hand. He had been to the farm the previous day and he could have said he needed the hatchet at the farm. Abby would have had no reason to disbelieve him and he could have approached close enough to her to swing it before she could even cry out. He could have left for Weybosset Street after her murder and made it in plenty of time by using the streetcar.

If he took an earlier streetcar than the 11:20 on his return, he could have arrived at the Borden house shortly after Andrew came home. With Lizzie in the barn, the screen door unlocked, and Bridget upstairs in her attic room, he would have free and easy access to the house. With the second murder over, he could have left, hidden the weapon in some vacant lot, empty building, or abandoned cistern in the neighborhood. His unconcerned stroll down the side of the house to a pear tree, with crowds already gathering in front of the place and Sawyer guarding the side door, was extremely odd. There was no close examination of his clothes for bloodstains, and certainly no scientific test was made of them. And for a man who had traveled to town without any change of clothing, a few more stains on his dark suit might have very well gone unnoticed.

What was the motive? There is no clear answer to that, for there was no financial gain for Morse. Perhaps it had something to do with the mysterious quarrel, but again, we will never know. That is, of course, if he had anything to do with the murders at all. He did, in fact, see his niece as he planned to do and she didn't notice anything unusual about his behavior, even though his visit would have occurred shortly after Abby's murder. When he had left the house that morning, he had promised to return in time for dinner, which was exactly what time he returned – no matter how bizarre he might have acted when he did.

So, *could* John Morse have committed the Borden murders? Yes, he could have, but there doesn't seem to be any clear evidence that he did. Even so, readers are asked to make note of the time period when the screen door was unlocked and Lizzie was conveniently absent in the barn.

Emma Borden

Emma Lenora Borden was born on March 1, 1851, and was 12-years-old when her mother died. We know nothing of her schooling, her activities in the community, any suitors that she might have had, or the reason for the implication that she had none. Her physical description was given as "slight," nothing more. Photographs of her are rare, and the courtroom sketch in which she appears shows her with her hand covering her face. Unlike her younger sister, she was never known to express her dissatisfaction with her lot in life, her "humble home," or her lack of material things that were so easily attainable for those with Andrew Borden's wealth. She did not, however, like her step-mother. She got along passably with her father, though some have suggested that his stingy ways were what had gotten in the way of her finding a suitable husband, thus dooming her to the life of a spinster. But Emma still didn't complain. Even after the falling out over Abby and the real estate a few years before the murders, Emma swallowed her anger.

When the murders were taking place, Emma was vacationing with the Brownells – friends and distant relatives – at a seaside cottage in Fairhaven, about 15 miles from Fall River. She had been at the cottage for two weeks prior to the crime and was notified of the murders by a telegram sent to her from Dr. Bowen. She arrived home in the early evening on the day of the murders.

Those who were at the Brownell cottage with Emma were questioned mercilessly by the police and harassed by reporters. The Brownells were unanimous and unequivocal in their confirmation of Emma's presence in Fairhaven at the time of the murders. In spite of this, there are still some who believe that Emma could have – and did – commit the murders.

It has been pointed out that Fairhaven was only 15 miles away from Fall River and there was frequent train service between the two communities. Emma was cleared as a suspect by the police, and yet there is some doubt about whether or not any officers actually went to Fairhaven to make direct inquiries about her alibi. The fact that Emma received the telegram that Dr. Bowen sent her appears to be the only evidence that the Fall River police thought was necessary to clear her as a suspect. By the time that she returned home, some of the officers were concentrating solely on Lizzie.

The attraction that Emma seems to have for those who name her as the perpetrator of the crime is that she is an unknown entity. Emma, who seldom left the house unless she was calling on one of her small circle of friends, was the least-known member of the family. Theorists maintain that she could have slipped into town unnoticed. During the trial, she admitted frankly that she had never been very cordial with her stepmother after the house incident. Even though Lizzie became a suspect when she referred to Abby as "not my mother," Emma had never referred to her stepmother by anything other than her first name. This seems to show that her resentment of the second Mrs. Borden was deep and of long standing. There are no indications of any affectionate bond between Emma and her father to match that between Lizzie and Andrew. Most historians have portrayed Emma as weak-willed, self-effacing, and ineffectual, but, as had been shown, she could be as strong-willed as her sister when she wanted to be. Knowlton had learned this quickly enough when he discovered that she was a match for him in his efforts to shake her testimony. Emma, of course, knew the house well enough to conceal herself between the two murders.

What was Emma's motive? Money, of course. Because her father's often-mentioned-but-never-seen will was never probated, Emma knew that Abby had to die first. If the carnage had been reversed, Abby's sisters, Sarah Whitehead and Priscilla Fish, would have claimed a major share of Andrew's wealth. By eliminating Abby, Emma insured that they would inherit only the paltry sum that had been Abby's estate.

Immediately following the murders, Emma, being the elder daughter, applied for her father's fortune. In accordance with the law, her application had to be published for three weeks in succession in the *Fall River News*. Then, 29 days after her father and stepmother were butchered, she gained possession of Andrew's entire estate. Emma was now in control of half a million dollars.

According to the theorists, Emma's control of the fortune was a new source of fear to Lizzie. Following Lizzie's arrest, the argument which jail matron Hannah Reagan had overheard between Lizzie and Emma concerned the inheritance. Mrs. Reagan thought she heard Lizzie say, "Emma, you have given me away, haven't you?" But there was nothing about Lizzie that Emma could have given away since Emma, of course, was the killer. The crux of Lizzie's anger was that Emma had applied to become the sole administrator of the estate, with none of the money going to Lizzie. She believed that if she was convicted, even if she escaped the death penalty, she might never see a penny of her father's money. The courts would side with the innocent sister, rather than the convicted murderess, and Emma would keep it all.

There are a myriad of problems with the scenario of Emma as the killer, not the least of which Mrs. Reagan denied that the jailhouse argument ever occurred. The whole thing was the invention of an unscrupulous newspaper reporter.

There is also the subject of the estate, of which Emma became the sole heir by necessity, not avarice. The irony in this situation is generally overlooked. The daughter with no expressed desire for her father's money now had it all, while the daughter who wanted it so desperately was now ordering meals from a jailhouse menu. There was no question that Emma, like Lizzie, would have liked to live in a better part of town and have nicer things, but she was silent in her complaints, unlike her sister. All trial expenses were Emma's to govern. Admittedly, she had the constant, diligent, and effective assistance of Andrew Jennings, but she took good care of Lizzie. Just how many decisions were deferred to him is not known, but between them, they did everything right.

When Lizzie was declared not guilty, the estate was split down the middle, and Lizzie was presented with her share with no opposition from her sister. This has been used by those who believe in Emma's guilt as proof of her fear of exposure, and thus, her guilt. But this makes little sense because once tried, Lizzie could not be tried again. If Emma had killed Andrew and Abby, Lizzie would have known it and could have taken all of the estate by betraying her sister.

In truth, Emma was a good friend to her sister and a supporter of Lizzie's cause with no sinister or secret motives. It was more than 10 years after the trial before she declared some independence and separated herself from Lizzie.

By then, the person who was likely the real murderer had been dead for almost two years.

Lizzie Borden

As mentioned, although she was acquitted at trial, Lizzie remains the prime suspect in the minds of many readers, historians, and in popular culture. Books, articles, films, television shows, and even comic books have painted a picture of a bloodthirsty maniac with a hunger for her father's wealth. In the preceding pages, I have attempted to be as open-minded as possible as to the idea of what Lizzie knew, when she knew it, and how involved she was.

There have been many theories produced that name Lizzie as the killer. The earliest writer to expound on her alleged guilt was Edwin H. Porter, police reporter for the *Daily Globe*. He was an observer of both the investigation and the trial and for whatever reason, called for her arrest, trial, and a guilty verdict. He later wrote a book on the case and on the day of its publication, Lizzie, on advice of Andrew Jennings, bought all of the available copies and burned them -- although this is an assumption, since there is no direct evidence that she was the purchaser. A few copies survived and until a reprint was done many years later, four of the surviving copies were in the possession of the Fall River Historical Society, and one other was said to be in private hands. Oddly enough, Porter never wrote anything again. His byline never appeared in any newspapers across the country. It has been suggested that he was paid off to disappear and never refer to the damning book again. Truth or legend? No one can say for sure.

Writers have proposed that Lizzie committed the murders while naked, and then washed off in the basement; that she committed the murders while in a fugue state; or committed the murders after being caught in a lesbian tryst with Bridget Sullivan. Abby discovered the two together and when she reacted with horror and disgust, Lizzie killed Abby with a candlestick. When her father returned and she confessed to him, he reacted in the same way and so she killed him with a hatchet. Bridget disposed of the murder weapon later. Another prominent theory suggests that Lizzie was physically and sexually abused by her father, which led to murder. There is, of course, absolutely no evidence to support this theory either.

Some believers in Lizzie's guilt state that she escaped by sheer luck, based on how poorly structured and presented the prosecution's case was during the trial. Lizzie's deliverance was due mostly to two judicial rulings: the exclusion of her inconsistent statements made under oath at the inquest, and the exclusion of the prussic acid evidence. A second piece of luck for Lizzie was the sensational axe murder of Bertha Manchester in her Fall River home, five days before jury selection began. The implication was, of course, that whoever had murdered Bertha might have also murdered the Bordens. And while such theories explain how Lizzie achieved a not guilty verdict, it does not explain how she could have committed the murders in the first place.

Could Lizzie have been guilty? I don't believe she could have murdered Abby and Andrew. I do believe that Lizzie had knowledge of the murders, although it was not her hand that wielded the axe. It was impossible that she could have done so. In Chapter 4 of this volume, we explained the 11–15 minutes that were available to Lizzie to commit the murders. Starting from the moment that Bridget went to her room, Lizzie could not have gone to wherever the hatchet was hidden, returned to the sitting room, murdered Andrew, hidden the hatchet, inspected herself, combed her hair and washed away the inevitable bloodstains, gone back up to her room, changed clothes, hid the bloody garments somewhere, gone back downstairs, out to the yard, picked up pears, entered the barn, gone up to the loft, eaten the pears, come back down, returned to the house, and, finally, called out to Bridget. It is impossible, physically, to do all of those things in that short amount of time. Even if we extend that time to include the trip to the barn (and we only have false testimony from a police officer to say that the dust on the floor of the loft was undisturbed), she still could not have have committed the murders.

But we can't be finished after that. Even though it is physically impossible that Lizzie could have committed the murders, this has not ended the speculation. Let's look at this closer…

There are six statements made by the prosecution that the Commonwealth believed pointed to Lizzie's guilt. They are as follows:

1. Lizzie was involved in an earlier effort to poison her family.
2. Lizzie disliked her stepmother, Abby Borden.
3. Lizzie stood to profit from the crime.
4. Lizzie's actions after the murders showed consciousness of guilt.
5. Many of Lizzie's statements about the case were untrue.
6. No one except Lizzie had the opportunity to commit the crime.

We'll explore these contentions, beginning with the alleged poisoning. How likely were these previous acts of violence (as prosecutors called it) toward the victims? It seems unlikely that this was true. Abby Borden had told Dr. Bowen that she thought she was being poisoned, but he dismissed the idea. After the murders, the autopsies found no evidence of poison. So, why did the prosecution pursue it? Needless to say, if Lizzie had poisoned her family, it would certainly make her look guilty at trial and so to continue with the suggestion, they relied on the testimony of Eli Bence, the pharmacy clerk who claimed that Lizzie tried to buy prussic acid on the day before the murders.

How reliable was his testimony? As it turned out, not very. Oddly, it is common for people to come forward in cases that excite the public imagination and say all kinds of things, many of them untrue – in fact, most of them untrue. The clerk did not know Lizzie before the attempted purchase; he stepped forward in the investigation in response to murders. He appeared to be just an excitable gossip who inserted himself into the case. If we set aside the murders, was his testimony enough to convince a jury beyond a reasonable doubt that Lizzie tried to poison her family? Definitely not. There is no evidence of a history of violence on the part of the accused. Lizzie may not have liked her stepmother, but she was never cruel or abusive toward her and she had no issues with her sister or her father, making the accusations of poisoning rather hard to believe.

As mentioned, it's true that Lizzie did not particularly care for Abby, but she loved and revered her father and was never known to have spoken ill of him. The Borden house was not a particularly happy one – you have four adult women, aged 25 to 65 living in a relatively small and shabby house with a dour, old miser – but there is tension of some kind in most families. The animosity between Lizzie and

Abby was not the kind that turns violent; they just didn't really like one another. A murder conviction cannot be obtained on the fact that two people just don't get along.

Lizzie's "profiting" from the crime means little in the confines of this case. Andrew Borden was a wealthy man, but there are few people who are greedy enough to murder their parents in order to inherit their parent's money. Again, this was a mild-mannered young woman with no history of violence. The idea that she could suddenly go mad and murder her parents because she was greedy is impossible to believe. Those who manifest this kind of greed usually give off pretty clear signs of unusual avarice. Lizzie was not in need. She did not have a gambling habit or huge, unpaid bills at the local stores. She did not have a drug habit to support. Did she want nice things, and to live in a nicer house in a better part of town? Did she want her father to spend some of the money on the family? Yes, to all of those questions, and yet, Lizzie was going to inherit the money anyway. She didn't have to kill anyone for it and there is no record of her talking a lot about money in the days before the crime.

To say that Lizzie would profit from her parents' murder is taking a narrow view of the facts. The murders turned Lizzie's life into a living hell. She was ostracized, ridiculed, and imprisoned for a better part of a year, stood trial for murder, and was a social pariah for the rest of her days. To assert that money was a motive for murder, one must assume that she saw the money coming to her and nothing else. Certainly some people (and most murderers) are so shortsighted that they do not plan for the "negative side-effects" of the murder.

However, the money does provide a motive for people other than Lizzie to have committed the crime. Andrew may have been killed by someone who felt he had cheated them in a business deal. On the board of several banks, he could have uncovered wrongdoing by someone involved in one of the banks, or in one of his other businesses. He may have been murdered by someone who rented a house or apartment from him.

Or, it's even possible that he may have been slain by some other relative with whom he was less than generous.

The prosecution was quick to focus on the idea that Lizzie's behavior after the murders showed a consciousness of guilt. They believed this "consciousness" was revealed in three ways: her emotional affect was flat and seemed to some people to be inappropriate to the situation; she burned a dress on the Sunday after the murders; and she made numerous statements about the case that were untrue or were at odds with testimony from other people, which was the fifth statement the prosecution made about Lizzie's guilt.

As far as Lizzie's emotions went, there has already been quite a bit written about that in this book. People react to alarming and horrible events in all kinds of different ways. There are so few people who have an experience like "discovering your father's mutilated body only minutes after he was murdered" that it is difficult to generalize how a person should behave, even assuming there is some kind of predictable behavior for such a scenario.

The vast majority of statements about Lizzie being an emotionally "flat" person were generated by reporters, and specifically Edwin H. Porter, who have some agenda in painting Lizzie as a monster. After the crime, people expected to see her distraught, and she was – sometimes. Lizzie was a quiet, dignified woman and was not prone to emotional outbursts, long before anyone ever accused her of murder. Nevertheless, when she reported the murder to her neighbor, she was crying and shaking. During the inquest, when she read a description of the injuries suffered by her father, she wept until she vomited. During the trial, the prosecutor revealed the skull of her father and she fainted. At other times, she seemed by some people to be unnaturally composed, but she could not be expected to dial her emotions to a certain point and leave them there for weeks on end because that was what people expected to see. If she had been able to do that, we would have to have cause for concern that she might truly be the killer.

Lizzie's emotions went up and down, she went into shock, and she became unpredictable at times. All of this was normal behavior for a person who endured what she was going through. Lizzie was given sedatives shortly after the murder, and was heavily sedated with morphine for several days after that. This could have caused the inappropriate emotional affect that some claimed to see, but it was certainly not consciousness of guilt.

The burning of the dress was the trigger that caused Lizzie to be arrested and brought to trial, there is little doubt about that. As soon as the judge and the grand jury heard about the burning of the dress, they ordered Lizzie to be bound over for trial.

But, based on the testimony at trial, there was nothing to the incident. Emma testified that the dress in question was faded and had been spotted with paint from when the house was painted some months earlier, and that she asked Lizzie to burn the dress after she was unable to find a hook on which to hang a newer dress. The dressmaker who made the dress confirmed that it had been spotted with paint not long after it was made.

Further, the idea that the dress might have had small spots of blood on it (Alice Russell described the dress and never mentioned seeing any blood) because of the murders is fairly preposterous. It is clear that Lizzie had virtually no blood on her in the minutes after the murders. All of the people who saw her at that time, without exception, stated that there was no blood on her dress. If Lizzie had been wearing that dress when she committed the murders, the dress would have been soaked with blood. The crime scene looked like a slaughterhouse. Whoever killed the Bordens was unquestionably covered in gore. She could perhaps, conceivably, have had a wrap of some kind around the dress, through which some small amount of blood could have seeped, but the police had thoroughly searched the house before the dress was burned, to the extent of tearing apart the woodpile log by log to look for the murder weapon, and had closely examined every garment in the house, looking for bloodstains. They found nothing. The police could easily have seized this dress before Lizzie burned it, but they did not.

Lizzie's burning of the dress was turned into something more unusual than it was. Was it poorly timed? Yes, it was, but, in my opinion, it shows that she was not thinking like a killer because she did not consider the idea that it would make her look guilty.

The burning of the dress might have been the incident that sent Lizzie to trial, but it was not what prosecutors focused most heavily on. They were more intrigued by what seemed to be untruths in so many of Lizzie's statements. They believed that her obvious misstatements were clearly designed to avoid being named as a suspect, but in truth, misstatements like the ones that Lizzie made have happened in just about every murder case that has ever been tried.

What happens in murder cases – and happened scores of times in this case alone – is that the defendant is repeatedly asked questions that are designed to confuse her and designed to elicit inconsistent statements that can be used against her. A series of events happened that were, at the time, quite trivial – Abby went out, or Lizzie thought she went out, the maid was washing some windows, Lizzie was ironing handkerchiefs, Andrew came home, Lizzie went to the barn to get some metal for fishing sinkers. These are not the kind of events that cause a person to check a clock and make note of the time. All of the sudden, Lizzie returned to the house, found the screen door wide open and her father horribly murdered. Shocked and heavily sedated, she was then questioned relentlessly for days without a lawyer about this series of trivial events, which had occurred before the most horrific experience of her life. While undergoing this interrogation, she was intermittently accused of the crime because a policemen didn't like the way she referred to her stepmother as "not her mother." It is virtually impossible to avoid making inconsistent and inaccurate statements under those conditions. Specifically:

* Lizzie said that she had gone out to the barn and to the hayloft of the barn to look for lead for sinkers, and that she found her father murdered when she returned. Two police officers, however, said there was a thick layer of dust in the hayloft of the barn and it didn't appear that anyone had been up there for weeks.

But the young boy who testified at Lizzie's trial said that, hearing about the murders, he and a friend went to the house and attempted to see what was going on. Turned away by the police, they had gone out to the barn and had watched the spectacle from the hayloft – within an hour of the murder and before the police had even examined it. It turns out that it was the police – lying outright – who were in error about the hayloft, not Lizzie.

* Bridget Sullivan said that she heard Lizzie laugh from the second-floor landing as she was unlocking the door to let Andrew into the house about 10:45. However, Lizzie said that she was in the kitchen at that time, later that she was in the bedroom on the second floor, and later (again) that she was in the kitchen.

The noise that Bridget heard while unlocking the door was almost certainly some noise made by the murderer, be that Lizzie or someone else. However, if you think about it as evidence against Lizzie, Abby was already dead by this time, probably dead for about an hour. It is difficult to imagine that Lizzie murdered her stepmother at 9:45, was laughing a few feet from the body an hour later, hacked her father to death a few minutes later, and yet, appeared stunned, pale, and shaken when she called for help a short time after that.

A laugh, particularly coming from a different area in the house at a different elevation, is a relatively indistinct sound, easily mistaken for some other noise. A cat, a creaking door, a rustling of cloth… any of these can, at times, be mistaken for laughter. The noise that Bridget heard was fairly trivial at the time and she expected it to be a laugh in response for her swearing as she fumbled with the door locks.

* Lizzie said that on the morning of the murders Abby Borden had received a note asking her to visit someone who was ill. No such note was ever found. Lizzie said that perhaps she burned it or perhaps Abby had burned it, but no one came forward to say that they had sent such a note, and it seems extremely unlikely that Abby ever left the house that morning.

Lizzie's answers on this issue are very troubling. Looking at it from Lizzie's standpoint, she may have heard someone at the door, which may have been Abby admitting the murderer to the house, and she may have noticed soon afterward that her stepmother did not seem to be about. She may have guessed incorrectly that Abby had gone out to visit someone. She did tell Bridget, before the murders, that Abby had been called away on a sick visit. Questioned about this later in a confused, drugged state, she may have attempted to give an explanation that fit what she could remember, and may have filled in the mental gap with a non-existent note.

The judge at Lizzie's trial, in the process of demonstrating profound bias in Lizzie's favor, speculated that perhaps the note was written by the murderer, who took it with him when he left. However, neither of these is a very satisfying explanation, and Lizzie's lack of forthrightness about this issue remains troubling even today.

* A neighbor said that she sat before a window facing the Borden house with a clear view of the back door from 10:00 to 10:55 and saw no one come or go from that door. This conflicts with Lizzie's testimony that she went out to the barn which, by the way, was confirmed by a peddler who stated that he saw a woman crossing the yard, heading for the barn, just before 11:00 a.m. Did the neighbor just miss Lizzie leaving the house and going to the barn? Or was the peddler mistaken?

Lizzie was accused by the prosecutors of lying or giving inconsistent statements about dozens of other issues – for example, at one point she said that she had been home all day the previous day, and at another time that she had been out, at one point she had visited Emma in Fairhaven and at another point she had not, at one point she had overheard a conversation between her father and uncle and another point she had not, at one point that she had eaten a meal with the family and at another point she had not, at one point the door was locked and at another point it was not, and at one point she had gone out to the barn at about 10:00 and had stayed for a half-hour and at another point she gone to the barn just before 11:00 and had stayed only a few minutes. These conflicts can only be characterized as normal confusion, in many cases centered on immaterial facts. In the greater scheme of things, none of what happened on the day before the murders mattered to the investigation, but prosecutors focused on these trivial items to make Lizzie look guilty.

There is no question that Lizzie did make a number of statements that appear to be inconsistent with other testimony. However, evidence that can be "created" in a case is not real evidence, and in many cases, these types of conflicts can be and are generated by the police and prosecutors in every murder case.

A favorite police and lawyer's interrogation method in these circumstances is to ask the accused to *characterize* something which has no precise description – and then later, in different words, ask them to characterize it again. One day Lizzie might say that relations between her and her stepmother were "cordial," another day that they were "distant." Why were they "distant?" Weren't they "cordial" just yesterday? Was it cordial, or was it distant?

But the real question remains – was Lizzie lying? Do her mistakes reflect consciousness of guilt? Lizzie was questioned for many, many hours, without an attorney and under the influence of morphine, by police and by highly trained prosecutors who were convinced that she had committed the crime. She never confessed to the crime, she never came close to confessing to it, and she never found herself trapped in a maze of lies. She made no truly damaging admissions. She answered every question. She said nothing that could be construed as a clear and deliberate falsehood.

In the end, the jury believed that she was innocent. Lizzie was acquitted after a very brief deliberation and her innocence was believed by most of the press who attended the trial. No matter what, though, it's clear that the case presented against Lizzie was inadequate to sustain a conviction.

The harder question is, was she innocent in fact? While it's physically impossible that she could have actually carried out the murders, was she involved? In order for that to be the case, this means that an intruder would have had to enter the house, unseen or otherwise. This relates to the prosecution's assertion that no one but Lizzie could have committed the crime, but this definitely is not the case.

To believe that someone else committed the crime, you have to believe seven things:

1. The intruder entered the house unseen by any of the occupants or any witness outside of the house: This is not that difficult to believe, since there are many possible explanations for this. A door may have been left open as Andrew or John Morse departed that morning. He could have entered the house while Bridget was going in and out, washing the windows. He could have been admitted to the house by Abby Borden. He could have broken into the house during the night by jimmying open a door or window, or during the day through the basement. The murderer entering the house unseen is not really an obstacle.

2. The intruder murdered Abby in a gruesome, violent manner without making loud noises that would have attracted the attention of Lizzie and Bridget: It's difficult to believe that this is possible since the timeframe of Abby's murder has never been precisely pinned down. She may have been murdered not long after 9:00, or she may have been murdered as late as 10:30. The doctors thought she had been dead for an hour or so before Andrew was killed because her blood had coagulated by the time her body was found, but this is an imprecise way of timing the death. Since Lizzie and Bridget were moving around throughout the house, there may have been a few minutes when neither of them was in a position to hear the attack or to hear the body hit the floor, no matter how heavy Abby was.

3. Abby then lay dead in the house for an hour without anyone being aware of it: The prosecution made this seem very difficult, but, in fact, it was not, as one of their own witnesses performed a test to show that it was almost impossible to see Abby's body from anywhere other than inside the guest bedroom.

4. The murderer remained hidden inside of the house without anyone knowing he was there: While this is eerie, it is not otherwise difficult to imagine. Both Bridget and Lizzie were busy with chores and even after Andrew returned home, he was not feeling well and went into the parlor to lie down on the couch. No one was looking for an intruder because no one knew that Abby had been attacked.

5. He then murdered Andrew with equal violence, again with no one being aware that the attack was happening: This seems difficult to believe, but it is possible with Bridget in the attic and Lizzie out in the barn, which is where both women testified that they were.

6. The murderer then left the house unseen and unnoticed in a busy neighborhood, covered in the blood of his victims: Again, this is difficult to imagine, although it could happen if he was wearing dark clothing or if it simply happened that none of the people who might have seen him chanced to be paying attention at the moment.

7. The killer avoided the attention of the police and avoided being associated with the crime for the rest of his life: This is also difficult to believe, but the intruder theory remains a possibility. The neighbor's testimony about being able to see the back door from 10:00 to 10:55 does not conflict with the intruder theory, since the intruder would have been in the house before 10:00 and departed just a few moments after 11:00.

The intruder theory, on the whole, seems difficult to believe perhaps, but the alternative explanation – that Lizzie committed the murders – is more difficult to believe, and, I believe, entirely impossible. As discussed, Lizzie was entirely clean and there was no murder weapon in the house. The time frame of Andrew's murder cannot be changed. No matter how you look at it, Lizzie had no more than 10 minutes to commit the second murder, clean herself up, and dispose of the murder weapon. It's impossible. Some have suggested that she committed the murders wrapped in protective sheets, and then burned the sheets. That hardly seems possible. She could cover her clothes, but her hair, her face, her hands, and her feet? There was no blood on her – anywhere. She could have completely wrapped herself up, but blood would have seeped through. Even if it didn't, she would have gotten blood on her hands and arms when she pulled it off and put it in the fire – and there was no time to do it. She didn't have time to put her shoes back on. She didn't have time to wash her hands. She didn't have time to make a fire. If she had tried, there would have been blood all around the stove and a trail of bloodstains in a path to the stove, and she didn't have time to clean it up – even assuming that she came up with this remarkable plan in advance.

In the 1975 television movie about Lizzie Borden starring Elizabeth Montgomery (who happened to be a distant relative of Lizzie), it was suggested that she committed the murders in the nude, then washed herself off quickly and re-dressed before calling to Bridget. Again, this is impossible. First, for a Victorian Sunday School teacher, the idea of running around the house naked in the middle of the day is just as inconceivable as committing a couple of hatchet murders. Second, the only running water in the house was a spigot in the basement. If she had been naked when she committed the murders, there would have been bloody footprints leading to the basement – and there is no time for them to have been cleaned up. There isn't enough time for her to have washed herself off and gotten back into her clothes, even if that was all she had to do.

Bridget saw Lizzie after the first murder and before the second. She wasn't covered in blood then. She would have had to clean herself up twice. She couldn't have gone through the house to the basement and washed herself off in the basement while Bridget was cleaning the windows without Bridget being aware of that. And, where did the murder weapon go? The police tore the house apart looking for the murder weapon. When they couldn't find it, they took a broken-handled hatchet out of the basement, its head covered with ashes or dirt, and suggested that perhaps Lizzie had broken off the handle during the assault, then burned the handle in the kitchen stove. Of course, this blew up in Knowlton's face when one of the policemen confessed that the broken-off handle had been in the box with the hatchet when it was found, and when the prosecution's expert witness testified that there wasn't a trace of blood on the hatchet, and that it couldn't have been easily cleaned off. Further, the prosecution's "murder weapon" had been dull and rusted, whereas the real murder weapon was new, and razor sharp.

The murderous attack on Andrew Borden probably occurred between 10:55 and 10:58, and Lizzie probably called for help about three minutes later. That leaves her with essentially three minutes to clean herself up, get her shoes and stockings back on, get back into her dress and underclothes, dispose of the murder weapon, and pull herself together. Even if you make that timeframe six minutes, or double that, or triple that – even then, it's not enough time. In a modern investigation, Lizzie Borden would have been almost immediately excluded from suspicion, because a modern investigator would know immediately that the perpetrator would have to be covered in blood.

Simply put, Lizzie could not have swung the hatchet that took the lives of her parents.

But, on the other hand, just because she didn't swing the hatchet doesn't mean that she bore no guilt in the murders. Because none of the seven things that have to be believed about the "intruder theory" have to be true if Lizzie already knew the murderer was in the house.

The Killer
One of the most compelling theories about the killer of Andrew and Abby Borden is that he was someone known to them, known to Lizzie, and even had help from

Lizzie herself when he entered the house. This suspect was William Borden, an apple farmer and horse renderer who lived several miles north of Fall River. For many years, he was rumored to be Andrew's Borden's illegitimate son. The Borden family denied such talk, but his mother was a woman named Phebe Hathaway, with whom Andrew allegedly had a relationship. Andrew never publicly acknowledged William, but this did not stop the strange young man from going around town talking about rich men and rich sisters and of the wealth that would someday be his. When he was drunk on "ice cider," a kind of homemade applejack liquor, such claims would become even louder. William was said to be mentally handicapped and there is evidence that he spent some time in an insane asylum.

William's occupations left him marked in strange ways. For example, since he made cider he needed to clean his casks frequently with a mixture of lye soap and axle grease. As a horse renderer, he would have to come and cart off dead horses, many of whom had died of Blister Beetle Poison, a disease that attacked the bladder and urine of the animal. Both activities left him smelling so frightful that his wife frequently forced him to sleep in the barn. Was this the indescribable odor that Ellan Eagan encountered when she spotted the man in the Borden yard on the morning of the murders?

If William Borden was the killer, then what was the reason for his rampage? It has been speculated that William had begun making demands of his father, who was in the process of making his will, and that these demands were rejected by Andrew. William, mentally ill and filled with rage, killed Abby first, hid in the house, and then killed his father. Lizzie, with the help of Emma and her attorneys, either paid William off, or threatened him, or both, and decided that Lizzie would allow herself to be suspected and tried for the murders, knowing that she could always identify the real killer, should that be necessary.

But why would Lizzie allow this to happen? I'm not totally convinced that she did, not on purpose anyway. I believe that Lizzie had good intentions that morning to settle a problem that was plaguing the family. Instead of settling things, though, she let a killer into the house.

When the Bordens were murdered, a strange man was reported by Dr. Handy, by Officer Hyde, by Ellan Eagen, and by several other witnesses, hanging around the house. Officer Mullaly testified that in his early interrogation of Lizzie she told him of a man that she had seen that morning outside of the house. She never mentioned that man again. She couldn't mention him. If she had, she and Emma would have had too much to lose.

At the time of the murders, William Borden was making demands of his father. For whatever reason, John Morse was the mediator between Andrew and William, his presence required when William insisted on meeting with Andrew. Lizzie, too, was involved in the arrangement as a go-between of some sort. John Morse was on the scene when Mrs. Borden's watch and jewelry were stolen, a robbery likely committed by William. Lizzie had not been home at the time, but to divert suspicion from William, she went so far as to allow herself to become suspect, just as she did for the murders. When Andrew learned the truth about the crime, he dismissed the police investigation. In August 1892, when William was becoming erratic again – leading to Lizzie's warnings of extreme danger – John Morse again returned to town and was in such a rush that he brought no luggage with him.

On the morning of the murders, someone was supposed to arrange for a note to be delivered to Abby that would cause her to leave the house, thus providing Andrew and William the freedom for an open and uninterrupted conversation without fear of Abby's negative reactions. It is safe to assume that Abby would have been opposed to Andrew's dealings with his illegitimate son. Even if she didn't speak up, though, Andrew would not have wanted her to have any knowledge of what was taking place. My guess is that John Morse was supposed to arrange for a note to be delivered, but for some reason, did not do it, or forgot to do so. This is the reason that Lizzie was convinced that the note had been delivered that morning. The nonexistent note was, of course, never found and no one ever came forward to tell the police that they had sent it.

With no note delivered, Abby was still in the house when William Borden arrived.

Andrew drew up a will that was unacceptable to two of this children and maybe unacceptable to all three of them. He was giving $25,000 each to Lizzie and Emma. William Borden may have been getting some money, but it's likely that it was far less than what his half-sisters were going to receive. And since the money paid out to the children was only a fraction of Andrew's entire estate, it is safe to assume that the bulk of it was going to Abby. The children would see none of her share until her death. Was this what sent William over the edge?

On the day he was murdered, Andrew had an appointment to speak to his son. John Morse was in full sympathy with his nieces and didn't want his brother-in-law to give any of his money to his illegitimate son. Emma had washed her hands of the entire affair, letting others negotiate her inheritance with her father. Doing this, she uncharacteristically left Fall River and went to stay with friends. Andrew and John were at odds about what Andrew intended to do, and on the eve of the murders, they had an argument about it. Long after the trial had ended, Prosecutor Knowlton gave an interview in which he said that if he could have known exactly what subject was discussed between the two men that evening, he could have gained a conviction against the person responsible for Andrew's death. He couldn't have meant Lizzie since she was no longer eligible for conviction.

On that August morning, William likely entered the house unseen through the cellar door – a door that Lizzie had unlocked for him. At the time, Bridget was outside at the front of the house, and Lizzie, believing that a note had been delivered to her stepmother, thought Abby had changed her clothes and left the house on some imagined errand of mercy.

Lizzie wisely feared her half-brother. She knew that he would be in the house alone with her until her father returned, which likely prompted her declarations of fear to Alice Russell. Although she had every reason to fear William, she was also convinced that she could control him. If she truly attempted to buy prussic acid, it may have been as a defensive weapon against William if one was required.

This placed William Borden in the front upstairs bedroom when Abby unexpectedly went into the room and surprised him as he waited to see his father. Why William killed Abby is open to speculation, but hatred and insanity can seldom be reasoned with. In William's mind, Abby, as the wife of his father, had usurped the position of his own mother, Phebe Hathaway, who had been divorced by her husband and had fallen into poverty. After years of hatred and resentment, the deranged young man simply snapped. It has long been suggested that Lizzie killed her stepmother because she hated her, but it is far easier to imagine William doing it for the same reason.

Whether from surprise, from fear of discovery, from insane hatred, or from some combination of all of these, William killed Abby. Perhaps he had planned to commit the murder all along since he brought a hatchet with him to the house, or perhaps he was just carrying it with him at the time. William Borden was said to have an unnatural attachment to his hatchet. He carried it with him all the time, spoke with it, and even called it by name.

Lizzie had no idea that William had killed his stepmother until she found her father's body and wondered aloud whether Abby might not be in the house after all, in spite of the note she was supposed to have received. There was no way that Lizzie could not have known she had not left the house. Her defense at the inquest, that she could not have killed Abby because she did not know Abby was in the house, was the simple truth.

Lizzie undoubtedly kept her distance from William while he waited upstairs for his father to return that morning. She was in the kitchen when Bridget, fumbling with the front door lock, heard William, upstairs, laugh at her expletive. Bridget assumed it was Lizzie she heard since, as far as she knew, only she and Lizzie were in the house.

Andrew came into the house, exchanged a few words with Bridget, took his bedroom key from the mantle, and went upstairs, possibly to his safe. Whatever Andrew brought home with him that morning, it was likely connected in some way to William. It was the size and shape of bank notes, but it could have been papers, deeds, or even a copy of the will that favored the rest of the family over William. Andrew may have had it in his hand ready to give or show to William, or he may have changed his mind and placed it in the safe. After the murders, when the safe was opened under the watchful eyes of Andrew Jennings and Officer Harrington, its contents were noted as "a large amount of cash and a great many papers," but "nothing incriminating."

When Bridget went upstairs for her nap, Andrew ordered Lizzie out of the house while he met with his son. Later, Lizzie testified that after leaving her father, she went out of the house, picked up some pears that had fallen off the pear tree, and then went to the second story of the barn where she spent 15–20 minutes first eating pears while looking out the window and then looking for lead for fishing sinkers. But as already pointed out from the timeline of the murders earlier in the book, not only did Lizzie not have time to murder her parents and clean up twice, she also didn't have time to wait around in the barn.

Unfortunately for the police officers involved, they chose to lie in their testimony about something that Lizzie didn't do. She never went to the barn, although they had no idea of that since they lied. She did spend a few minutes in the backyard, eating pears, but not long enough to disrupt the timeline of the murders, as a trip to the barn might have done.

When Lizzie came inside from eating pears, she checked her ironing flats, found the fire in the stove had gone out, and decided to wait until Bridget started the fire to make dinner before heating up the flats again. The fact that she checked her flats *before* discovering her father's body indicates that she did not expect to find him dead. Although she knew that Andrew had met with William, she did not know the meeting ended in murder. Her panic, her grief, and her horror were genuine.

Obviously, the meeting between Andrew and William did not go well. The history of Andrew's murder has always stated that he was killed when napping, but this was not the case. Lizzie testified that her father had removed his shoes before lying down for his nap, but the testimony of Officer Allen and crime scene photographs taken on the day of his murder contradict this story. Officer Allen's first impression when he saw Mr. Borden's body was, "I noticed how Mr. Borden sat on the sofa." It's obvious in the photographs of Andrew's body that he would not have been in a comfortable position for sleeping.

Andrew Borden was not napping when he was murdered. He was engaged in a conversation with his murderer. The first blow of the blunt side of the murder weapon killed him while he was sitting up. The blows that followed were delivered in an uncontrolled rage. Dr. Bowen had noted at the preliminary hearing that the photograph showed Andrew's body had slid down on the couch before the photograph was taken. The doctor's observation was that, initially, Andrew's head and body had been higher on the sofa. Officer Allen, who saw Andrew's body just a few minutes after Dr. Bowen, also had the first impression that Andrew was sitting.

The legend has always claimed that Andrew was murdered while he slept, and 10 or more blows landed on his head while he was lying down with his head on the arm of the sofa. If this was true, it would seem logical that the blows his head received would have driven it into the sofa, and a photograph taken later could possibly show a spring-back action with the head higher, rather than lower than first observed. But Dr. Bowen stated that when he first saw the body, "the head was a little higher on the arm" than it was in the picture.

There are a couple of other things about the photograph that are worthy of mention. At the trial, George A. Pettee, a spectator who was shown Andrew's body by Dr. Bowen just after the doctor returned to the house, said Andrew's feet were crossed. They are obviously not crossed in the photograph. This discrepancy was never questioned, even though it seems significant since a sitting person crossed his legs, not a reclining one. The unprovable conclusion is that Andrew was sitting up when he was killed and was later lowered into the position shown in the photograph. In addition, Andrew's hands in the photograph are clenched into fists. It would be extremely rare for someone to sleep with his hands clenched into fists. Fists generally connote aggression or are the first reflex action of defense.

It's also likely that a modern examination of the crime scene's blood spatter would show that Andrew was sitting when he was first struck, but that kind of science did not exist at the time. The poor quality of the existing photograph – combined with the pattern of the wallpaper – makes a careful study of the photograph today nearly impossible.

With all of that said, it's likely that Andrew was seated on the sofa when the meeting began. It's possible that William may have cleaned himself up somewhat after Abby's murder. If not, then very few words would have been exchanged between them. Most likely, William struck Andrew in a downward swing and then followed the first blow with several more. The parlor had been turned into a slaughterhouse.

After killing his father, William left through the open cellar door, first being seen by Ellan Eagen before fleeing to the backyard and leaving the property. Lizzie may have just missed him, entering the house while William was in the front and going inside just as he was crossing the backyard, probably covered with blood. He soon vanished into the alleys and streets on his way out of town.

After raising the call of murder, and the initial investigation that followed, Lizzie enlisted her uncle's aid in contacting her half-brother William, and with threats, money, and promises, convinced him to stay out of the way. If he did, he was told, everything would be taken care of. In return for giving up his claim to his father's fortune, William was guaranteed that he would not be charged with murder.

Lizzie's concern now became Andrew's fortune. If the will – often talked about, but never produced in the legal wrangling that followed – was kept hidden, her father's entire fortune would *all* go to Lizzie and Emma, rather than the $25,000 that Andrew had deemed adequate. But the silence of William Borden was essential. The course of action that Lizzie chose was drastic and dangerous, but it was foolproof as long as she had the identity of the real murderer at her disposal. Lizzie had to become the prime suspect. She must be tried and she must be found guilty. Should anything upset that plan, then all that was necessary was for her attorney's detectives to "discover" the man and hand the actual killer over to the authorities.

But, as we know from his own letters, Prosecutor Knowlton never truly believed the case against Lizzie was winnable. A more jaded observer might wonder if Knowlton knew more about what was going on in the politically charged district – where the town mayor was known to put a suspect under house arrest, where alleged killers were never offered an attorney by police officers who lied on the stand, and judges coaxed jury members into findings of reasonable doubt – that he was letting on as he paraded back and forth in the courtroom each day. Did he have orders from higher up that Lizzie Borden was meant to be found not guilty? Did her attorneys, as some have claimed, offer substantial payments to many of the officials involved to make sure that Lizzie never went to the gallows?

It's unlikely – probably impossible – that we will ever know for sure.

At some point after Lizzie's trial, William was apparently confined at the State Hospital for the Insane in Taunton, although no official records of this have been discovered. There was a note on the *Taunton Daily Gazette* that reported on his suicide in 1901, and it contained the mention that "he was undoubtedly insane. He spent a period in our asylum some years ago." We do not know who ordered his commitment, or when it was done, but it's not far to guess. Like the contents of Andrew's safe, the hospital records that would cover that period of time, are missing.

In 1901, William Borden committed suicide in the New Boston Road woods outside of Fall River. His body was found hanging from a tree, after first drinking a six-ounce bottle of poison. He placed the empty bottle and his hat side by side on the ground, climbed a tree, secured a logging chain around his neck and to the limb of an overhanging tree in such a manner that he would be suspended about four feet from the ground. He then either jumped or fell from the limb, breaking his neck, or lowered himself down the chain hand over hand until it tightened around his neck and choked off his air.

It took two days for his body to be identified as William Borden, an East Taunton farmer with a wife and an apple orchard that produced cider. He sold it throughout the area, which was what brought him to Fall River on the night of April 18. Early the next morning, he took the chain from a wagon that belonged to William Meachim – one of his customers – and then hung himself after drinking a bottle of carbolic acid. His body was discovered the following morning.

The newspaper noted that Borden had two sisters in the Taunton asylum and added, "It is established that Mr. Borden was very erratic, though it is not known here that he ever before exhibited suicidal tendencies."

In the end, the mystery of what William Borden did, or didn't do, remains open to speculation. Many people believe that he was the killer of Andrew and Abby Borden. Quite possibly, he was also guilty of more serious crimes, such as making impossible demands of the wrong people. He may have been greedy. If nothing else, he was a major threat and a serious danger, not to Lizzie directly, who had been acquitted of the only crime of which she was ever accused, but the fortune that she had inherited from her father.

What do we make of all this? It's an intriguing theory and one that I feel, after delving into the case for two decades or more, likely the closest one to the truth. Is every part of the theory accurate? Who knows? But I do feel that it contains many elements of the truth: Lizzie did not commit the murders (nor did Bridget or anyone else in the family; an intruder (which she likely let into the house) carried out the crimes; Lizzie knew who this person was; political corruption both brought her to trial and insured that she was set free; and finally, no matter who we *think* might have done it, the murders of Andrew and Abby Borden remain unsolved.

Did someone else kill the Bordens? If so, it's highly unlikely that we will ever really know who that person was. It's also unlikely that we will ever discover just what Lizzie, and her defense counsel, really knew about the events in 1892. The papers from Lizzie's defense are still locked up and have never been released. The files remain sealed away in the offices of the Springfield, Massachusetts, law firm that descended from the firm that defended Lizzie during the trial. There are no plans to ever release them.

The history of the Lizzie Borden case lingers in our collective imaginations, much like the spirits that are still believed to linger at the former Borden house in Fall River, Massachusetts, which now serves as a bed and breakfast. More than one overnight guest has claimed an encounter with one of the ghosts that remain from the brutal murders. The truth behind such stories remains as elusive as the killer of the Bordens – but the speculation will certainly never end.

But before we get to the ghosts, we should finish the story of Lizzie Borden. Because her story – and the stories of those whose lives were mired in this case – were not yet at an end.

10. MISS LIZBETH OF MAPLECROFT

Americans have long believed in the myth that when a jury returns with a verdict of "not guilty" in a murder trial, a defendant walks out of the courtroom a free person, entitled to resume his or her rightful place in society. This is true – at least as far as the courts and law enforcement agencies are concerned. But in the eyes of many, their reputation has been permanently destroyed, and as long as the murder remains unsolved, they are never free from suspicion. There will always be those who will disagree with a verdict of acquittal in a murder trial, not on the basis of facts or evidence, but on the basis that the police must have known something or they would not have made an arrest in the first place. Yet those same people will recoil at the suggestion that we abandon jury trials and convict simply because the police made an arrest, which is the logical conclusion of their reasoning.

Permanent suspicion is but one of the enduring blights an acquitted person has to face. He or she has become a public figure and is fair game to the press, having lost their precious rights to privacy.

For Lizzie Borden, she walked out of the courtroom that day – and into American legend.

Lizzie and Emma were surrounded by a joyous mob when they left the courthouse in New Bedford. Judge Dewey was interviewed by the *Boston Globe*. He boasted, "I am perfectly satisfied with the verdict. I was satisfied when I made my charge to the jury that the verdict would be not guilty, although we cannot always tell what a jury will do." In Fall River, the news, which flashed over the wires, of Lizzie's acquittal was met with stunned amazement. Immediately, a crowd began to gather in

front of the house on Second Street, awaiting a glimpse of the released prisoner.

When the sisters arrived on the 8:15 train from New Bedford, they had planned to go directly home, but friends intercepted them with the news that a crowd was surrounding the house. They traveled by carriage to the residence of banker Charles J. Holmes, where they had been offered refuge for the night. The first person to step down from the carriage was Holmes, followed by Lizzie and Emma. Lizzie did not wait for Holmes to escort her, but hurried up the steps and disappeared into the house.

A United Press reporter succeeded in getting into the house that night and newspapers proudly announced the next day that he had obtained an exclusive interview with Lizzie, wearing a black silk dress and laughing joyously that she was the "happiest woman in the world." The so-called interview turned out to be questionable since there were no other words in the article that could actually be attributed to Lizzie.

There was a party later that evening, during which guests pored over newspapers collected from everywhere in the country, showing sketches of Lizzie at the trial. More were terrible likenesses, and even Lizzie chuckled a few times as she looked at them.

At the house on Second Street, the number of people in front of the dark, empty Borden home had swelled to over 2,000. For the people of Fall River, the warm night was the finale of months of sensationalism, of waiting for the grim tragedy to be over. Emotionally, it had taken its toll on everyone. The gossip, the stories, the solutions, the theories had been incessant. The Fall River police officials had been vilified and the gaze of the world had been focused on their daily lives.

Shortly after 10:00, a band arrived and began playing. The voices of the crowd chimed in, singing "Auld Lang Syne."

During the trial, Emma had continued to live in the house on Second Street, but Lizzie firmly decided that she could not return to the place where the murders had occurred. Seeking some privacy after the trial, Lizzie appealed to a friend, the former Sarah Remington, who turned over to Lizzie an isolated cottage on a wooded point near Newport. Lizzie managed to slip away from watching reporters and spent several weeks there by herself. While there, Lizzie decided that she would not return to Second Street.

For the first years of her life, Lizzie had lived in her grandfather's old house on Ferry Street and for the next 21 in a converted two-family dwelling located in the downtown business area so that Andrew could be near the bank and mill that he owned. The dream of living in the fashionable district of town known as the Hill had once seemed impossible, but now it was a reality. Emma fulfilled her sister's wishes by purchasing a 13-room, gray stone Victorian house at 306 French Street, which they moved into five weeks later.

It was the happiest day of Lizzie's life when she and Emma arrived at the fine, rich home. It stood at the top of a quiet hill that looked across the fields toward Providence. She must have felt that the Borden legacy had come full circle. Andrew had recaptured the lost wealth of his predecessors and now Lizzie was able to take her position beside the descendants of the other founding families of Fall River.

Lizzie and Emma Borden's new home, Maplecroft

The house must have seemed extravagant when compared to the crowded home that she had known for so many years. Elegantly situated on extensive grounds, the east and north sides of the house were flanked by a row of towering maple trees. The front steps led into a long, curving, glassed-in porch, which opened into a spacious front entry hall. Connected by cherrywood stairways, three floors of rooms were heated by six coal-burning fireplaces. There were Italianate arches, oak mantelpieces, iron gratings, parquet floors, and even the laundry room had exquisite dark wood wainscoting. There were windows everywhere, through which light continually radiated, giving the house a refined, pastoral feeling. And there were bathrooms -- four bathrooms -- not like the primitive plumbing and chamber pots that had been contrived to accommodate the family on Second Street.

Lizzie furnished each room, bordering the first-floor windows with heavy rose silk drapes. On either side of the buffet, she installed mother-of-pearl light fixtures. She fashioned a comfortable breakfast room and a well-equipped kitchen. On the glass pane that formed the upper part of the door leading from the kitchen to the backyard, a glazier cut a subdued, but definite, letter "B."

Finally, her new home was christened. One word was carved with bold block letters into the top stone riser of the steps facing the street: *Maplecroft*.

Within the same week that Lizzie moved into her new home, Hosea Knowlton's young prosecutor, William Moody, received an unusual package. It contained press clippings of the trial and pertinent illustrations, including photographs of the bodies. It was accompanied by a polite note from Lizzie. She had sent them "as a memento of an interesting occasion."

It had been, indeed, an "interesting occasion," but the murders had not been solved.

When a murder and trial have aroused the kind of enormous interest as did the Lizzie Borden case, the public's desire for information did not end with the verdict. A trial like this one increased the newspaper circulation for dozens of papers, and as long as there was public interest, no editor was going to sit back and pull back his reporters. Lizzie found this out first-hand when she stepped out of the courtroom after the trial and was immediately surrounded by reporters, all of them demanding to know her future plans. With the exception of Mrs. McGuirk, who had been successful on the basis of friendship and knowing Lizzie personally from charitable causes, Lizzie had rebuffed repeated attempts by reporters to interview her, and she made little effort, while awaiting trial, to sway public opinion. She would not talk to reporters, and worse, never bothered to deny stories no matter how patently false they were. She continued this practice for the rest of her life. If the theory which I believe about this case is true, it served her well to simply stay quiet, but if not, she would have been far wiser to have acted otherwise, particularly during the first weeks after the trial. Reporters could have gotten their follow-up stories, the public's curiosity would have been somewhat satisfied, and she would not have been watched so closely.

In the first excitement immediately after the verdict, Lizzie did speak briefly to the newsmen who crowded around her in the courtroom. Julian Ralph of the *New York Sun* quoted her as saying, "A good many persons have talked to me as if they thought I would go and live somewhere else when my trial was over. I don't know what possesses them. I am going home and I am going to stay there. I never thought of doing anything else."

This statement was typical of the Borden stiff-necked pride, stubbornness, and arrogance, which Lizzie had inherited from her father. She was always blunt and forthright when she spoke, even when it did her more harm than good – such as when she told a police officer that Abby was "not her mother." Her direct way of speaking, without softening her words, antagonized people and helped to build the legend that began to swirl about her.

There would be writers who would claim that some newspapers were quite maudlin and sentimental in the way that the press went after continuing news about Lizzie. Determined to get their follow-up stories, reporters kept the house on Second Street under watch and shouted questions at anyone who appeared outside the door. Lizzie was unable to resume any normal activities, which led to her escape to Newport. Some of the reporters who were hard-pressed for news were not above inventing a few stories to keep their far-off editors happy, and these reports often found their way into legend. For instance, when Lizzie later made a trip to Taunton to see Mrs. Wright, matron of the county jail, wife of the sheriff, and long-time friend of the family, the editor of the local paper there sent out a dispatch saying that Lizzie had surrendered herself to Sheriff Wright. He later explained, somewhat lamely, that he had put out a "jocose statement."

Undoubtedly, Lizzie found no humor in it, but again, legends are much easier to start than to stop. She was already being harassed with the four-live verse about the axe, which had become a great favorite with children in Fall River who sang it while jumping rope and playing other games. It didn't matter that no one had been given "40 whacks," or that Lizzie had been acquitted of the crimes. The children didn't stop using it, and adults laughingly continued to repeat it.

But through it all, Lizzie said nothing.

The legend had been building during the months before the trial, and while the acquittal temporarily halted the stories, Lizzie's continued cold-shouldering of the press resulted in incidents that swelled the legend. The *Fall River Globe* was quiet for a time after the trial, but emboldened by Lizzie's silence, the paper returned to its private war against her and printed every rumor that its reporters could gather. It also began a custom of celebrating the anniversary date of the murders with stories filled with innuendo and carrying such headlines as *Perhaps Murderer or Murderess May Be in the City. Who Can Tell?* The paper still aimed its editorial appeal at those who had grievances, real or imagined, against Lizzie.

When a reporter from the *Providence Journal* called at Maplecroft for an interview and was turned away, he began an ugly, one-sided battle with Lizzie. In an editorial on June 21, 1893, the paper wrote, "There is no reason now for Miss Borden's silence; let her speak! Let her spare no effort to bring this horrible case to a more satisfactory conclusion than it now has reached, which so much evidence barred out by the Court, and the presumption of innocence so strenuously insisted upon by the Judge in his charge to the jury." The *Journal* was one of the most widely-read newspapers in the region and its effect on public opinion was chilling.

Two days later, the dismissed reporter struck again. He assaulted "Lizzie's other kind of champion, the Reverend W. Walker Jubb, who obviously thinks that the fact of Miss Borden's attendance at his church should immediately hush all inquiry into her connection with the murders."

Even though she did not attend Reverend Jubb's church, he was a close friend, and Lizzie and her defenders were emerging as objects of ridicule as other newspapers joined in on the attack. Lizzie may have been found "not guilty" in the court of law, but the court of public opinion was turning out to be another story.

After moving into her new home, Lizzie, for the first time since her acquittal, attended services at the Congregational Church on Rock Street, where she had devoted so much of her time and energy over the years. She had grown up in the church and it had been the center of her social life. Here she had taught Sunday

School before the murders, and from its pulpit, Reverend Buck had vigorously defended her after she was arrested.

Entering through the side door, Lizzie sat in the family pew, just as she had so many hundreds of times in the past. Immediately, those sitting near her got up and began moving away, leaving her surrounded by empty pews.

Lizzie never went back.

Even though when she was in jail, no one wanted to see Lizzie sentenced to death for murder, but as the press lampooned her as "the self-made heiress," it was glaringly obvious that whoever was responsible for the deaths of Andrew and Abby Borden had gotten away with murder. Either Lizzie, or someone very clever, very lucky, or very protected from prosecution had fooled the police, the press, and the law. Now they were stymied. Lizzie could not be tried again and no new evidence had been discovered to open the case. Marshal Hilliard had officially marked the investigation "closed."

Seven months after the acquittal, on January 22, 1894, Emma filed documents that gave Lizzie her portion of their father's inheritance. The papers, witnessed by Andrew Jennings, were filed at the courthouse in Taunton.

It was also in 1894, soon after the inheritance was divided, that the deceitful reporter Edwin H. Porter of the *Fall River Globe* published his account of the murders and the trial, calling it *The Fall River Tragedy*. It was printed privately by a small company in Fall River and was the first book on the subject that was written – from Porter's bitterly skewed viewpoint. In the preface, Porter stated "the desire to give the reading public a connected story of the whole case, commencing with the day of the tragedy and ending with the day that Miss Borden was set free. That the grand jury indicted the young lady was no fault of the author, and the story of what brought that indictment about is important – therefore it is given without prejudice." Of course, as has been pointed out throughout this volume, Porter's book – along with his newspaper articles during the investigation and trial – were highly prejudiced. He was one of the first to call for Lizzie's indictment in print and painted her in the most unflattering manner possible, almost single-handedly creating the legend of her lack of empathy and emotion after the murders.

Porter's presentation of the evidence made a strong case for Lizzie's guilt, but his book ends on a face-saving note: "Thus ended, on the thirteenth day, the famous trial of Lizzie Andrew Borden, and she returned guiltless to her friends and home in Fall River." His sarcasm dripped from the page.

Legend then has it that Lizzie immediately bought up all the available copies of Porter's book and had them burned. In truth, no one can say for certain that it was Lizzie who bought them, but she most likely did. Regardless, all but four copies of the book were destroyed and the text remained very hard to find until recent years, when it was reprinted.

At the same time, Lizzie was also being snubbed by the group of women who had once staunchly defended her – the Women's Christian Temperance Union (W.C.T.U.), which had rented space in the A.J. Borden Building from her father. According to an article in the *Fall River News*, Lizzie "felt that she should not put up with insults from her tenants, and accordingly, the W.C.T.U. has been compelled to seek quarters elsewhere. The affair has caused considerable indignation among the eighty members of the local branch." What transpired between Lizzie and her one-time supporters will never be known, but this was one more incident to upset Lizzie's already frazzled nerves.

Meanwhile, a judge from Plymouth, Massachusetts, named Charles Gideon Davis had just published a series of articles in the *Boston Daily Advertiser*. In them, he accused Judge Dewey of acting not as an impartial judge, but as Lizzie's advocate during the trial, "by teaching the jury to distrust every important item of evidence offered by the prosecution in the case." Davis did not accuse Dewey of corrupt motives, but he charged that Dewey had been unconsciously overcome by bias and prejudice in Lizzie's favor. Judge Davis' overall view of the case was that "it was not the prisoner but the Commonwealth which did not have a fair trial." He published an attack on everyone who had believed Lizzie innocent in the case, even before she had been put on trial and the evidence against her had been presented:

There is a natural and uncontrolled repulsion against the barbarism of coldly putting to death a fellow human being... this repulsion is warping the law of criminal evidence in capital cases... This feeling exalts a prisoner charged with a crime into a hero, and sends flowers to him. It induces philanthropic women, whose life is spent in going about doing good, to volunteer during a trial their unsworn testimony to the character of the prisoner, even to deposing without cross-examination that women burn their clothes three months old in stoves.

A little more than a year before, the *New York Times* had commented on the legal officers who had secured Lizzie's indictment and conducted her trial:

They were guilty of a barbarous wrong to an innocent woman and a gross injury to the community. And we hold it to be a misfortune that their victim has no legal recourse against them and no means of bringing them to account. Her acquittal is only a partial atonement for the wrong that she has suffered.

Public sentiment for the demure Sunday School teacher had certainly taken a downward turn.

Early one morning, Lizzie's carriage and coachman were recognized outside of Fall River's largest dry goods store, E. S. Brown and Company, at the corner of Main Street and Franklin. When Lizzie emerged from the store, more than 30 curiosity-seekers were waiting to catch a glimpse of her. They began calling out remarks and pointing at her as she quickly got into the carriage and drove away.

As Joe Howard had once written: "The great Beecher used to say that a public man couldn't blow his nose on his doorstep, without its report being echoed through the entire city, and so it has been with Lizzie Borden, whether she washed her face, wiped her eyes, blew her nose, puckered her mouth, or raised her hand, whatever she did, wherever she went, she was an object of curiosity and unmitigated assault by the gossips of the time."

Lizzie likely thought back to the remarks that she had made to the reporter when she stepped out of the courtroom on the day of her acquittal. "I am going home and I am going to stay there," she said. "I never thought of doing anything else."

Looking back, she probably wondered if that had been a mistake. Since the incident at the Central Congregational Church, she had been shunned by those who had once rallied to her side. Even though the legal trial was over, she was now being tried by the people of the town where she had spent her entire life. They were people who no longer considered her a woman they were proud to know. They had been relieved when she had been acquitted, but only so that there would be no more scandal. So many who had watched her grown from a young girl to a fine woman, and then witnessed the upheaval of the past few years, remained tight-lipped, but were firmly convinced that she had murdered her parents.

Shortly after the acquittal, Lizzie, with her curly hair still gathered into auburn waves and dressed expensively in the latest fashions, was often noticed on the streets of Fall River. But now, threatened with mounting recriminations in the press, Lizzie's defense was to withdraw from the public eye.

But, in so doing, she became even more famous.

At the Fall River railroad station, hackers met the trains from Boston and advanced on the passengers yelling, "Come see the notorious Lizzie Borden home – where she now lives!" Carriages of sightseers would pull up in front of Maplecroft as the tour guide, taking out his whip and pointing at the house, would deliver a history of Lizzie and the bloody details of the murders. For this, each tour guest was charged 25-cents.

Maplecroft was Lizzie's refuge – and her prison. She was determined to become self-sufficient. Unable to shop without being followed by staring crowds, she had all of her groceries delivered to a box at the back of the house. When she did leave the house, she dressed in a formidable black outfit with a veil for excursions into town. She knew that people were whispering and pointing at her, but she carried herself like an actress on the stage.

But the press would not leave her alone.

On December 10, 1896, a brief article that appeared in the *Boston Globe* was picked up by newspapers throughout the country:

Is Lizzie Borden to Marry?

Fall River, Mass., Dec. 10 – Friends of Lizzie Andrew Borden, who was once accused of the murder of her father and stepmother and whose trial was one of the most famous the country has known, are congratulating her upon the approach of her marriage. The husband-to-be is one Mr. Gardner, a school teacher of the village of Swansea, which lies a few miles across the bay to the west of the city. He has been a friend of Miss Borden since childhood days, which they spent upon adjoining farms. The engagement has been rumored about for weeks, but it lacked confirmation until a few days ago, when it was learned that Miss Borden has given to a well-known dressmaker an order for a trousseau. Mr. Gardner has had erected in South Somerset a fine new house. It is said that the wedding will probably take place about Christmas.

The residents of the farm adjacent to the one which Andrew Borden had owned in Swansea were named Gardner. And the eldest son was a school teacher. But the rest of the story of Lizzie's romance and impending marriage had been fabricated.

Soon after the article appeared, reporters from out-of-town newspapers flooded into Fall River. Gardner went into hiding and Lizzie vanished behind the locked doors of Maplecroft, where she was harassed by the reporters. She was both disturbed and infuriated by the incident, which had all of the markings of a cruel prank. Two days later, she wrote to Mrs. Cummings, a dressmaker that she and Emma had long done business with, and the woman who was allegedly making her wedding gown. The letter's significance was that it revealed the strain that Lizzie was under. Lizzie wrote:

My dear Friend,

I am more sorry than I can tell you that you have had any trouble over the false and silly story that has been about the last week or so. How or when it started I have not the least idea. But never for a moment did I think that you or your girls started it. Of course I am feeling very badly about it and I must just bear as I have in the past. I do hope you will not be annoyed again. Take care of yourself, so you can get well.

Yours sincerely,
L.A. Borden

The strange story soon faded from the news, but within two months, Lizzie made the front pages of newspapers again --- a warrant had been issued for her arrest on another charge.

In September of 1896, Lizzie had entered the Tilden–Thurber Company, a stylish art gallery located on the upper floor of the Westminster Street building in Providence, Rhode Island. Since 1790, its collection of silver and art replicas had been considered the finest in New England.

On the day that Lizzie visited, Miss Addie B. Smith was in charge of the sales floor. After she was informed who her famous visitor was, Miss Smith paid particular attention to Lizzie as she waited on her. Lizzie asked to see a vase, which Addie had to go to the back of the building to find. When she returned with it, Lizzie decided that it was not what she wanted and hastily left the gallery. At that time, she had been the only customer in the gallery.

Lizzie spent years harassed by reporters and curiosity-seekers after the trial. The public had turned against her.

A few moments after Lizzie left, Addie Smith noticed that one large and one small porcelain painting were missing from the stand where they had been displayed. Addie also recalled that Lizzie had been wearing a voluminous fur coat. Perplexed, she immediately reported the matter to her employer, Mr. Henry Tilden.

Tilden told her that there was nothing that could be done about the situation.

Five months later, in early February 1897, a lady unknown to Miss Smith entered the art gallery. Walking up to the counter, she opened a package that contained the larger of the two missing paintings. She explained that she had received it as a Christmas gift from Lizzie Borden. It had been damaged and she brought it in to be repaired. Of course, Addie recognized the stolen painting but she told the woman that she would find out how long it would take to have it repaired, then excused herself. Hurrying at once to find Mr. Tilden, Addie told him what had happened. He instructed her not to let the woman know that she was suspicious, just to take her name and address and tell her to come back in two weeks. Addie did as she was told. The lady wrote down her information and left the gallery.

Immediately, Henry Tilden notified the Providence police. Chief Detective Patrick H. Parker was given all of the necessary information and he agreed at once to leave for Fall River.

Lizzie was shaken when Parker appeared at her front door. She immediately denied that she had stolen the paintings. They were hers, she said, and she had a right to give them to whoever she chose.

When Parker returned to Providence the next day, Henry Tilden swore out a warrant for Lizzie's arrest. Tilden's associate, Morris House, was called in to confer as a member of the firm. He advised that Lizzie should be asked to visit Tilden-Thurber in an attempt to clarify the situation.

The following evening, in the darkened, after-hours offices of Tilden-Thurber, Lizzie met with Henry Tilden, Morris House, and William G. Thurber. Indignantly denying all accusations of theft, Lizzie claimed that she had legitimately purchased the items. She asserted that she was being hounded because of her association with the murders of her father and stepmother. As the three men were undecided about what to do next, they asked her to return for another conference. Before she left, Tilden told her, "Unless this situation is resolved, we shall have to publicize the incident."

Henry Tilden had been an avid follower of Lizzie's trial, and he – like many others – was firmly convinced that she had committed the murders, and had gotten away with it. A day later, he met with Stephen C. Metcalf, an editor at the *Providence Journal*. Tilden confided to his friend that he had an opportunity to succeed where everyone else had failed. He was convinced that because he had the power to send Lizzie to jail as a shoplifter, he could make her confess to the murders. Metcalf was dubious, but Tilden said that with the newspaper's ability to publicize the affair, he could make it work. She would, he believed, exchange her freedom now for a confession about what she did in 1892. Metcalf doubted the outcome, but Tilden was persuasive, and he eventually agreed to go along.

With that agreement, five men – Henry Tilden, Morris House, Detective Parker, Stephen C. Metcalf, and William Thurber – began a confidence game against Lizzie Borden.

Metcalf ordered a portrait of her to be drawn by a *Journal* artist. Beside it was an article that was type-set with a headline reading:

LIZZIE BORDEN AGAIN
A Warrant for Her Arrest Issued From a Local Court
Two Paintings Missing from Tilden-Thurber Co.'s Store

They put together several mock-ups of this newspaper article, picture, and headline and when Lizzie returned to the store, Tilden showed them to her. As soon as Lizzie glanced at the proofs, she became angry and stated that they wouldn't dare print the story, adding that she would sue them if the article actually appeared.

Tilden replied that she could sue them, but she would never win. He could serve the arrest warrant at any time, but there was a way out of the situation, he told her. If she would clarify the question of the Borden murders, she could avoid jail. Sign a confession that she had committed them, he said, and the theft charges would disappear.

Lizzie refused. She rushed out the room and left the building.

The following morning, the story was on the front page of the *Providence Journal*. The humiliating news was given to Andrew Jennings by a reporter and his response appeared in the same edition:

Andrew J. Jennings of Fall River, who was engaged as counsel by Miss Borden when she was first suspected of murdering her father and mother, and who defended her in the Second District Court at the preliminary hearing of the case, would have nothing to say yesterday when informed that it was reported that a warrant has been issued for her arrest on a complaint charging his former client with shoplifting. That is, Mr. Jennings said nothing to indicate that he had the slightest knowledge of any such offence on Miss Borden's part, and intimated that he did not believe there was any foundation for the story.

As soon as the paper came out, Detective Parker returned to Maplecroft. He showed Lizzie the front page. "I am authorized to serve the warrant, but a postponement is possible if you return to Tilden-Thurber's with me now."

When Lizzie again threatened to sue, the detective scoffed at her. She could try and sue, but if she did not leave with him in a half hour, he was going to serve the warrant.

Blustering and fuming, Lizzie finally calmed down and left the room. Five minutes later, she returned in her coat and went with Parker to Providence. At 6:00 that night, the five men and Lizzie were once more seated around the conference table.

Amateur detective Tilden threatened Lizzie again, warning her that they had already taken the first step to ruin and that if she did not confess that the acts of August 4, 1892, were hers, and hers alone, she would be arrested for theft. If she confessed, she would be a free woman. She could, of course, never be tried for the murders again because of the rules against double jeopardy, but Tilden would have achieved some sort of fame for being the man who gained the confession of the infamous Lizzie Borden.

He told her, "You will be in serious trouble and in jail if you don't sign it. You have my word and I speak for the others as well. I'll never reveal to a living soul what you write on that piece of paper that I have put in the typewriter."

Somewhat startled, Lizzie looked at the typing machine in front of her. There was a piece of blank white paper rolled into it, awaiting her confession. Unnerved by it, she became defiant once more and sat at the table, staring at the men in silence. Hours went by, and by 10:00, all of them were weary. Lizzie looked exhausted – and increasingly desperate.

At 11:15, William Thurber stood up and gestured for Henry Tilden to follow him out of the room. They conferred and decided to make one final try. When they returned, Thurber sat down next to Lizzie and spoke to her: "Miss Borden, anything you do in this room tonight will never be revealed in the lifetime of any of us here. All you have to do is exchange a piece of paper for a jail term of possibly several years. Come, I'll type it out if you wish."

Again, Lizzie refused. A hurried consultation was whispered on the other side of the room.

Thurber returned to the table. "Miss Borden, it is now eight minutes of twelve. I am authorized to state that if you don't sign within eight minutes Detective Parker will serve you the warrant and you'll go to jail. Eight minutes are left."

Lizzie sat very still, looking at William Thurber. The hands on the clock ticked ever closer to midnight, and then finally reached it. The five men looked at each other. Their gamble had failed. Thurber gave a nod to Parker, who stood up and started across the room for the warrant that was in the pocket of his overcoat.

From her silent side of the table, Lizzie hissed a whisper, "Just a minute." She got up slowly from her chair and stepped to the typewriter. Every eye was upon her as she sat down. The room soon echoed with the clack of the keys as she slowly worked the machine. Satisfied, she unrolled the paper and laid it on the table top. A minute later, she reached for a pen, dipped it into the inkwell, and scratched her signature.

She stood up and walked across the room to her coat. Morris House helped her into it. She stood there, silent for a moment, apparently uncertain about what to say. At the door, she paused. Detective Parker was shrugging into his own coat, getting ready to drive her to Fall River. A moment later, she vanished into the hallway. No additional words had crossed her lips.

The four men crowded around the typewriter as soon as she had left, anxious to read what she had written and signed. Across the bone-white paper, only one sentence had been typed:

Unfair means force my signature here admitting the act of August 4 1892 as mine alone.

Lizbeth A. Borden

The next day, House decided to have a copy of the "confession" made, in case the original was lost or destroyed. He went to Boston to have the copy made, perhaps fearing that the story of the secret incident might be leaked. But while in Boston, he did a curious thing – he told the photographer making the copy the whole story of what had occurred. The photographer promised to never reveal what he had been told and, unlike House, actually kept his word. He didn't tell the story to author Edward Rowe Snow until 1952, after all of the men and Lizzie Borden were dead.

House, he said, ordered one print and took it and the negative with him. The photographer did not tell him that he had retained a first print that had not turned out well. A copy of this print was given to Snow, who later discovered that the original had been destroyed in the Tilden–Thurber safe during the New England Hurricane of 1938. The copy was believed destroyed in a fire in 1913.

Snow, along with historian Edward D. Radin, were skeptical of the story, especially since the photographer had asked for $100 to give Snow the poor copy. Snow offered $50 and bought it for that amount, more as a literary curiosity than because he had any belief in it. Snow checked into the validity of the man's story, going no further than to make sure he really had been a photographer in Boston at the time in question. He later turned over the confession copy to Radin, who delved much more deeply into its authenticity.

He noted that the confession was signed "Lizbeth A. Borden." Lizzie began using the name Lizbeth some time after the trial but signed most of her letters "L.A. Borden." No letters had been signed as Lizbeth as early as 1897, when the confession was supposedly written. He also compared the signatures with letters written in 1897. The latter were firm, clear and flowing; the confession signature was shaky and ragged. If the confession story was true, this might be explained by her emotional state at the time, so he made another comparison. Since few samples of her writing were readily available, he decided to track down a public document: her will. Lizzie had actually signed it twice, once as "Lizbeth A. Borden" and then with her legal signature of "Lizzie A. Borden."

He obtained a copy of the will and compared the alleged 1897 signature on the confession with the Lizbeth A. Borden signature on the will, written 29 years later, in 1926. They were remarkably similar – too similar. Except for the fact that the confession signature was written with a broader pen than the one Lizzie used to sign her will, the signatures were identical. The "confession" was a fraud. There was no way that she could have written the confession in 1897 at the age of 37, and then duplicated it so exactly on her will, 29 years later when she was 66, ill, and facing a major operation.

Radin took the two signatures to his editor at Simon and Schuster, Clayton Rawson, and they enlarged them to the same size. They superimposed them one on the other and held them over a light. The two signatures coincided perfectly. The two signatures that were alike suggested only one thing: one must have been traced from the other. The confession signature had been traced from the signature on the will, signed many years later.

Radin had the signatures studied by a handwriting expert named Ordway Hilton, who produced a six-page report that detailed what he already suspected: the confession was fake. He noted that the print in the typed portion of the confession was worn and faded. Hilton believed that it had been typed on an old Caligraph machine, with a type face that was first introduced around 1895. The forger had managed to locate a machine of the proper period, but overlooked the fact that the typewriter would have been almost new in 1897. The type should have been clear and sharp. Instead, the type and roller on the machine that was used were so worn that only many years of use could have accounted for the condition.

The "confession," and the entire story that went along with it became just another part of the legend of Lizzie Borden, a skewing of the facts to make it appear that she had been guilty.

One has to wonder whether or not – if Lizzie truly did go along with a plot to protect her half-brother from prosecution – she took into consideration the damage that would be done to her reputation, her life, and her mental health in the years that followed?

The story of the confession may have been a myth, but the truth is, Lizzie did, indeed, steal the paintings from the art gallery. Why would she have done it? She was a wealthy woman, worth at least a quarter of a million dollars at the turn of the last century. She lived in a large, elegant home in the richest section of Fall River. She owned the A. J. Borden Building, the Union Savings Bank, and her father's share in the mills.

The two porcelain paintings were worth less than $100.

Lizzie's theft of the two paintings seems to have been a classic case of kleptomania – the inability to refrain from the urge to steal items and done for reasons other than personal use or financial gain. Those who suffer from this disorder often feel a sense of release following the act since they also usually suffer from great levels of stress, guilt, and remorse. Whether or not Lizzie ever felt compelled to steal in other instances is unknown. Perhaps she was never caught. She certainly had no logical reason to steal the paintings. She could have easily afforded them. That she may have suffered from some type of mental disorder can hardly be a surprise, though. She had been shunned by many who once supported her, ostracized by the community, harassed by reporters, believed to be a brutal killer by most of the general public, and had few left who loved her, other than her sister – and that would not last much longer.

Lizzie Borden had become an outcast in the town where she had been born and raised. Even though the story of the confession was a lie, the article that had appeared on the front page of the *Providence Journal* about the theft had damned her forever. There was no one left for her to turn to. She no longer went to church. Even Reverend Jubb had deserted her.

After the incident, fewer and fewer of her friends called and she began to spend her days sitting idly in the sun behind the walls of her property. Lizzie Borden had retreated from the world, but in far too many ways, the world refused to leave her alone.

On the twelfth anniversary of the murders, as it had for each of the prior 11 years, the *Fall River Globe* lashed out at Lizzie:

August 4, 1904
A DOZEN YEARS
Since the Bordens were Brutally Butchered, and Yet the Horrible Crime is Unpunished,
Perhaps Murderer or Murderess, May be in the City – Who Can Tell?

The long article that followed stretched down the *Globe's* front page:

A dozen years!

What a long time it seems, yet how quickly passed in this busy, practical world, where so few people have the time to devote to retrospection or reflection, on all the good, and all the evil that is encompassed in the historic chronicle of such a period of time.

Twelve years ago this morning, when God's radiant sunshine was dispelling its August warmth, and casting its brilliant reflection over all in this peaceful community, the just and the unjust, the rich and the poor, the contented and the envious, the Pharisee and the publican, there sallied from the midsummer peace, on outrage bent, a demon in human form, who quickly accomplished hellishness, was destined to make Fall River occupy a place in the centre of the state under the entire country's observation, such as has been the misfortune of few civilized communities to stand in.

The *Globe* recalled every detail of that August morning, as it urged the residents of Fall River to never forget that a disgrace to their lives had occurred and that someone was still out there who needed to answer for it. But the insinuations in the attack left no doubt as to who the editors believed that "someone" might be:

Who that recalls that sultry, sickening day of an even dozen years ago, will ever forget the day of the deed? Who knows, even now, that the vile-minded murderer may not be at large in the community walking, stalking, or driving about in carriage or in car, seeking the opportunity to make new criminal history?

Perhaps the good people of Fall River maybe daily meeting him – or her – in hall or store, or railroad train, and, oh, what a frightful contemplation there arises, if such be the fact, that it is due to a miscarriage of justice in the grand old state of Massachusetts, the cradle of liberty, of advancement, of just judges and historic statesmen! And what a saddening and solemn reflection it must be for those who were near and dear to the murdered pair in life, to think that they have never been called upon to pay out the $5000 reward for the detection of the murderer, where they would have been so happy to spend that small portion of his hoarded wealth in hunting down those who robbed them of their father and mother – no, step-mother, please!... And how the good and kindly disposed people of the town were shocked to hear the people who know what they were talking about, mention their suspicions as to the identity of the murderer – or murderess! ... Perhaps before another year rolls around, self-accusing conscience may have taken up the task laid down by the criminal law authorities of the state and the man – or woman – who shocked the people of two continents with one of the most ghastly, cruel, selfish, and brutal double murders 12 years ago, deliver himself – or herself – into the hands of the avenging law, as an escaped criminal. What can tell?

The *Fall River Globe* had always been one of Lizzie's greatest enemies. From the day after the murders, when it published Hiram Harrington's interview that strongly suggested that Lizzie had committed the crimes, the *Globe* had never ceased trying to convict her in print.

By now, though, it was 1904, early in a brand new century. Most of the police officers, officials, and characters in the case had either died or faded into history.

Lizzie's trial had caused the press to focus almost continually on five of them – Andrew Jennings, former Governor Robinson, Hosea Knowlton, William Moody and Judge Dewey. During the 13 days of testimony leading up to Lizzie's acquittal, drawings and depictions of them had appeared in every newspaper in the country.

Although unable to convict Lizzie – a frustration that was prepared to face before the trial ever began – Prosecutor Knowlton realized his ambitions. One year after the trial, he replaced Arthur E. Pillsbury as Attorney General of Massachusetts. He served as the Attorney General for eight years before retiring into public practice. After an injury that he suffered falling from a streetcar in 1902, he had a serious stroke later that year and passed away on December 18. He was only 57-years-old when he passed away.

Ironically, Andrew Jennings succeeded Knowlton as District Attorney of Bristol County. In exchange for his defense of Lizzie, Jennings was named by Emma and Lizzie to the board of directors of the Globe Yarn Mill, a company that their father had owned. He also remained in the District Attorney's office until 1898. Jennings had been retired for some years and was enjoying private life when he suffered a small stroke. He was hospitalized, but never recovered. He died 10 weeks later on October 19, 1923.

Governor George Robinson collected the lavish sum of $25,000 for his defense of Lizzie. After the trial, he returned to his private law practice in Chicopee, Massachusetts. Oddly, he also suffered a stroke, which occurred in February 1896 and he died peacefully a few days later at the age of 62.

William Moody, the passionate young district attorney from Essex County who had assisted Knowlton, gained national prominence. He was elected to the U.S. House of Representatives from Massachusetts, and served from 1895 until 1902. During President Theodore Roosevelt's administration, Moody served as the Secretary of Navy and then was appointed Attorney General in 1904. Two years later, after failing to convince William Howard Taft to take the seat, Roosevelt nominated Moody as an Associate Justice of the U.S. Supreme Court. Moody was confirmed December 17, 1906. By 1908, Moody suffered from severe rheumatism, which affected him to such an extent that his last sitting on the bench was May 7, 1909, when he left for a brief rest and never returned. Moody was only 55, but President Taft encouraged him to step down. After Taft successfully lobbied Congress for a Special Act to grant Moody retirement benefits not normally granted unless justices reached age 70 or served for 10 years, Moody retired from the Court on November 20, 1910. He died in Haverhill, Massachusetts, July 2, 1917.

Criticized by the anti-Lizzie faction, as well as fellow judges like Charles Davis and John Wigmore, Judge Dewey survived the attacks and remained an associate justice until his death in 1900.

But the people of Fall River had not forgotten the case, and neither had the *Globe*, which grimly reminded its readers:

He – or she – is enjoying at least the waking hours of daily life very much as the neighbors, well fed, well dressed, well waited on, however the still hours of the night may be passed, whether in the solace of refreshing slumber, or in the viewing of phantom pictures of the hideous scenes of twelve years ago this morning. Who can tell?

And it's likely that Lizzie was haunted by "phantom pictures of hideous scenes" as she lay restless in her bed at night. If you accept the theory that the murders were committed by Lizzie's estranged half-brother, who committed the bloody acts without Lizzie's knowledge, leaving her to find the slaughtered corpses, then you understand how traumatized she must have been and how the horrific events of that August morning would have haunted her sleepless hours. In these pages (as well as in other books), it's been proven that Lizzie could not have carried out the murders herself. So, even if the William Borden theory seems like bunk to you, you have to accept the fact that Lizzie walked into the parlor of the house on Second Street and came upon the brutalized corpse of the man she loved most in the world. Cold and uncaring to most, Andrew Borden was Lizzie's beloved father. Try and put yourself in her place and then imagine what it would be like to have a vision of your own bloody father waiting for you in your dreams.

And then there was the stigma of the trial, the fact that the murders were unsolved and made Lizzie look suspicious, the shunning by the towns people, the betrayal of her friends, the cold shoulder from the congregation at her church, the constant badgering by reporters, the incessant, thinly veiled accusations printed in the newspapers, and that song – that damnable piece of doggerel, made up by an unknown source, and repeated in singsong by children as they played in the streets of town. It was a simple rhyme that left no doubt that Lizzie had murdered her parents. Even Theodore Roosevelt confessed to being amused the first time that he heard it. There seemed to be no one who hadn't heard it – just as there seemed to be no one who didn't accept it as fact.

Lizzie Borden took an axe,
And gave her mother forty whacks.
And when she saw what she had done,
She gave her father forty-one.

Is it any wonder that Lizzie Borden was driven half-mad?

Lizzie made an attempt to reinvent herself, or at least to depict herself more elegantly. Ridding herself forever of the childish sounding "Lizzie," she changed her name to Lizbeth A. Borden.

In spite of the feelings of many of the people in Fall River, Lizzie had a full staff at Maplecroft – and she paid them well. There was a housekeeper, a cook, second maid, and a coachman. Besieged by reporters eager to concoct a story that they could spin into an "exclusive" revelation about her life, Lizzie ordered the glazed windows of the cellar barred so that no intruder could get inside. Needless to say, her neighbors were dismayed – one did not put bars on the windows of a house on The Hill.

In the basement, hidden away from the world, surrounded by various small rooms for storage, Lizzie installed a billiards rooms with felt cue holders lining the walls. On the second floor, the ceilings of all the rooms were covered in white linen, except for one: the front sunroom leading from Lizzie's bedroom. It was done in gold leaf. The walls beneath it were covered with chocolate brown wallpaper, embossed with bright pink flowers. In this room, which looked out over French Street, Lizzie kept a large library of leather-bound books, collected over the years.

In the adjacent room, near her bed, was a brick fireplace. Carved into the cherry mahogany mantelpiece, was a phrase from a little-known Scottish poem:

The green leaf of loyalty's beginning to fall.
The bonnie White Rose it is withering an' all.
But I'll water it with the blood of usurping tyranny.
And green it will grow in my ain countrie.

In 1901, Lizzie had thousands of pounds of stone carted in to build a fireplace onto the back of the house. It became part of a private bedroom with a separate staircase that she constructed to move her farther away from Emma's room and give her seclusion to look out over the multitude of bird feeders below. Each morning, cardinals, woodpeckers, catbirds, orioles, and black-capped chickadees gathered in the yard, offering her perhaps more pleasure than she experienced at any other time of her day.

But even so, none of that fulfilled her. The restlessness and loneliness that had grown over the years since the trial caused her to disappear from Fall River for days at a time. Alone, she journeyed to Washington, New York, and Boston. In Boston, a carriage driver met her at the Back Bay Station and drove her to the Bellevue Hotel, near the State House. It was always the same driver, paid handsomely to remain at her disposal. The staff at the hotel discreetly pretended not to know who she was.

Lizzie went out in the mornings to go shopping. In the afternoon, she visited the art museums. Finally, in the evening, she went to the theater. The theater had always been one of her great loves, ever since her trip to Europe, where she had seen Sarah Bernhardt and Lillie Langtry perform.

In February 1904, she attended a performance of *Macbeth* at Boston's Colonial Theatre. In the part of Lady Macbeth was an actress that Lizzie had never seen before. She was cool and beautiful, a tall, light-haired young woman with veiled, haunting blue eyes. Onstage, as the young actress wildly encouraged her husband to murder the king, she suddenly became fiery and incredibly emotional. The *Boston Daily Transcript* had noted the actress' ability to bring audiences "a portrayal of supreme power, a rage bordering on madness."

Lizzie went back to see *Macbeth* over and over. As her fascination with the young actress grew, she began to slowly, brick by brick, build the wall that would cut her off from her sister for the rest of her life.

Like Lizzie, Emma had not fully recovered from the ordeal of the trial and murder, but unlike her sister, Emma made little attempt to do so. She continued to wear black, years after her father's death. She clothed her small, slim body in long, severe, silk dresses. Much of her time was spent on the second floor of Maplecroft in a white, cell-like room. In one closet, she kept her few personal belongings. She rarely traveled and took no part in social activities.

Prior to the murders, she had seldom gone to services, but now she steadfastly attended the Central Congregational Church. It was seven blocks from French Street and each Sunday morning, she walked there. Sitting alone in the Borden family pew, Emma prayed and sang hymns with all of the members of the congregation who had shunned her sister. Religion had become her life. It may have allowed her to deal with the terrible guilt that she felt if she truly knew who had killed her father and stepmother, as I believe that she did.

Emma had never been a problem to the community. Even though she defended Lizzie at the trial, her own innocence was never questioned. Those who knew her could only sympathize with the terrible strain under which she had been placed as a result of her notorious sister – a sister that Emma could never truly forgive for allowing the horrible crimes to take place.

But soon she would be pushed to her breaking point and Lizzie would be out of her life forever.

On a summer day in 1893 – oddly around the time of Lizzie's acquittal – a 19-year-old teenager from Oakland, California, walked into the Alcazar Theater in San Francisco. The stage-struck young girl's name was Gertrude Lamson. There was a new drama about to go into production and the young woman had brought with her a letter to the director, McKee Rankin, from a family acquaintance who was a newspaper critic. It read: "Here is a young friend of mine who wants to go on the stage. Kindly discourage her."

Rankin did as he was asked and tried to discourage her, but Gertrude was insistent. Finally, he allowed her to audition. Within moments, the brilliant young woman had her first role in Rankin's version of *Trilby* from the du Maurier novel. He signed her to play the heroine.

Shortly before the play opened, Gertrude decided to change her name, combining the names of two famous actresses: the eighteenth-century British actress Nance Oldfield, and the Irish actress Eliza O'Neil. When *Trilby* premiered in San Francisco on October 16, 1893, the billboard announced the debut of a new actress named Nance O'Neil.

The opening-night audience went into an uproar. The young woman had chosen to play one of the scenes, which took place in an artist's studio, with bare feet –

something that was simply not done at the time. McKee Rankin was arrested and hauled into court, where he finally agreed to drop the play from his repertoire.

But Nance O'Neil was unfazed by her troublesome debut. In 1896, she arrived in New York for the smash play *True to Life*. The critic for the *New York Sun* raved, "Where has she gained her stage experience? New York has never heard of Nance O'Neil before, but surely the art of giving such a finely graduated performance does not come by instinct alone. But wherever she hails from, and whoever she may be, Miss O'Neil is an actress with a future." The critic from the *New York Times* added, "I didn't expect such a wonderfully clever girl as Miss O'Neil proved herself to be. How anyone can call her crude passes any comprehension, unless crude means being perfectly natural, for that she certainly is, and may remain so. Naturalness is one of the greatest charms of an actress, and one of the most rare as well."

At the age of 22, Nance began a tour of the country in the role of Hedda Gabler in Henrik Ibsen's play. The critic for the *St. Louis Post-Dispatch* was enthralled with her. He found her to be a "real woman. Her hair is tawny, her thick, well-refined eyebrows are brown, and there is a golden glint in her eyes – eyes that have not decided whether to be grey, green, blue, or brown, but are soft, clear, and expressive. Her mouth is small and exquisitely formed. She is probably five feet five inches tall, slender, and graceful in figure. Her hands are small and soft, and crumple like rose leaves in her grasp."

In 1899, she traveled to Australia, where she was immediately acclaimed as one of the greatest actresses in the world. She appeared in New Zealand, South Africa, and Egypt, where she performed by royal command for the khedive in Cairo. Her next challenge was in London. On September 1, 1902, Nance opened at the Adelphi Theatre in the title role of *Magda*. The critic for the *London Sphere* wrote, "Miss Nance O'Neil made a daring attempt at the Adelphi Theatre on Monday by challenging the comparison with Eleanora Duse, Sarah Bernhardt, and Mrs. Patrick Campbell in the role of Magda. But her boldness won, and the audience, inclined to be critical at the outset, was fairly conquered." One week later, she starred in the tragedy *Elizabeth, Queen of England*, and the *London Morning Post* added to her many accolades, "Miss O'Neil showed that she had fully grasped the character of the great Queen. She played with a passion and often with a subtlety that completely captured her audience."

When Nance traveled to Boston in October 1903, a reporter from the *Herald* asked to visit her in her hotel suite. He found her sitting in the middle of the floor, playing with her Boston terrier and an angora cat. She invited the reporter to join in the romp. He later wrote: "In her sun-flooded apartments her masses of glorious golden hair were caught loosely on top of her shapely head, and held in place by a huge Spanish comb. Nance O'Neil is not always tragic, nor even serious-minded. She impresses from the start as a girl, a very, young girl. She is as unaffected by her great

Nance O'Neil

success as a child. It may be truthfully said that she is even more interesting personally than she is as an actress – and that is saying a very great deal."

The *Herald* reporter asked her why she never smiled onstage and Nance replied, "I can't very well tell why. I have a sense of humor, though people may not believe it, and I love fun, though I may not appear to. But in most of my plays I have no occasion to smile. I am usually in tears."

The reporter concluded his piece with these words: "She is subject to melancholy. She is decidedly moody in temperament. There is a constant intermingling of sunshine and shadow in her nature. And this is what makes her so entirely fascinating."

She told the reporter that her role as Lady Macbeth would be her greatest challenge. She would be opening at the Colonial Theatre in Boston on February 23, 1904 – the performance that was attended by Miss Lizzie Borden of Fall River.

It was not until six months after the performance at the Colonial Theatre that Lizzie actually met Nance O'Neil. The meeting occurred at a large summer hotel in Tyngsboro, Massachusetts. Nance was about to star in the play *Judith* at Boston's Tremont Theatre and had purchased a beautiful summer home nearby, known as Brindley Farm.

Unfortunately, she could barely afford the down payment. Despite her success, she was in desperate need of money. Her finances, managed by her mentor, McKee Rankin, were in chaos. Most of the expenses of the acting company in which she toured had been deducted from her share of the profits. In December 1903, all of her properties and costumes had been attached by a theatrical manager in Chicago, William Cleveland, who claimed that she and Rankin had defrauded him of several hundred dollars. She had been forced to borrow money to open in Boston. Heavily in debt, she was now being sued by E.J. Ratcliff, a Boston manager, for commissions that he alleged she owed him when he attempted to raise more money for her company.

Nance and Lizzie hit it off immediately. Lizzie was so taken with her new friends that she began to shower her with gifts. In time, she not only paid off all of Nance's legal expenses in the suit filed by Ratcliff, but accompanied her to the courtroom throughout the proceedings.

The two women became inseparable. Was it simply the case of two lonely women who found another lost soul in the other, creating a deep bond of friendship? Or was it, as many have suggested, a romantic affair? It was an era when such things were certainly not discussed in the open.

They were very much alike, and yet markedly different too. Nance could be as unpredictable and rebellious as Lizzie, yet there was a difference. She was from the West and possessed neither the Puritanical moralism nor the tense prudishness of a New Englander. She could be wildly eccentric and colorful, fiery, and uncontrollably passionate. She was an actress at a time when this was not seen as a respectable profession, and Nance threw herself into her art with such blinding emotionalism that she never considered her lifestyle as anything other than normal, despite the fact that it was usually considered unseemly work for a young woman in the early 1900s.

Perhaps for this reason – as well as many others – Emma Borden despised Nance. As the intimacy between Lizzie and Nance grew, Emma became more resentful. With her proper nature, Emma couldn't help but disapprove of what Nance did for a living. She would never be socially acceptable to her because, at that time, social attitudes still regarded an actress as a loose woman, no matter how well regarded she was while she was on the stage. It's also likely that Emma was jealous of the relationship between the two of them. Lizzie had, for the first time in her life, a close friend. Prior to that, Emma had really been her closest confidante. They had shared everything, but the murders and the trial had ruined all of that and they had never been close again. Emma had retreated into her own private world and Lizzie had been trapped into a forced seclusion that she so desperately wanted to escape.

And it may have been more than that. Emma was still haunted by the murders and the secret that she shared with her sister over exactly what had happened on that August morning. She hated the constant publicity that Lizzie had attracted. Lizzie had withstood the trial, the accusations, the waves of newspapers articles, but Emma was terrified by them. She wanted to forget what had happened – even if the world would not. She only wanted to be left alone, but Lizzie was making that impossible.

Finally, after several months, Lizzie's invitation to Nance to stay with her in Fall River was more than Emma could stand. Emma had attempted to isolate herself in her cell-like room on the second floor of Maplecroft, but Lizzie ended her attempts at seclusion when she threw a tremendous party for Nance and the entire acting company one night at Maplecroft. Caterers arrived with lavish trays of food, there were hired palm trees and an orchestra. Maplecroft blared with music and life. It was the fulfillment of Lizzie's childhood dreams: the beautiful home that her father could have afforded to give her, but had not, filled with interesting, exotic, talented people.

Emma was furious and left the house that night. For a while, she stayed with Reverend Jubb's sister, who had befriended her, and then with friends in Fairhaven. Finally she moved to Minden House, a residential hotel in Providence.

Meanwhile, Lizzie remained entranced with Nance. She followed her to Tyngsboro, where the parties and music continued. Subsequent reports of wild behavior and alcoholic improprieties reached the people of Fall River and were discussed by the members of the Women's Christian Temperance Union, of which Lizzie had once been a member. Rumors spread throughout town that Lizzie's "friendship" with Nance O'Neil was something much more than that. It became common knowledge that Lizzie and her sister had parted ways because of it. Even newspaper articles hinted about their relationship, telling the story of Emma and Lizzie's split and noting that Lizzie was "a warm friend of Nance O'Neil."

But if there was a romantic relationship, it was destined not to last.

After years of touring on her own, Nance was suddenly "discovered" by David Belasco, the famed director. He had recently lost his major leading lady, Mrs. Leslie Carter, and immediately needed a star to replace her. Belasco offered Nance a part in his new play, *The Lily*, with the stipulation that he sign her to an exclusive contract so that he could manage her career.

In order to join with Belasco, Nance parted ways with McKee Rankin in December 1909. Rankin immediately sued her in New York. The *New York Times* reported: "Counsel for Miss O'Neil contended that Mr. Rankin had no claim on her exclusive management. Mr. Rankin, counsel said, had borrowed money on her jewels, and the last thing he did was require seventy-five dollars a week from her." Finally, to make the lawsuit go away, Belasco had settled with Rankin for Nance's contract.

Nance had left Lizzie's life as well.

There is no evidence as to what occurred between the two women, although we do know that Nance's financial situation continued to worsen and Lizzie was not around to bail her out this time. In February 1906, the mortgage for Brindley Farm was due, but Lizzie did not assist her. Nance lost the farm because she could not come up with the $7,500 necessary to avoid foreclosure.

It's possible that Nance began to see her association with someone as notorious as Lizzie as detrimental to her career, or perhaps she just felt so stifled in the relationship that she had to free herself from it. She may have felt trapped by the strict New England morals that looked upon both actresses and unconvicted murderesses as social pariahs. Or, maybe she just didn't want to be tied down. Nance was, among other things, a free spirit and perhaps no relationship, even one as unconventional as the one she would have had with Lizzie in that era, could make her happy.

We will never know for sure, but we do know that Lizzie and Nance's relationship had destroyed all hope of Emma and Lizzie ever being reunited. The two sisters had not spoken to each other since the night Lizzie had given the party for Nance and the acting company, and Emma had fled from Maplecroft in a rage.

Emma gave some explanation as to what had happened to Edwin J. Maguire, a reporter for the *Boston Sunday Post*, in 1913, the twentieth anniversary of Lizzie's famous murder trial. At first, Maguire had attempted to see Lizzie. As he approached Maplecroft, he noticed that the shades were drawn on all of the windows. He repeatedly rang the front and rear doorbells, but there was no response. Leaving the house, he found a telephone. When he called, the maid summoned Lizzie to the phone. Maguire asked if he could come and see her, but Lizzie curtly told him that she had nothing to say. When he badgered her a little further, she slammed down the phone.

But Maguire was persistent. He learned that Emma was staying in Fall River at the home of Reverend Buck. He called the house on Rock Street that was adjacent to the Central Congregational Church and was stunned to be granted an interview – "the first declaration to the outside world that either sister has made regarding that most notable murder mystery – a butchery on which the faintest light is yet to be shed."

He described Emma as "a gentle-mannered woman, who unhesitatingly led the way from the front portal of the Buck resident to the quaint parlor at the left. She was courtesy and gentility personified. Her tranquil face, sweet of expression and enhanced by a pink and white complexion that a debutante might envy, was crowned with heavy, snow white hair, parted in the center and rippling to the side of the head in curly billows. There was a look of sadness, even of resignation in Miss Borden's large brown eyes. They seemed to reflect the sorrow and grief that were part of the heritage she received through the untimely death of her father. A gray dress, rich in material, but unostentatious in style, bespoke the quiet, retiring character of the woman."

In a parlor decorated with framed scriptural texts and religious paintings, Emma admitted to Maguire that Reverend Buck was "my best friend in the world." It was he "who advised me when matters reached such a pass that I could not stay longer in the same house with Lizzie."

When asked why she had parted with her sister, Emma refused to divulge the details. However, she commented, "I did not go until conditions became absolutely unbearable. I consulted Reverend Buck. After listening to my story he said it was imperative that I should make my home elsewhere. Under the agreement we entered into, Lizzie is to occupy the house as long as she lived, and is to pay me rent for the use of my half." She added, "I do not expect ever to set foot on the place while she lives."

When Maguire asked her about the stories involving Lizzie and Nance O'Neil, Emma had a ready reply: "Nance O'Neil has for years been a close friend of Lizzie, and she holds that relation to this very day." Although since Emma had not spoken with her sister in many years by this time, she had no way of knowing this.

Emma decided to set the record straight about what she knew of the murders: "The day the crime took place I was at Fairhaven on a visit to friends, I hurried home in response to a telegram and one of the first persons I met was Lizzie. She was much affected. Later, when veiled accusations began to be made, she came to me and said, 'Emma, it is awful for them to say that I killed poor father and our stepmother. You know I would not dream of such an awful thing, Emma.' Later, after her arrest and during her trial, Lizzie many times reiterated her protest of innocence to me. And after her acquittal she declared her guiltlessness during conversations that we had at the French Street mansion. Here is the strongest thing that has convinced me of Lizzie's innocence. The authorities never found the axe or whatever implement that it was that figured in the killing. Lizzie, if she had done the deed, could never have hidden the instrument of death so that the police could not find it. Why, there is no hiding place in the old house that would serve for effectual concealment. Neither did she have the time."

To that point, the purpose of Emma's words seemed to be that she wanted to defend Lizzie. But gradually, it became apparent that she was attempting to unburden her own feelings: "Perhaps people wondered why I stood so staunchly by Lizzie during the trial. I'll tell them why. Aside from my feeling as a sister, it was because I constantly had in mind our dear mother. She died when Lizzie was only three years of age, while I had reached twelve years. When my darling mother was on her deathbed, she summoned me, and exacted a promise that I would always watch over 'baby Lizzie.' From childhood to womanhood and up to the time the murder occurred, I tried to safeguard Lizzie… I did my duty at the time of the trial and I am still going to do it in defending my sister even though circumstances have separated us. The vision of my dear mother is always bright in my mind. I want to feel that when Mother and I meet in the hereafter, she will tell me that I was faithful to her trust and that I looked after 'baby Lizzie' to the best of my ability."

Emma's words to Maguire seemed to dramatically affect her. As the reporter listened, Emma's voice became a low moan and then she convulsively began to sob. Clutching the arms of the rocking chair, she abruptly stood up, began pacing back and forth, and attempted to control herself as she pressed a black-bordered handkerchief to her face.

Maguire wrote, "For several minutes the paroxysm of grief continued. Then the little figure straightened slowly to dignified posture, the remaining traces of tears were removed by soft dabs of the handkerchief, and Miss Borden became quite herself once more."

Quietly, she went on, "I intend to defend Lizzie against the harsh public so that Mother will say I have been faithful to my trust. Every Memorial Day I carry flowers to Father's grave. And Lizzie does not forget him. But she generally sends her tribute by a florist."

Suddenly, Emma asked that Maguire leave. The interview was over.

As she led him to the door, he noted the words that Emma murmured under her breath, "Though we must live as strangers, I am still the little mother..."

But the sisters never reconciled. In October 1925, newspapers noted that a legal battle had erupted in Taunton, Massachusetts, between attorneys for Lizzie and Emma Borden. Emma was attempting to sell her share in the A.J. Borden Building, once owned by her father, located in the heart of Fall River's business district. Andrew had constructed the office building two years before his murder. Emma had petitioned the Probate Court at Taunton to sell the property and make an equal distribution between herself and Lizzie.

The significant fact of the story was that the world had not forgotten Lizzie Borden. The news articles that were immediately published revived the story of her trial as if it had just occurred, despite the fact that just about everyone involved – Andrew Jennings, Hosea Knowlton, Governor Robinson, William Moody, Alice Russell, Adelaide Churchill, Dr. Bowen, the police detectives, patrolmen, and medical examiners – were all dead.

But not Lizzie Borden, who personally appeared in the Taunton courtroom. She was 66-years-old, overweight, white-haired, and wearing small wire-rimmed glasses. She was furious at Emma for trying to have the building sold. Like her father, she felt that the roots of the Borden name should be kept intact. That was the reason she had stayed in Fall River all these years, despite the dislike of her neighbors. She was a Borden and her family had founded the town.

As reporters descended on the courthouse, Lizzie settled the matter by quietly buying Emma out.

When the matter was over, she returned to her seclusion at Maplecroft. She had surrounded the mansion and its rolling lawn with a wrought-iron fence and a locked gate. Her driveway led to a sleek, windowed coach house, where she kept her black Packard limousine. In one corner was a gas pump, the only privately owned one in town. Even though Fall River's dislike of Lizzie had not wavered in three decades, she did have a few friends. Librarian Helen Leighton said that Lizzie often spoke longingly of how lovely it would be to take trips to Boston, New York, and Washington, to be in places where nobody recognized her. But her days of travel were over.

Another who liked Lizzie was a young neighbor, Russell Lake. He spoke of her years later: "She made a big hit with me by being my best customer when I had a lemonade stand. Later on, when I left for boarding school, she gave me my first fifty cents. I was one of the privileged children who could run through her yard and climb over the wall to get away from the neighborhood bully... Most other children reflected their parent's views and treated Miss Borden and her house like she was a witch or some person to fear."

Animals became Lizzie's passion, especially the helpless, the stray, or the abused. There were always several cats and litters of kittens around Maplecroft. She purchased peanuts regularly and fed them to the squirrels who roamed her lawn. She took in stray dogs and when they died, had them buried in Pine Ridge of the Animal Rescue League, near a marker she erected that read "Sleeping Awhile."

Occasionally, she would allow a number of children to wander through her backyard, reciting the poetry of Tennyson and Longfellow. Lizzie would listen from an enclosed porch. If it was a cold day, she would invite them inside. Some would be too afraid, but to the brave ones, she offered hot chocolate.

As he got older, Russell Lake recalled, "I still continued to go across the street and visit with Miss Borden whenever I came home from boarding school. She was very generous and kind to anyone who worked for her or was associated with her. A Mrs. McFarland was Miss Borden's dressmaker, as well as my mother's. I know that Miss Borden helped her out financially. Miss Borden also helped her coachman buy a house. Mother told me that she helped his children through college. As kind and good a woman as Miss Borden could never have committed such a gruesome murder.

An elderly Lizzie at Maplecroft. Her later years were dedicated to her care for animals.

It would have to be done by someone with a great hatred and absolutely furious at their victims. Miss Borden was never that kind of woman."

Death eventually came for the Borden sisters, although certainly not with the violence that ended the lives of their father and stepmother – or their half-brother, William, who may have committed the crime that shaped their lives after that August morning in 1892.

Emma Borden eventually reappeared in the tiny town of Newmarket, New Hampshire, more than 100 miles from Fall River. It was a quiet place, hidden away, and not a place that was known as a destination for travelers.

On Main Street, near the railroad tracks that ran through the center of town, stood a large, white, two-story house. On November 9, 1915, the house was purchased from its owner, George K. Leavitt, by Miss Mary Connor for $2,500. But there were certain puzzling elements surrounding the purchase. Mary Connor and her sister, Annie, were middle-aged spinsters who had lived all their lives on a 65-acre farm in Wadleigh Falls, New Hampshire, about two miles from Newmarket. Neither of the Connor sisters had ever been employed and between them they possessed only a small inheritance of a few hundred dollars, left to them by their father, Patrick J. Connor. Consequently, there seemed to be no practical reason why the older sister, Mary, should purchase a second home for her sister and herself – a much larger house in town – while continuing to own the farm and residence in Wadleigh Falls.

Immediately after the Connor sisters moved into their new house, in 1916, a third woman, whom no one in town had ever seen before, quietly joined them, taking over the second-floor front bedroom facing the street. Her identity was unknown, or, as one long-time resident of the town expressed it, "No one made it their business to know who she was."

The mysterious woman never went out in public, although she immediately had installed a modern bathroom leading from her second-floor bedroom, and steam heating throughout the house. The Connor sisters did all of the shopping for the house, while the identity of the woman living with them remained a secret.

But then postman Robert Bennett began receiving letters addressed to her and the people of Newmarket learned that the stranger sharing the house with Mary and Annie Connor was Emma Borden, sister of the notorious Lizzie Borden.

A number of residents of the town recalled seeing Emma, wearing pale dresses and with her white hair piled up on her head, usually rocking and looking out the window, or seated on the porch. When friends of the Connor sisters came to call, she would slip away and disappear upstairs.

Eva Edgeley, a 17-year-old girl who lived across the street, was haunted by Emma. There was a screened-in porch on the side of the house where Emma sat day after day, watching the street. Eva would notice that, sometimes at night, Emma would slip out through the screen door and stand for several moments in front of the house. But she never came out in the daytime.

Eva remembered, "She was alone, always alone."

In 1921, Mary Connor died. At the time of probate, when it was revealed that Mary's entire financial worth was $365 in savings, her younger sister, Annie, made an astonishing statement. She maintained that Mary had only put up $500 for the purchase of the house in Newmarket – Emma had paid for it. Emma had concealed her arrangement with the Connor sisters. She had chosen to hide away in Newmarket, an obscure little town where no one knew her, and as the sisters' constant guest, she could be a shadow in their home, while still maintaining an official presence at the Minden House in Providence.

Ione Kent lived nearby and was a close friend of Annie Connor. At different times, she had asked Annie about the woman living with her and her sister, and Annie finally confirmed the fact that it was Lizzie Borden's sister. She also told her two odd things about Emma, which Ione never forgot.

The first was that Emma was addicted to cubes of sugar, which she sucked on continually.

The second fact was more disturbing. When Emma moved into the house, besides installing an upstairs bathroom and steam heating, she paid for the construction of a second stairway down the back of the house to the kitchen. The stairway was hidden by a closet door, next to which was a narrow pantry where a large axe was kept for chopping wood. On the wall next to the pantry was an extremely unusual lighting panel, which would instantly illuminate the entire downstairs. With a single movement, the panel lit the foyer, parlor, living room, hallways, kitchen, dining room, porch, and the front of the house.

The light panel was a protective measure.

Emma told Annie in terror, "One night they will come for me."

Startled by this, Ione asked Annie who *they* were. Who was Emma afraid of?

Annie admitted that she did not know.

Emma died on June 10, 1927. Dr. George Towle, her physician, when completing her death certificate, noted "contributory cause of death – senility. Duration – unknown." Perhaps the horrible need to keep the secret about the murders eventually drove Emma mad.

Lizzie had died eight days before her sister.

In 1926, she had entered Truesdale Hospital in Fall River for a gallbladder operation. She had herself admitted under the name "Emma Borden of the Hotel Biltmore, Providence." Her attempt to disguise herself proved ineffective, though. After her admission attracted reporters, the south corridor of one floor had to be cleared for her privacy.

The nurses found her to be an uncooperative patient. They had difficulty in keeping Lizzie, her bed, or her room in proper hospital order. She would not eat the food, so her chauffeur brought her daily meals from Laura Carr's, a well-known caterer, and her maid brought her dressing gowns from home. The hospital seemed as confining as the time she had spent in the Taunton jail, awaiting her trial.

But there were gentle moments during her stay. A Fall River woman who was in the hospital at the same time had just given birth to her second daughter. Lizzie asked if she could see the infant. As she caressed the child, she remarked to the nurses that it was the first baby she had ever held.

The operation was a difficult one and it took Lizzie several months to recover. Eventually, she returned to Maplecroft, but she was never the same. She suffered drastic complications on the night of June 1, 1927 – the same night that something terrible occurred in a dark house in Newmarket, New Hampshire.

Emma Borden had no idea that Lizzie was dying.

During the early morning hours of June 2, Emma awoke as she heard a noise on the first floor. The night before, her sleep had been interrupted by terrible dreams and so Dr. Towle had given her a sedative before she went to bed. But the drug had not kept her asleep and now she was sure that someone was breaking into the house.

Overcome by terror, Emma pulled herself up out of bed, got to her feet, and crept silently through Annie Connor's back bedroom. Annie appeared to be asleep as Emma started down the dark, secret stairway leading to the kitchen. She knew that she had to reach the bottom of the stairs and find the panel of switches that would flood the first floor with light. Next to the panel of switches, she knew, was the small closet that contained the axe.

She descended the steps one by one. There was no bannister and the stairway was narrow and curved. Almost halfway down, she lost her footing and tumbled down the wooden steps. As she hit the bottom, she shattered her hip.

Annie Connor woke to the sound of screaming in the darkness and she went to search for Emma. The poor woman died just over a week later.

Lizzie died just hours after Emma's accident, on the morning of June 2. The *Fall River Globe* published her obituary and for the first time, wrote about her with no hint of condemnation or malice:

June 2, 1927
Lizbeth Borden Dies After Short Illness, Age 68
Miss Lizbeth A. Borden died this morning at 306 French Street, where had made her home for about 30 years. She had been ill with pneumonia for about a week, although for some time she had been in failing health.
A member of the one of the old Fall River families, having been the daughter of Andrew J. and Sarah (Anthony) Borden, she had lived here all of her life. With her

two maids, she lived a quiet, retired life, paying occasional visits to out-of-town friends and receiving a few callers, whose staunch friendship she valued highly.

Taking an intense pride in the surroundings in which she lived, she did much to improve the locality, purchasing adjoining property that the same refined atmosphere might be maintained. Greatly interested in nature, she was daily seen providing for the hundreds of birds that frequented the trees in her yard, taking care that the shallow box where they gathered was filled with crumbs, seeds, and other foods that they favored. She had miniature houses erected in her trees, and in these, frivolous squirrels made their homes. Her figure as she visited with her wild callers, many of whom became so friendly that they never seemed to mind her approach, was a familiar one in that section.

Another pastime in which she greatly delighted was riding through the country roads and lanes. She made frequent trips about the town in her motor car but was never so pleased as when riding through the shady country by-ways.

Surviving Miss Borden is a sister, Miss Emma Borden of New Hampshire, formerly of Providence.

The obituary was unrecognizable as coming from the same newspaper that had relentlessly called for Lizzie's arrest and trial, railed about her guilt, and hounded her for years after her acquittal. It seemed the old days had now been forgotten in Fall River, by the newspaper at least.

Mrs. Vida Pearson Turner sang in the choir at the Congregational Church on Rock Street. On the night before Lizzie's funeral, she received a call from the undertaker asking her to come to Maplecroft the following morning to sing "In My Ain Countrie."

When Mrs. Turner arrived, the undertaker unlocked the door, let her in, and then locked the door behind her. Mrs. Turner was startled. There was no one else in the house except for the two of them. She was led into the parlor – where the undertaker left her.

All alone, surrounded by all of Lizzie's fine things, Mrs. Turner began to sing. It was Lizzie's favorite song, the title of which had been carved into the fireplace mantel of her bedroom after her acquittal in 1893. The words, taken from a verse by an obscure Scottish poet, Allan Cunningham, epitomized Lizzie's feelings of sorrow. When she finished, Mrs. Turner was paid and ushered out of the house. She had no idea that Lizzie had already been buried during the night.

"Go straight home," the undertaker told her, "And don't tell anyone where you have been."

The story was now over, expect for the money. It was money that had driven a deranged man to kill his father and then bind the two sisters together in a terrible secret. Money had turned Andrew into a cold, tight-fisted man and it had eventually gotten him killed. Money had built the prison that Lizzie spent the next 35 years of loneliness and solitude trapped in. And finally, money was all that remained.

Not surprisingly, Lizzie's will provided well for animals, not for people. To the Animal Rescue League of Fall River, she bequeathed $30,000 and all of her stock in the Stevens Manufacturing Company, left to her by her father. An additional $2,000 was left to the Animal Rescue League of Washington, D.C. She commented in her will, "I have been fond of animals and their need is great and there are so few who care for them."

She left other gifts: a parcel of real estate adjacent to Maplecroft and $2,000 to her driver, Ernest Terry, $2,000 to his wife, Ellen, and $2,000 to their daughter, Grace. To Charles Cook, her business manager, she left $10,000 and some land across the street from her home. There were also bequests of $5,000 each to two friends she had made outside of Fall River, Margaret Street and Minnie LaCombe of Washington, D.C. To her most faithful friend, Helen Leighton, and her favorite cousin, Grace Howe, she left the A.J. Borden Building, in addition to all of her jewelry and furnishings. Finally, $500 was given to the city of Fall River, which was to be invested and the income used for the perpetual care of her father's grave in Oak Grove Cemetery.

Toward Emma, Lizzie made no gesture. She wrote, "I have not given my sister, Emma L. Borden, anything as she had her share of her father's estate and is supposed to have enough to make her comfortable."

Emma, on the other hand, became known as one of Fall River's greatest humanitarians. Her estate, which almost doubled Lizzie's, bestowed large bequests to children's homes, homes for the aged, the Girl Scouts, Boy's Club, the Y.M.C.A., and the Society for the Prevention of Cruelty to Children. There were scholarships to Durfee High School and gifts to hospitals. She allotted $1,000 for the perpetual care of the "family burial plot," $1,000 to Andrew Jennings, "as a remembrance in appreciation of all that he has done for me," and $1,000 was left to Lizzie.

Immediately after Emma's death, Annie Connor sold the house in Newmarket, and moved back down the road to the farm in Wadleigh Falls. No evidence has ever been found about the connection between Emma and the two spinster sisters, how they met, how the living situation was arranged, or what the connection was between the three of them. That remains another mystery of this story, largely because, a short time later, Annie Connor lost her sanity. She would wander the roads, a neighbor named Renata Dodge said, no longer knowing who she was.

The story ended among the trees of Oak Grove Cemetery, a place where the founders of Fall River were laid to rest. Among the famous are the infamous. Sheltered under the branches of four large oak trees is a row of slim granite stones, which stand above the graves of Abby Durfee Borden, Sarah Morse Borden, and Sarah's second child, Alice, who died as an infant.

Between Sarah and Abby is Andrew's plot, containing his headless corpse.

And at Andrew's feet are two small plaques, embedded in the earth, side by side. They mark the graves of Andrew's other two daughters, Lizbeth, and her sister, Emma.

But does the Borden family truly rest here in peace?

EPILOGUE:
THE HAUNTING ON SECOND STREET

When Lizzie Borden was born in 1860, Fall River was a busy port where a procession of steamboats loaded vast shipments of textile goods to be carried to the markets of New York, Boston, and beyond. The boom times lasted until the early years of the twentieth century. World War I provided an increase in the demand for textiles but the post-war economy quickly slowed, and production quickly outpaced demand. In 1923, Fall River faced the first wave of mill closures. Some mills merged and were able to limp along for a while, but the Depression sounded the death knell for the industry in Fall River. The mass exodus of workers left the huge brick buildings deserted and useless. Life in one of America's leading textile manufacturing centers changed forever as the era of wealth came to an end. In the decades that followed, the aging mills continued to decay and the town decayed with it.

In the 1960s, the city's landscape was drastically transformed with the construction of the Braga Bridge and Interstate 195, which cut directly through the heart of the city. In the wake of the highway building boom, the city lost much of its history. A large portion of the Quequechan River was re-routed and filled in. The historic falls, which had given the city its name, were diverted into underground culverts. Steel viaducts that were constructed to provide access to the new bridge forced the destruction of many of Fall River's historic buildings, including the old City Hall, from which Bridget Sullivan heard the clock chime on the morning of the murders, the old Troy Mills, and many other structures.

Although new development has come to the city over the years, it has never gotten away from its connection to the Borden murders.

Second Street does not resemble to elm-lined carriage way of the 1890s. The gracious wood frame homes have vanished. The block that Andrew Borden climbed on his way home that sweltering August morning was long ago replaced by commercial buildings. The narrow house where the murders occurred still stands, although the yard, barn, and surrounding fence are gone. The house had changed hands many times since it was sold by Lizzie and Emma. At one time, after the Fall River police discovered that it was used as a headquarters for a gambling operation, they raided the place. It was later renovated and turned into a commercial printing business by John

McGinn. He and his wife maintained the second floor as an apartment for an elderly relative. McGinn built a large printing plant in the south yard of the property, where the barn once stood, but it has also become part of the house's history.

In 1996, the house was renovated again and this time, was turned into the Lizzie Borden Bed and Breakfast. Now the only question about the house is not who committed the murders, but who haunts the house where the Bordens lived and died?

The stories of ghostly encounters at the Borden house do not date back to the days that immediately followed the crime. They are of a more recent vintage, likely stirred up by the renovations that took place to convert it from a commercial business to a bed and breakfast – and to restore the house to what it looked like at the time of the murders in 1892. Most paranormal enthusiasts believe that restoration work can cause a location to become "active." In many haunted locations, an event may occur – two murders in this particular case – that leaves an impression on the atmosphere of the place. Often, a haunting can be dormant for many years before becoming active when the energy is displaced by remodeling. Paranormal literature is filled with accounts of hauntings that begin in buildings that were previously quiet and then suddenly, seem to be haunted. The disturbance caused by the renovations can often cause effects to occur that are related to the history of the place – including sounds of voices, footsteps, cries, and even physical effects like doors opening and closing, windows rattling, and knocking sounds. Is this merely a "recording" of the past that has been activated again by a change in the physical presence of the house, or could there be an actual spirit that lingers at the site? In some locations, like the Borden house, it may be both.

The Borden House today

The Borden house has been turned into a colorful time capsule of 1892, the ghastly murders that occurred there, and the mystery that remains as to the killer's identity today. The walls hide many secrets and these secrets bring scores of visitors to the door. Some of them come hoping to learn about the house's history, others to experience the atmosphere of the place where the infamous murders took place, and many come looking for ghosts. Guests come from all over the country to sleep in the room where Abby Borden was murdered, but not all of them sleep peacefully.

If there are truly spirits here, they are not restful ones.

Ever since the Borden house was opened as a bed and breakfast in 1996, ghost enthusiasts, curiosity-seekers, hardened paranormal investigators, and even so-called paranormal television "celebrities" have flocked to it in droves. They all come seeking the strange, the unusual, and the haunted. Guests and staff members alike have had their share of strange experiences in the house. Some have reported the sounds of a woman weeping, and others claim to have seen a woman in Victorian era clothing dusting the furniture and straightening the covers on the beds. Occasionally, this even happens when the guests are still in the bed. Others have heard the sounds of footsteps going up and down the stairs and crossing back and forth on the second floor, even when they know the house is empty. Doors open and close and often, muffled conversation can be heard coming from inside otherwise vacant rooms. One visitor witnessed an old framed photograph that lifted into the air, flipped over a few times, and then traveled halfway across the room, propelled by an unseen force.

One man, who had little interest in ghosts, claimed that he accompanied his wife to the inn one night and had a very strange experience. When they first arrived, he carried their luggage upstairs and placed it in what was their bedroom for the night. The room had been perfectly made up when he entered, the bed smooth, and everything put in its place. Over the course of a few minutes of unpacking, he happened to look over to the bed again and saw that it was now rumpled, even though he was in the room alone and had not been near it. With a start, he also noticed that the folds of the comforter had been moved so that they corresponded to the curves of a human body. On the pillow, there was an indentation in the shape of a human head. His wife found him a few minutes later, waiting in the downstairs sitting room. His face was very pale and he seemed quite nervous. When she asked him what was wrong, he took her back upstairs to show her the strange appearance of the bed. However, when he opened the door, the pillow had been plumped and the comforter looked just as it did when he first entered the room -- the room where Abby Borden had been murdered.

The current owner of the house is Leeann Wilber, who first visited the place with her boyfriend on Valentine's Day 2003. By mid-June of 2004, they had purchased the house and now Leeann runs it by herself. She wasn't sure what she was getting into at first – especially after the encounter in the basement, where a former owner claimed to see a misty apparition. It was her first week as the owner of the house and she had gone down to the basement to switch over some laundry. When she went down the steps, she turned to her left to go to the laundry room. As soon as she took a step forward, she felt like she had walked into a freezer. She stumbled two more steps and walked out of the other side of the cold. She reached out her hand for the door to the laundry room and it felt like someone had traced her back with two cold fingers. She recalled, "I stopped dead in my tracks, I turned around, and I went trotting right back up the stairs."

Since that time, weird noises and ghostly phenomena have become almost commonplace for Leeann. She admits that "something's going on here," and speaks of phantom footfalls and unexplained gusts of wind. She has been downstairs and heard someone walk across the floor above her. And she was alone in the house at the time. "It didn't sit well with me," she said, "But after a while you get used to it."

Leeann is used to it, but not all of her guests are. While most come looking for ghosts, there are often those who are afraid when they find them. She has had many cases of people fleeing the inn at 2:00 a.m., rattled by the whispers, strange voices, and footsteps.

If the house is as haunted as so many claim, who lingers here? The obvious suggestion would be Andrew or Abby Borden, still demanding that justice be served. Or could it be Emma, her life ruined by the events that occurred that morning?

Or could it be Lizzie herself? She was the person who could not have committed the crime and yet bore the blame for it. Persecuted, ridiculed, arrested, placed on trial, and even though she was acquitted, was ostracized by the community, attacked by newspapers, hounded by reporters, and was forced into seclusion for the rest of her life. Countless books, stories, and poems have been written about how she murdered her parents, even though she could not have wielded the axe.

A.L. Bixby wrote:

There's no evidence of guilt,
Lizzie Borden,
That should make your spirit wilt,
Lizzie Borden;
Many do not think that you
Chopped your father's head in two,
It's so hard a thing to do,
Lizzie Borden.
You have borne up under all,
Lizzie Borden.
With a mighty show of gall,
Lizzie Borden;
But because your nerve is stout

Does not prove beyond a doubt
That you knocked the old folks out,
Lizzie Borden.

Is it any wonder that she might not rest in peace? Or that her ghost might still be steeped in the torment that she suffered in life? But you might say that Lizzie didn't swing the hatchet, but she knew who did. And perhaps this is true.

I believe that Lizzie and Emma kept a terrible secret between them for the rest of their lives. Even when Emma was so shocked over Lizzie's behavior, she refused to reveal what happened on that hot August morning and never told about the horrendous crime that William Borden committed.

But I also believe that Lizzie was just as tormented by guilt as Emma was. She loved her father and the soul-crushing pain of his brutal death, followed by her arrest and trial, and finally the suspicion that followed her for the rest of her life were more than enough to keep her spirit from finding peace.

Andrew and Abby Borden – their lives cut short in the walls of the house on Second Street – may linger there. But I don't believe they haunt the rooms and hallways alone.

BIBLIOGRAPHY

Adams, Barbara Johnston – "The Fall River Murders" in *Crime Mysteries;* 1988

Austin, Joanne M. – *Weird Encounters;* 2010

Ayotte, John – "The Unfathomable Borden Riddle" in *Yankee Magazine;* 1966

Booth, Robert – "Vengeful Daughter" in *American History Magazine;* 2013

Brown, Arnold R. – *Lizzie Borden,* 1991

Chapman, Sherry – *Lizzie Borden: Resurrections;* 2014

De Mille, Agnes – *Lizzie Borden: A Dance of Death;* 1968

Early, Eleanor – "Did Lizzie Do it?" in *A New England Sampler;* 1940

Gibson, Walter – "The Last of the Borden Case" in *The Fine Art of Murder;* 1965

Hunter, Evan – *Lizzie;* 1984

James, Bill – *Popular Crime;* 2011

Lester, Henry – "Lizzie Borden" in *Unsolved Murders and Mysteries; 1955*

Kent, David – *Forty Whacks;* 1992

------------- with Robert Flynn – *Lizzie Borden Sourcebook;* 1992

Lincoln, Victoria – *A Private Disgrace;* 1967

Nash, Jay Robert – *Open Files;* 1983

Pearson, Edmund – *Trial of Lizzie Borden;* 1937

Porter, Edwin H. – *The Fall River Tragedy;* 1893

Radin, Edward D. – *Lizzie Borden: The Untold Story;* 1961

Samuels, Charles and Louise – *The Girl in the House of Hate;* 1953

Snow, Edward Rowe – *Piracy, Mutiny and Murders;* 1959

Spiering, Frank – *Lizzie;* 1984

Sullivan, Robert – *Goodbye Lizzie Borden;* 1974

Special Thanks To:

April Slaughter – Cover Design and Artwork

Lois Taylor – Editing and Proofreading

Lisa Taylor Horton and Lux

Rene Kruse

Rachael Horath

Elyse and Thomas Reihner

Bethany and Jim McKenzie

Orrin Taylor

Derek Bartlett

Haven and Helayna Taylor

CPSIA information can be obtained
at www.ICGtesting.com
Printed in the USA
JSHW010002051019
1754JS00004B/1